THE STALIN PHENOMENON

THE STALIN PHENOMENON

Edited by ALEC NOVE

Weidenfeld & Nicolson · London

Weidenfeld & Nicolson Ltd
Orion Publishing Group
Orion House
5 Upper St Martin's Lane
London WC2H 9EA

British Library Cataloguing in Publication Data
for this title is available upon request.

Typeset by Deltatype Ltd, Ellesmere Port, Cheshire

Printed in Great Britain by
Butler & Tanner Ltd, Frome & London

ISBN 0 297 82108 3

Contents

CHAPTER 1

Stalin and Stalinism – Some Introductory Thoughts

Alec Nove

Stalin will be argued about for centuries yet. His career, his crimes, his achievements, raise so many problems. Thus: the role of personality in history (what difference did *he* make?). How far were his policies shaped by circumstances? What was the role of ideology, of Marxism-Leninism? How far did he modify or distort the received ideology? His role can be seen in the context of Russian history and political culture, or within a model of rapid economic development, or of Asiatic despotism. As the former USSR struggled to shake off those aspects of the stalinist legacy which conflicted with today's needs, it is necessary to face up to the facts of the stalinist past. But this calls into question the legitimacy of the regime, of rule by the Party, even of the October revolution itself. So arguments about Stalin and his system have also a direct relevance to the collapse of the Union.

The émigré historian Alexander Yanov once wrote an interesting paper about attitudes to and interpretations of Ivan the Terrible: from these, much can be deduced about the given author's attitude to despotic government in more recent times. For Yanov, Ivan and Peter, along with Stalin, were the evil geniuses of Russian history. It is therefore worth noting that, in the course of his discussion on the origins of Stalinism (*Istoki*, *Novyi mir*, No. 5, 1988), V. Selyunin takes a very similar line: he, too, sees them as enslavers of the people, sharply criticizing those historians who see them as positive figures.

The present book reflects some differences of view among its authors, but let us be clear: none are in the business of defending Stalin.

I hold firmly to the view that *tout comprendre* does NOT imply *tout pardonner*: to understand is not to forgive, but it is better than the only alternative, which is not to understand. We all agree that Stalin was personally responsible for many crimes, that millions died as a result of policies adopted and ruthlessly pursued when he was supreme ruler. As we shall see, even wider differences can be found among Soviet participants in a debate that, at long last, rages freely in the former USSR itself, even among those who take a strongly anti-Stalinist position.

This variety reflects, among other things, the authors' conscious or unconscious historical philosophies. One recalls E. H. Carr's well-known set of lectures on 'What is history?', his discussion of free will versus determinism, the way in which he applied his own ideas (to the discontent of many reviewers) to the history of the Soviet Union. My own first work on this subject was entitled 'Was Stalin Really Necessary?', and this earned me a reproof from that much-respected scholar Alexander Gerschenkron: there is, he insisted, no such thing as necessity in history. I tried in vain to convince him of the contrary: 'necessary' does not mean 'inevitable'; thus it could be said to have been necessary to alter the Polish constitution, with its liberum veto, in the eighteenth century if Poland was to survive, but it was not altered and Poland did not survive. Carr was right to say, in an ironic aside, that no historian ever says that anything is inevitable until after it has happened. All this relates to the meaningfulness of the question: was there an alternative to Stalinism? If alternatives existed, why were they eliminated, defeated, not implemented? In my own reviews of Carr's many-volume history, I several times expressed the view that he went too far in rejecting or ignoring the possibility of alternatives – though I also defended him from the exaggerated attacks by Norman Stone and Leo Labedz. Among the Soviet anti-stalinist historians it seems to me that Igor Klyamkin holds views closest to Carr's. I shall be quoting him later on.

There is another, related point. It can be illustrated by reference to another of this century's sanguinary despots: Hitler. Here too one can list the circumstances which made him and the Nazi regime POSSIBLE: German nationalism, romanticism, the Versailles treaty, anti-semitism, the effects of the hyper-inflation and of the great depression, the divisions and weaknesses among his opponents. But here too there is a danger of accepting as conclusive 'explanations' which could fit a quite different outcome and appear equally plausible. Thus important elements in German history and culture, philosophy, bureaucratic traditions, could have been invoked to explain Hitler's failure, had he failed. Indeed many of Hitler's victims, including Jews, refused to believe that so civilized a nation could spawn so murderous a regime. If intelligent men, German and non-German alike, had been asked in 1930 whether a fully-fledged Nazi totalitarian regime was likely to come into existence within just a few years, the vast majority would surely have answered 'no'. And the independent Soviet historian Roy Medvedev argued likewise: even as late as 1927, it seemed in the highest degree unlikely that Stalin would soon wind up NEP, forcibly collectivize the peasantry and eliminate the bulk of the old Bolsheviks (plus millions of others). The underlying causes were no doubt already present, but to the actors of the time such an outcome seemed not at all likely, let alone predetermined.

Explanations that list antecedent circumstances are, of course, both useful and necessary. However, this in no way implies inevitability, and leaves untouched the vitally important question of responsibility, including that of individuals. The point is frequently and rightly made, in and out of the former Soviet Union, that if circumstances predetermine outcomes, it becomes pointless to 'blame' Stalin or anyone else for these outcomes, since he or they turn out to be mere pawns in the onward march of historical necessity. In his book on Stalin, Randall made a valid point: 'In a sense the cause of human freedom rides with Stalin', since if even his actions were predetermined by antecedent circumstances, then none of us are free! A number of historians take the view that discussion of foregone alternatives is pointless, that it is a waste of time to consider the what-might-have-beens of history, we should expound and explain what actually occurred.

However, in my view they cannot be fully consistent in this position. For example, suppose we say that Stalin's misunderstanding of Hitler's intentions had a catastrophic effect in June 1941, or that Zhukov showed consummate skill in organizing in the nick of time the defence first of Leningrad and then of Moscow in that same year. By so doing we imply that if other decisions were made, and/or other decision-makers appointed, the outcomes would have been different. Therefore Stalin and Zhukov can be held responsible, praised, blamed, for what they did or failed to do. Needless to say all sorts of circumstances – information and disinformation, organizational deficiencies, training, the quality of equipment, mobility, communications, not to mention the actions of the enemy, all played their part. Just as in the October revolution itself, the outcome was decisively affected by war-weariness, the weakness and divisions among the forces opposed to Bolshevism, the quality of Lenin's leadership, and so on. Even Trotsky, despite his orthodox Marxist views on the role of the individual in history, had to admit that without Lenin the Bolshevik revolution might well have failed to materialize.

The question of Stalin's responsibility extends beyond the (undoubted) fact that circumstances gave him the opportunity and to some degree set the agenda, the problems to be solved. And of course he could not act alone. His associates, men like Molotov, Kaganovich, Mikoyan, Zhdanov, carried out his policies, but could have minds of their own and might have influenced events. But one also recalls that many who were thought of as loyal stalinists perished in the purges: apart from the still-argued-about case of Kirov, there were Kosior, Postyshev, Eikhe, Rudzutak, Chubar, and such old comrades of Stalin's as Ordzhonikidze and Yenukidze. The OGPU/NKVD chiefs Yagoda and Yezhov seemed to have been doing his bidding until he chose to destroy them. Then there were the postwar victims at the top, Voznesensky and Kuznetsov. One cannot overlook the fact that the wives of some members of the politburo were imprisoned, and their husbands were unable to help. Does not all this support the view that Stalin, once in power, tolerated only totally obedient satraps around him?

But even if this were so, the fact remains that there are only 24 hours in a day, and even despots must sleep. The number of decisions to be taken vastly exceeds the possibility that one man can consider them personally, and influence is inevitably wielded by whosoever filters information, drafts proposals, reports on implementation of orders, and so on. This is true of any despot anywhere. One recalls the story of 'Lieutenant Kije', the subject of Prokofiev's excellent music. The English title is misleading: the point was that Nicholas I overheard two staff officers talking, and one of them said '*Poruchiki-zhe*' ('as for lieutenants'). The Tsar thought they referred to an officer named Poruchik Kizhe. So, rather than explain, they invented such an officer, created a file for him – and ultimately killed him off. The entire episode was not willed by Tsar Nicholas, but its (fictional!) occurrence was, so to speak, a byproduct of his autocratic rule and the fear it inspired. A nonfictional episode, described in Evgenia Ginzburg's admirable *Into the Whirlwind*, may be seen as similar in its motivation: one interrogator in Kazan is heard to say to another interrogator: shall we charge this man with Trotskyism? The other replied: we have fulfilled our plan for Trotskyists, the man is a Tartar, so we shall charge him with bourgeois nationalism. To say that this happened because Stalin ordered it is no more true than that Lieutenant Kije was 'born' because the Tsar ordered it. The Tsar, and Stalin, can be said to be responsible for the system and for the policies which engendered a pattern of behaviour in subordinates. But it can also be argued, with some force, that Nicholas and Stalin were in a sense the creations as well as the creators of the system.

This last point is often argued by reference to the human material with which Bolsheviks ruled Russia in the twenties, and, most important, to the impact on Bolshevik officialdom of the experience of brutality and arbitrariness in the years of civil war. Thus in the collection of articles edited by Yuri Afanasyev, *Inogo ne dano* (Moscow, 1988), V. Frolov stressed the low level of education of so many party cadres. Thus of the delegates to the 14th party congress (1926), 5.1 per cent had higher, 22.3 per cent secondary and 66.1 per cent elementary education (which leaves 5.5 per cent who presumably had no education at all). Yet 70 per cent of the delegates were 'party officials of all levels'. He argued: 'having no life or work experience for coping with their new circumstances, this stratum in a certain respect had no confidence in tomorrow, which engendered the need for a leader who would clearly and surely determine the rules of life and behaviour, whose judgments were always correct (*bezgreshnye*) and required only unhesitating obedience, preferably without prior thought' (p. 395). A similar point had been made by Roger Pethybridge in his *Social Prelude to Stalinism*, and also by Otto Latsis, whom we shall be quoting at length later. All this is, of course, relevant to our theme. It helps us to understand why Stalinism came to be. There were indeed a whole number of circumstances – not least the historical traditions of Russian autocracy, the sense of dangerous isolation in a hostile world (and much else, to be further discussed) – which facilitated the rise of Stalin and of his system. However, as Roy Medvedev argued long ago (in the first version of *Let History Judge*), whatever reasons explain the rise of the cult of personality, once he has achieved power much depends on the personality.

It is also too simple to assume that Stalin's triumph was due to mass support for his extremist policies. In his rise to power he presented himself initially as a moderate, opposed to Trotsky's alleged super-industrialization, opposed even to action against the *kulaks*, against 'those comrades who think it possible and necessary to deal with the kulak by administrative measures through the GPU' (this in 1927 – quoted by O. Latsis in *Znamya*, No. 6, 1988). As Klyamkin pointed out (*Novyi mir*, No. 2, 1989), Stalin adapted policies to the need to keep a majority in the politburo and the central committee, which were not yet under his full control.

All this said, let us now turn to a more detailed examination of the origins, causes, preconditions, rationale, essence and nature of the stalinist system, and of the role of Stalin himself. It will not be my concern to attempt a historical description of the steps by which Stalin achieved his personal dominance – but the degree of that dominance, and the origins and purposes of policies he pursued after 1929, will be. It is notable, and encouraging, that differences of view can be almost 'impartially' ascribed to Soviet and Western scholars and publicists. Freedom of discussion in the former USSR has reached a level which seemed unthinkable five years ago. There was only one exception, and even that (as we shall see) is only partial: Lenin was still a difficult theme on which to be totally frank and critical.

So – let us begin with what Selyunin and others refer to as *Istoki*, origins, sources, to history.

The Legacy of Tsarism: 'Stalin the Peter-the-Great of Today'

The poet Maksimilian Voloshin wrote: 'Peter the Great was the first Bolshevik.' The philosopher Nikolai Berdyaev wrote: 'Peter's methods were purely Bolshevik.' Stalin could be, and has been, interpreted as a twentieth-century modernizing despot. Efforts to fit him into the traditional marxist view of Oriental despotism (for instance by Wittfogel) break down when one recalls that for Marx the oriental despot ruled over a static society, whereas Stalin did preside over a vast revolution from above. So did Peter. There are numerous parallels. Thus both sought to mobilize society, from the highest to the lowest, in pursuit of the aim of catching up the more developed West. Both, in doing so, strengthened serfdom (Stalin's *kolkhozniki* could be seen as serfs), used forced labour on a big scale, promoted men from below, distrusted and disrupted the then-existing ruling strata (the boyars and the old party cadres respectively). One had his son tortured to death in prison, the other let him die in (German) captivity. I also noted, in an early article ('History, hierarchy and nationalities', *Soviet Studies*, July 1969) the close parallel between Peter's *tabel' o rangakh* (table of ranks) and the *nomenklatura*, i.e. the official hierarchy which alone gave power and status in the service of the tsar/general secretary.

Peter had been presented by early Bolshevik historiography as a cruel tyrant, as may be seen in the works of Pokrovsky. Stalin changed all that. In 1934 history was rewritten to make Peter (and Ivan) positive figures. This was part of the cultural counter-revolution of those years, which also saw the restoration of tradition in many spheres (education, the arts, family, etc.). In his remarkable novel *Deti Arbata*, Anatoli Rybakov has Stalin soliloquize about Pokrovsky's view of Peter: it was all rubbish, Peter was great, the builder of the modern great Russian state. A backward people had, and has, to be guided, forced, a ruler must be cruel, he must also be absolute (see *Druzhba narodov*, No. 5, 1987). Vasili Grossman had also noted the tragic association in Russian history between modernization and unfreedom, which is demonstrated by Peter and Stalin. So did V. Selyunin in his *Istoki* (*Novyi mir*, No. 5, 1988).

Along this line one sometimes encounters Stalin-apologists, in and out of Russia: Yes, he was crude, cruel, many of his acts were counter-productive, but on balance he did lead the country kicking and screaming into the twentieth century, he did force the creation of modern heavy industry which saved the country in the war. Theodore von Laue, in his 'Stalin in focus' (*Slavic Review*, February 1983), also places Stalin in the context of Russian modernization, 'both Western and anti-Western'.

There was an interesting counter-attack on such ideas from V. Kozhinov, writing in *Nash sovremennik* (No. 4, 1988, No. 1, 1989) from a neo-slavophil position. Ivan the Terrible was really no more terrible than many of his contemporaries, such as Henry VIII of England and Charles IX of France. Peter's cruelties were directed *against* Russian tradition, he was a 'Europeanizer'. More recently, argues Kozhinov, the repressions that followed the 1905 revolution cost infinitely fewer lives than did the suppression of the Paris commune. The Russian penal code in the nineteenth century was far milder than its Western equivalents. For him, therefore, Stalin's sanguinary regime cannot be explained by reference to Tsarist precedents – but he does stress the bloodletting of the civil war, and also the anti-peasant policies of the regime in the twenties, making no exception for Bukharin. Save on the issue of Lenin he seems very close to the position adopted by Solzhenitsyn: that Bolshevism, most Bolsheviks, Stalin, were by no means to be seen as a Russian phenomenon, but rather as something alien. Kozhinov tends to stress the role of individuals with Jewish names. This contrasts with the views of such as the émigré philosopher Nikolai Berdyaev, for whom Bolshevism has deep-lying Russian roots.

Some Soviet analysts have sought the *Istoki* in the ultra-radical traditions of the Russian ultra-radical intelligentsia. The origins of such arguments go back to Dostoevsky's *The Devils*, and also to the famous symposium *Vekhi* ('Milestones') published in 1909. They can be seen in the ideas of A. Tsipko (in *Nauka i zhizn*, spread over four isues, Nos. 11 and 12, 1988, and Nos. 1 and 2, 1989). The Russian radical intelligentsia lacked restraint, it was 'much weaker than among people who had learned realism and sobriety under capitalism'. The Russian intelligentsia was almost wholly anti-bourgeois, had little experience of practical constructive work, was given to 'Messianism'. Alas, 'our Russian workers' movement failed to avoid the "christianization" of Marxism. Marxism was not only given a utopian interpretation, but it became a symbol of faith. . . . The workers and peasants who took part in the armed revolt and then in the civil war saw communism in a utopian and fatalistic way, as the Christians saw an earthly divine paradise.' Very sensibly, he adds: 'I do not assert that Russian revolutionary radicalism, the traditions of spiritual maximalism and messianism, inevitably led to Stalinism. . . . To the real world the philosophic concept of "necessity" is not applicable' (*Nauka i zhizn*, No. 1, 1989). (So he would agree with Gerschenkron on this last point. See p. 2, above.) But, while of course other factors played their role, 'it is legitimate to seek the origins of stalinism in the traditions of Russian left-wing radicalism'.

My own opinion is that, while Kozhinov is right to remind us that sanguinary despots were also to be found in other countries in past centuries, there are none the less some specific features in Russian history which must form part (but only part) of any explanation of the phenomenon of Stalinism. Other countries did not have so dominant a state, such weak spontaneous social forces, so late a development of a bourgeoisie, and of representative institutions, trade unions. Russian 'feudalism' did not resemble its Western counterparts, after the destruction by Ivan the Terrible of the territorial power-bases of the nobility, whom Peter finally merged with the service class, the *dvoryanstvo*. Serfdom ended only in 1861, the mass of the peasants were not even given the opportunity to become individual proprietors until the Stolypin reform of 1906–11. The intelligentsia was indeed imbued with an anti-mercantile spirit, even those among them who hated the radical revolutionaries (for instance Dostoevsky). The lack of political culture extended to even the more moderate members of the educated classes, as can be seen by the poor showing of the Provisional Government after the fall of the last Tsar, their lack of legitimacy in the eyes of the people. There was, too, the age-old concern for order, *poryadok*, which even found its expression in the legend of the foundation of the Russian state: a foreign prince (Rurik) was called in to establish order in the place of anarchy. There was a traditional yearning for a strong master.

This was doubtless reinforced by the appalling experience of the civil war. On the importance of the civil war almost all the rival theorists are agreed. Together with World War I, it led to the physical elimination of a large part of educated manpower, through death in war and emigration. It led to the rise among the Bolsheviks themselves of the ruthless commissar type, who dealt brutally with emergencies and held human life cheap. Soviet writers as different as Kozhinov and Tsipko are agreed that the terror of the civil war can be seen as a prelude to the Stalinist terror. 'The meatgrinder of the class struggle, or class war, is as disgusting as the slaughter of the stalinist repression' (Tsipko, *Nauka i zhizn*, No. 12, 1988). (I will have more to say later on about what I like to call 'revolutionary immorality'.)

Marx, Engels, Lenin: Stalin the Leninist or Stalin the counter-revolutionary?

Two subquestions should be distinguished. One is the role (if any) of Marxism-Leninism in the formation of Stalin's own ideas about power and what to do with it. On this there is widespread and fundamental disagreement among Western and former Soviet commentators, among

Marxists too. The other is the relationship between Stalin's policies and Lenin's legacy: was he in some sense the executor of Lenin's policies, or was he the executioner of Lenin's comrades, 'the grave-digger of the revolution' (Trotsky's words, apparently to Stalin's face, which helped to dig Trotsky's grave), and was his accession to power a 'counter-revolutionary coup'?

A prior point to establish: I agree strongly with the remark made on this very theme in a percipient essay by Leszek Kolakowski, eminent former marxist philosopher, in a symposium edited by R. Tucker: 'No society has ever been entirely begotten by an ideology or may even be accounted for by the ideas of people who contributed to its origin; anybody is Marxist enough to admit that.'[1] Marx certainly inspired Lenin, his ideas had profound effects on the minds of the intellectuals who seized power in the October revolution. However, as also in the case of the French revolution, one must beware of assigning sole or decisive influences to the fact that some of the leading actors had read books, be they by Engels, Rousseau or Montesquieu.

Let us begin by agreeing that Marx's vision of socialism was certainly very different from that of what could be called High Stalinism. V. Kiselev, in the already cited volume *Inogo ne dano* (p. 363), describes the following as

> characteristics of the Stalin model of socialism: total centralization of control over all spheres of social life; administrative-command methods combined with state terror, including the organization of mass repressions and forced labour camps; the extensive and regardless-of-cost (*zatratnyi*) economic and political mechanism, which ignores evaluation by reference to social effectiveness; rejection of the values of antecedent forms of democracy, the detachment of the masses from government and the turning of democratic institutions into empty form; the rejection of self-management; the consecration of Authority and the cult of personality.

Add the widespread use of capital punishment, the strictest of censorships, the strictest ban on any autonomous trade unions, and this is not even a caricature of Marx's vision, it resembles it in no way. And yet it is precisely Kiselev, and in this same paper, who devotes detailed attention to the role of Marx's and Engels's ideas. So, in the already cited series of articles, does A. Tsipko. So, in his own way, does V. Selyunin. The matter was well discussed, too, by Leszek Kolakowski (ex-Marxist) and by Mihajlo Markovic (neo-Marxist) in the symposium edited by Robert Tucker, cited above. Similar arguments were advanced in my own *Stalinism and After* and *Economics of Feasible Socialism*.

They all in their various ways relate to the utopian elements in the original Marxist vision of socialism. If the state was to wither away, no attention needed to be paid to constitutional guarantees or to such 'bourgeois' irrelevancies as separation of powers. This is one of the senses in which (to cite the thought of Markovic) Stalin could advance through gaps in Marx's argument. Marx and most Marxists until recently believed in a socialism without markets and without bureaucracy. Yes, wrote Tsipko, yes, Stalin committed errors and crimes, 'but we say nothing about those errors and misunderstandings for which he bears no responsibility. We say nothing of the tragedies and confusions of the revolutionary workers' movement. . . . Stalin and his activities are the creation of the revolutionary movement, which began long before Stalin came to power. In the beginning was the Word. We must relate the Word, i.e. scientific socialist doctrine, with Stalin's conception of a collectivist society, and then only compare what he had done with what Marx, Engels, Lenin, thought about socialism.' Allowing for the backwardness of Russia, slave psychology and the rest, we must face 'the doctrinal basis of the deformation of socialism'. Thus 'everyone criticises the deformed, barrack, equalizing (*uravnitelnogo*) socialism created in the thirties. But this criticism carefully evades the structural causes of the barracks (*kazarmennosti*). It avoids the central question: is it possible to build a non-barracks democratic socialism on a non-commodity, non-market basis? Marx did not see this difficult question, since for this there was no historical experience. Lenin did feel his way towards it (*nashchupal*) at the end of his life. Why do we not wish to think about this?'

'Can there by any firm guarantees of individual freedom or democracy when all members of society are employed by the proletarian state and have no independent way of earning their livelihood? Can one avoid coercion of the peasantry if one firmly believes that collective labour on the land is an economic necessity? Does not the idea of a revolutionary advance-guard lead to new forms of completely overcoming weltanschauung-pluralism, religious consciousness. . . ?'

He went on: 'Let us state clearly the known fact that, taken as a whole, Stalin's thought and his conception of socialism were typical among Marxists of that time. . . . Today it has become difficult even to say that Stalin as an individual was formed in a Marxist environment, that he tried within the limits of his ability to absorb the theoretical inheritance of the classics, that he never departed from the elementary propositions of Marxism in his articles and speeches.'

In his attitude to the market, Stalin was at one not only with Trotsky and Zinoviev, but even with 'the revisionist Karl Kautsky'. Stalin's conceptions of socialism 'were not greatly different from those of other Marxists of his time, since they were based on the same social and philosophical ideas'. So 'what Stalin proposed to us as socialism was at first sight remarkably similar to the projects sketched by Marx, Engels, Lenin'.

Selyunin also sees a connection between the refusal to accept the market and material incentives on the one hand and the totalitarian excesses of Stalinism on the other. In the already quoted *Istoki* (*Novyi mir*, No. 5, 1988) he notes that Engels saw no reason for any differentation in pay in a socialist society, and Marx saw the need for only a temporary inequality, which 'preserves bourgeois right', and so, remarked Selyunin, 'it is clear that so unnatural a thing could only be tolerated for a short time'. In a symposium on the occasion of the anniversary of Engels's *Anti-Dühring*, G. Popov and others also criticized Marx and Engels for their anti-market concept of socialism (*Voprosy ekonomiki*, No. 6, 1988). More challenging still was Kiselev, whom we have already quoted:

> Socialism, according to Marx and Engels, is a consciously regulated, planned, non-commodity [non-market] self-governing society, based on social ownership of the means of production. The dictatorship of the proletariat would be necessary only for the transition period, coercion would be applied only to the resistance of the bourgeoisie in the course of its overthrow. The toiling masses would be organized into self-governing associations similar to the Paris Commune. . . . The army and the police would be abolished. As a result of these revolutionary transformations, the mediating relationships of markets and politics would be replaced by directly social 'transparent' and 'rationally-clear' relations. . . . The law of value, commodity-money relations are incompatible with conscious regulation (of the economy) and lead to anarchy, to the dominance of the product over the producer. . . .

Kiselev contrasts this view with that of the object of Engels's *Anti-Dühring*, i.e. with Dühring's. The latter was criticized by Engels for imagining a socialism where there is still division of labour, competition (between communes), money, additional pay for skills, right of inheritance, and an army, police, courts. So, given all subsequent experience, was not Dühring right? And were the visions of Marx and Engels, that inspired Lenin and the Bolsheviks, not only unreal but dangerous? To cite Kiselev again:

> But the elimination of commodity-money relations creates preconditions for bureaucratism, for arbitrary power, since the working masses lose the means of economic control over the effectiveness of the actions of the state apparatus. This apparatus has a tendency to self-assertion [*samoobladaniye*], to self-distortion, to separate itself from the people, to redistribute the social wealth for its own purposes. The state bureaucracy becomes a kind of cancerous growth on the social organism in the absence of legal market relations.

Kiselev adds that Marx thought that the state and the law of value (markets) should both vanish (Kiselev, *op. cit.*, pp. 357–359). Interestingly, the point about Dühring (should we call it 'anti-Engels?') was also made by Lisichkin (in *Novyi mir*, No. 11, 1988) and by Klyamkin (in *Novyi mir*, No. 2, 1989).

Marx and Engels cannot, of course, be seen as pointing to Stalinism. One recalls a crack attributed to an NKVD officer during the Terror: 'If Marx fell into our hands, within a week we would have him admit to being an agent of Bismarck.' The point is rather that the vision of socialism in which there is no 'civil society', no representative institutions, with 'labour directly social' without the intermediacy of market or money, was so unreal as virtually to render necessary a set of unforeseen substitutes: a powerful and unlimited state, centralized bureaucratic planning, *enforced* unanimity in the place of the imagined (but impossible) unanimity of a classless society.

What, now, of Lenin, and of his link with Stalin and Stalinism? Here, as already noted, opinions differ widely. Among Western scholars, Stephen Cohen has been particularly eloquent in stressing the differences between the two. No doubt they existed, and certainly Cohen is right to point to the unique nature of the Stalin terror. True, as Solzhenitsyn has been pointing out in his *Gulag Archipelago*, concentration camps, the shooting of hostages and the excesses of the Cheka took place while Lenin was in charge. One can assemble a number of sayings by Lenin which urged his subordinates to ruthlessness. His intolerance of even mild opposition (outside the party) was notable. Thus, this in 1921: 'when the mensheviks say, you are retreating, we were in favour of retreat, let us retreat with you, we should reply: for open expression of menshevik views our courts will shoot you, or they are not our courts but God knows what!' (Lenin, Vol. 45, p. 89).

There is much support for this interpretation from Soviet published sources; thus Tsipko implicitly extends his critique to Lenin's time by referring to the killing (at that time) of 'children who had the misfortune to be born royal', priests because they were priests, officers because they were officers; this could be a prelude not only to mass deportation of alleged kulaks but also to the later slaughter of party dissidents. He also noted Lenin's violent opposition (until 1921) to trade, to the market, his acute distrust of the petty-bourgeois nature of all but the poorest peasants. Selyunin, too, in his *Istoki*, cites Lenin's demand that 'petty-bourgeois speculators be shot on the spot', and indeed both can refer to the party programme adopted in 1919, with Lenin's active participation, his belief in the suppression of private enterprise, the role (under Lenin's appointee Dzerzhinsky) of the Cheka not only in suppressing 'counter-revolution' but also in imposing labour discipline. Trotsky was backed by Lenin most of the way in imposing militarization of labour in 1920, as Klyamkin pointed out (*Novyi mir*, No. 11, 1987). And we have already cited Tsipko to the effect that Lenin 'felt his way' (*nashchupal*) towards a different view at the end of his life. Kiselev, too, stresses Lenin's commitment to the programme (in 1919) of abolishing money and outlawing trade. 'The policies of war communism . . . were not only the result of the conditions of civil war, intervention and ruin, but also of a vision of socialism, the attempt to realise it in its classical form' (Kiselev, p. 362). Indeed Lenin himself, in 1921, spoke of '*our* illusions' (emphasis mine), and at no time denied that he too was carried away, shared the notion of some sort of direct leap into socialism. Those who defended Lenin, and spoke still of a return to 'Leninist' norms and policies, stressed that he had the courage and wisdom to abandon these illusions, to advocate new policies, to learn from past mistakes.

This last point connects with another controversy to which we will return, on the nature and possibilities of NEP. Several Soviet writers, aware of Lenin's extremism during the civil war period, maintain that he was developing a very different conception of socialism after the 10th party congress (March 1921), but which he had no time to fully elaborate. True, as V. Sirotkin points out in his contribution to *Inogo ne dano*, Lenin at first envisaged no more than 'direct products exchange with the peasants'; it was not until October 1921 that he recognized that 'products exchange' had to turn to freedom of trade and the rest of the NEP package. This, he saw, was to be undertaken 'seriously and for a long time'. He spoke of 'learning to trade', advocated economic accounting, a 'society of civilized cooperators'. But he spoke also of 'retreat', used the Russian equivalent of *reculer pour mieux sauter*, used the parallel of Port Arthur: the initial Japanese assault on the fortress in 1904 was repulsed with heavy losses, but they learned from this and after a long siege the fortress fell.[2] So his successors could base very different policies on the post-1921 sayings of Lenin. And was not Tsipko right when he wrote: 'I will dare to assert that at the end of the twenties . . . Stalin was closer to party activists and the new Soviet intelligentsia than was the Lenin who had spoken of learning to trade and make profits. Vladimir Ilyich at the end of his life did reject the naive faith in pure socialism, thereby gravely disappointing most of the party's theoreticians' (*Nauka i zhizn*, No. 12, 1988). In the same article, Tsipko notes that the Bolsheviks as a whole shared many of Stalin's assumptions, that they failed to see the cost of suppressing all dissidence, 'they did not see the possible consequences of the total power of the party apparatus, a total power which they all sought'. Could *stalinschchina* have been prevented 'without radically changing the system which had arisen in the conditions of civil war, without restoring a legal order'? Clearly it was not enough 'to increase the number of workers in our central committee. . . .' This last point was Lenin's 'solution' to the bureaucratic abuses, clearly no solution. Indeed, a valid point was made by I. Klyamkin: Lenin's notion to include workers in the central committee was motivated 'not by the idea of democracy, as some now assert, but by the notion of unity, with the help of men who would put unity above democracy' (*Novyi mir*, No. 2, 1989). The priority of unity over democracy could be seen in Lenin's proposal to the 10th congress to outlaw factions within the party.

One can attempt a generalization: Stalin's vision of socialism differed widely from Lenin vintage 1919, which still had strong elements of utopian extremism, and from Lenin vintage 1922, though the latter was a contradictory blend of vintages – if a mixed metaphor may be allowed. One element in the blend could be, and was, used by Stalin. Gefter noted this contradiction too, that it took Lenin long, too long, to accept the need for NEP, that while he said that 'out of NEP-Russia will come a socialist Russia' (Lenin, Vol. 45, p. 309), 'We have the right to ask today: was he not wrong, was he still in the grip of utopia? We have the right to ask: was NEP identical with NEP-Russia? Is not here the spoke in the wheel, the contradiction which combined those who were against it, all that were ultimately combined in Stalin?'

One is driven back to the nature of the Bolshevik revolution itself, to the seizure of power in the name of socialist revolution in a backward, predominantly peasant country, to the notion that the preconditions for socialism were to be created *after* the seizure of power, and to the dictatorial (one-party) implications of such a vision. This, I believe, is what Klyamkin had in mind when he wrote of

> the false and ambiguous position in which the party old guard found itself at the conclusion of the civil war. This falsehood and ambiguity rested on the fact that the party majority, of whomsoever composed, was predestined to suppress inner-party democracy. . . . This became clear already in Lenin's time. . . . It became clear that democracy within a mass party without a democratic society cannot be sustained. . . . Finally it became clear that the party cannot survive and rule if there were serious differences of opinion at the top: the split at the top would seep down below, where, in the absence of democratic culture, everything would speedily fall apart . . . and the leadership (*nachalstvo*) would be blamed for failing to keep order. [*Novyi mir*, No. 2, 1989.]

All this is part of the reasons for the rise to power of the man who was placed (by Lenin) at the centre of the party machine. How could 'democracy' limit the power of the party *apparat* when the party knew it was an isolated minority in 'the petty-bourgeois swamp', and its survival in power required discipline and unity. It had been hoped by many that these dilemmas would somehow be resolved by revolutions in more advanced countries, especially in Germany. But such hopes were disappointed.

Stalin, argued some, seized power, overthrew the old Bolsheviks. This was argued (in *Inogo ni dano*) by I. Vinogradov. It was argued at length by O. Latsis in *Znamya*, No. 6, 1988. Latsis saw in Stalinism a drastic break with the earlier traditions of Leninism, and this was facilitated by the dilution of the party by large numbers of recruits of limited intelligence and of petty-bourgeois mentality. Trotsky also spoke of 'Thermidor', imagined an unholy alliance of bureaucrats, Nepmen and kulaks, and in a tragicomic misunderstanding saw the main danger as coming from Bukharin, while Stalin was a vacillating 'centrist'.

All such notions were vigorously (and in my view rightly) attacked by

Tsipko. Explaining his position in *Nedelya* (No. 11, 1989), he sarcastically referred to interpretations of thirty years ago (i.e. during Krushchevian destalinization): 'Everything was alright, the road taken was quite correct, but then came a bad man and distorted everything. Stalin was allegedly a product of petty-bourgeois reaction to October.' Nonsense, he asserts in his *Nauka i zhizn'* articles (the passage to be cited is in No. 11, 1988): no, he says, there was no counter-revolutionary coup or any sort of 'Thermidor' in or around 1929. The supposed petty-bourgeois nature of new recruits to the party is quite irrelevant. All these are ways of avoiding 'the question of doctrinal reasons for our failures in the building of socialism, of the responsibility of the party intelligentsia and the working class for Stalinism'. It is from Marx that they took the notion of 'overcoming small-scale private agricultural production, turning the peasant into a farm labourer', grain factories, 'pure non-market socialism based wholly upon nationalised property'. If what happened after 1929, if what Stalin did, had no connection with Marxism, 'then we have no right to consider Marxism in the light of our socialist history'. Yet in the world communist movement 'the command model of socialism, total socialization of the means of production, is seen as most adequately expressing the essence of scientific socialism'. Of course it is tempting to remove Stalin from the history of Marxist socialism, thereby preserving 'the purity of theory'. It is understandable 'that it is difficult to reconcile oneself with the fact that the failures of the movement, with which all our lives were linked, lie in the movement itself, its own miscalculations and failures'. One prefers to believe that enemies were to blame or some sort of external and accidental factors, or (here he quotes A. Butenko) to assert that Stalin and his colleagues 'usurped power in a bonapartist way', and so on. This helps us not to think 'about the revolution itself, its own internal objective contradictions, of the internal contradictions of left-wing radicalism, of the dialectic of revolutionary coercion, etc.' He went on: 'the deep contradictions of the task begun by us in 1917 have still not become the subject of thoughtful and responsible analysis'.

Tsipko then links all this with today. 'The whole complexity of the contemporary situation lies in the fact that in the works and slogans of our conservatives it is hard to see any inconsistency with the usual standard conceptions about Marxism, and indeed with the texts of Marx himself.' Stalin too was always careful to cite the classics. 'Were he unable to find Marxist ideas on which to base the expropriation of the village, he would hardly have obtained the support of the party.' When he attacked the right deviation in April 1929, 'he based himself on the Marxist view of the peasantry as the last capitalist class. . . . We have no right to forget that Stalin as well as Trotsky based on Marxism their conviction as to the need for finally overcoming small-scale commodity production.' It is essential to ask: 'What in Marx's theories has been confirmed and should be followed? Which of their teachings were applicable only for their time, in the nineteenth century? And what did Marx and Engels get wrong? . . . They considered themselves to be scientists. It is we who turned them into prophets.' He added: 'The old certainty that everything written by Marx is the final truth would hardly be useful today. Imagine what would happen to our country if we try yet again, for the third time (after war-communism and Stalin's anti-market offensive) to base our economy on Marx's model, i.e. on direct products-exchange and total directive planning from above.'

In his fourth article (*Nauka i zhizn'*, No. 2, 1989) he was even bolder and began thus:

> Stalinism is above all the tragedy of the Bolshevik old guard, its pain, and its historic guilt. It is this old guard that created that political mechanism, a weapon of absolute power, which Stalin utilized for his egoistical purposes. . . . After all it was precisely the old guard which already during Lenin's lifetime voluntarily handed over to Stalin the vast power created by the revolution. And then, after 1924, it was the old guard with its leftist impatience which pushed the country towards leaps which turned into a national tragedy.

An analysis of causes and experience requires a study of the nature of left-wing radicalism, beginning with 'the principles of organization of the Party, its beliefs and rules'. He stresses again the responsibility of the left-wing intelligentsia. The peasants had quite other aims, and indeed 'the attitudes and expectations of the vast majority of the working class were not as "red" as is customarily assumed'. Finally: 'why, when it is clear to all where the roots of Stalinism are to be sought, many avoid serious discussion on this theme? I think because the wave of renewal, which has brought to the surface the evil figure of Stalin, touches our basic beliefs (*svyatyniami*): October, socialism, Marxism.'

One can imagine Tsipko's opponents countering: even if the actions and ideas of the old Bolshevik guard were helpful in Stalin's rise to power, even if he did cite marxist-leninist scripture for his own ends, surely it was no coincidence that he had to kill nearly all Lenin's comrades? His terror (*pace* Solzhenitsyn) was on a quite different scale, had quite different purposes, was not linked with civil-war emergencies.

The debate continues. Its very nature excludes firm conclusions. There was a link between Stalinism and some elements of the ideas of Marx and of the practice of Lenin. Though perhaps more important still were the circumstances of revolution and civil war, the low educational level of party cadres, the logic of a one-party state, the logic too of revolution from above, or 'permanent revolution', to use Trotsky's phrase.

Trotsky: Reality and Legend

Where are we to put Trotsky? How can we evaluate his activities, his interpretation of history? Was there a 'Trotskyist alternative'?

Trotsky's 'class' analysis led him astray in his assessment of Stalin. That and his evident contempt for Stalin's type of mind. As already mentioned, Trotsky tried to fit his enemies into marxist class categories, and saw a 'Right' danger stemming from Bukharin. Of course he saw the bureaucratization of the Party, but even as late as the 13th congress (1924) was warning about 'too much' democracy, which might let in non-proletarian, petty-bourgeois elements. He, like the others, believed in the necessity of preserving party unity, and so chose to deny the very existence of Lenin's testament. Later, when already defeated, he saw virtue in democracy within the party, but his own actions when he was 'the prophet armed' gave a very different impression. In a pamphlet criticizing Kautsky he made an eloquent defence of revolutionary terrorism (not foreseeing the visitor who would come to see him eleven years later, with an icepick under his raincoat). He had no compunction in supporting the killing of hostages, or of the Tsar's children. He not only pressed for labour militarization because of the chaos of the time (in this he was backed by Lenin), but devised a whole theory of forced labour: 'man is by nature a lazy animal', and he/she must be compelled to work where the 'proletarian state' orders, and be punished, as a soldier would be, for desertion. This, he insisted, would last throughout the transition period, until men and women under socialism did what was needed out of a sense of duty. Some Soviet writers, for instance the novelist F. Belov, argued that Trotsky was thus the spiritual father of Stalin's later excesses. This, as was pointed out by I. Klyamkin (*Novyi mir*, No. 11, 1987), was totally unfair: Trotsky's ideas dated from 1920, were largely shared even by Lenin (though he thought Trotsky ultimately went too far, especially in wishing to militarize trade unions), and were also repeated and developed by Bukharin in his *Economics of the Transition Period*, with its attacks on 'so-called freedom of labour'. None the less, Trotsky did go very far, perhaps further than most other Bolsheviks of his time, in intellectual justification of both terror and forced labour, though like most of the others he took up much less militant positions on these matters after 1921.

His political ideas also were all too consistent with the concentration of power at the top, to change society from above by coercive means. Here are two quotations. Note how the second of them anticipates by a decade Stalin's much-criticized doctrine to the effect that class war and state power increase in intensity as one moves towards socialism.

The 'workers' opposition' puts forward dangerous slogans which fetishize the principles of democracy. Elections from within the working class, were put above the party, as if the party had no right to defend its dictatorship, even when this dictatorship was temporarily at odds with (*stalkivalas'*) the passing feelings of workers' democracy. . . . It is essential to have a sense of – so to speak – the revolutionary-historical primacy (*pervorodstvo*) of the party, which is obliged to hold on to its dictatorship despite the temporary waverings of the masses . . . and even of the workers.[3]

The road to socialism lies through the highest concentration of state-power (*gosudarstvennosti*). Like a light-bulb which, before extinguishing itself, flashes brightly, so the state, prior to its disappearance, takes the form of the dictatorship of the proletariat, i.e. of the most pitiless state, which coercively (*povelitel'no*) controls the life of citizens in all its aspects.[4]

Over and over again, when he was 'the prophet armed' Trotsky used arguments to justify extreme totalitarianism, and indeed also terror.

But there is a Soviet myth about Trotsky's subsequent behaviour. Thus even in the admirable symposium *Inogo ne dano*, V. Sirotkin claims that there was a clash between the 'supporters of "war communism" led by L. D. Trotsky and the supporters of NEP headed by N. I. Bukharin'. It is also argued that Trotsky and Preobrazhensky advocated 'robbing the peasants to pay for industrialization', that Stalin stole the left opposition's clothes in 1928–30, and thus that Trotsky was somehow responsible even for the horrors of forced collectivization (see for example F. Belov's assertion, in *Pravda*, 15 April 1988, that 'Stalin was the chief Trotskyist').

I have no wish to defend Trotsky, but this is really quite wrong. Trotsky accepted NEP as speedily as had Bukharin, indeed had advocated changes in this direction before Lenin's decision to abandon requisitioning of peasant produce. In his speech to the 12th party congress in 1923 he took a consistently 'Nepist' line, even asserting that the peasant should 'get richer' (*stal bogache*). He did place greater emphasis on the international division of labour, and also on planning, but planning *for the market*. Preobrazhensky did advocate 'unequal exchange' as a means of achieving 'primitive socialist accumulation', but never argued for impoverishing the peasants (he had the notion, as any reader of his *New Economics* can see, that cuts in the inflated costs of state industry be not matched by equivalent cuts in retail prices, and that taxes on the more prosperous be raised. Not a word from him or from Trotsky advocating *forcible* collectivization!).

The 'left opposition' (Trotsky, Zinoviev, Kamenev) did criticize Stalin's and Bukharin's alleged toleration of the *kulaks*, and what they believed to be the insufficiency of industrial investment. Bukharin certainly believed, and said, that their programme would have been inconsistent with the precarious balance which sustained NEP. My own view is that, given the strains to which NEP was already subjected in 1926–7, the 'left opposition' did not have a viable policy. But, firstly, as pointed out by Klyamkin and also by Stephen Cohen, Trotsky remained a 'Nepist', i.e. he wished to modify and not to subvert the basis of NEP, a mixed economy with market-based relations with the peasantry. And if the 'left's' attacks on *kulaks* were inconsistent with a healthy peasant-based agriculture (for who was the *kulak*? A successful peasant!), in 1927 Bukharin too was pressing for measures to restrict and oppose *kulaks*.

In fact the desire to make Trotsky (and also such as Kamenev and Kaganovich[5]) responsible for various horrors is part of a trend to blame the Jews whenever possible. Yet the real villain was also non-Russian, and, but for the well-established anti-semitic tendencies, blame would be attached to such as Dzerzhinsky (Pole), Beria (Georgian), Mikoyan (Armenian), Ordzhonikidze (Georgian), along of course with Dzhugashvili himself.

'Revolutionary Immorality'

By this term I mean variations on the theme, *salus revolutionis, suprema lex*, that ends justify means, that such traditional virtues as truth, justice, conscience, are mere bourgeois prejudices, and, in the present context, that the creation by Bolshevik intellectuals of such an atmosphere helped Stalin's extremist policies or even justified them in his own eyes. Thus if for decades one mocks the notion of 'art for art's sake', then one kills Gumilev, Babel, Meyerhold, Mandelshtam, with less hesitation. If Krylenko, the commissar for justice, could tell a prisoner that he knew he was innocent but that he had to plead guilty because the party's good demanded it,[6] what defence could he offer when he was himself charged with offences he did not commit, a few years later? It is also notable that when this same Krylenko spoke to the 15th party congress (in 1927) about the need to observe Soviet laws, he was heckled by many delegates. This was a measure of the lack of any sense of the need for legal order among party members. If communists were taught to disregard promises made to 'class enemies' whenever it suited them, the same soon became the case within the party itself. If goods and chattels could be confiscated at any time from the 'bourgeoisie', it was not long before they could be confiscated from workers and peasants too.

In his critical remarks in *Nedelya* (No. 11, 1989), Tsipko here too goes back to Marx. Lenin and his comrades

> never for a minute forgot that the [Paris] communards were destroyed by their fear of civil war, that if they were to be beaten, this was due, as Marx warned, to 'conscience' and 'generosity'. . . . Even when, in order to retain power, the leaders of the October revolution had to resort to terror, to instil fear in the class enemy, they derived confidence and strength from Marxist revolutionary theory. Did not Marx warn that 'to shorten, simplify and concentrate the bloodthirsty agony of the old order and the bloody birth-pangs of the new society one needed but one means: revolutionary terrorism.'

So one had Marx's own commitment to revolutionary violence, if only to shorten birth-pangs, his idea that under socialism law (like the state) would be unnecessary, and also the lack of regard for law and legal order so widespread among the Russian intelligentsia of all persuasions (duly stressed in *Vekhi* in respect of the radicals, but notable also in, for example, Tolstoy).

A childhood memory: when I lived in Moscow seventy years or so ago there were many beggars, and I recall being told by my parents that communists would usually refuse to give alms. Along with 'conscience', another word became ideologically unfashionable: *miloserdiye*, 'compassion'. Indeed, it is only within the last two to three years that I recall seeing it in print. Also the 'struggle against religion' was no invention of Stalin, though mass arrests of priests and the forcible closing of churches reached extreme heights (or lengths) in the thirties. Here again, no Bolshevik leader publicly sought to urge moderation.

Solzhenitsyn shows little sympathy with communist victims of Stalin's purges, clearly taking the view that they were also unscrupulous towards their opponents and deserved what they got. Even some Soviet critics took a similar line. Kozhinov cites a number of disagreeable sayings of Bukharin's. Sergei Yakolev, in a review of a book on rehabilitations (*Novyi mir*, No. 6, 1989), cites first from the denunciation of Stalin's crimes by Fedor Raskolnikov, published abroad in 1938: 'Afraid of free elections, as a leap into the unknown, which threatened your personal power, you stamped on the constitution, treating it as a scrap of paper, and turned the elections into a farce. . . .' He then follows it by citing the same Fedor Raskolnikov, this time dated January 1918. 'Today's counter-revolutionary majority in the Constituent Assembly expresses the past of the revolution. . . . We declare that we walk out of the Constituent Assembly, leaving it to the Soviet power to decide what to do with the counter-revolutionary elements in the Assembly. . . .' Similarly, Mikhail Koltsov, a short time before his own arrest, published an article in *Pravda*, entitled 'gang of bloody dogs', these being Rykov, Bukharin and Yagoda, praising the 'wonderful hard Bolshevik' Nikolai Yezhov.

Solzhenitsyn's *Zhit' ne po lzhi* ('Live without lies') is widely known in the USSR and has been published legally. Stalin and falsehood 'belong' together, but where did these habits, which became widespread, originate? In *Novyi mir*, No. 2, 1989, Klyamkin argues that the attempt to create an inherently unrealizable utopia led to a vast gap between 'is' and 'ought', which had to be sustained by lies. While for Stalin, in his view, lying was second nature, such men as Kamenev, Bukharin, Rykov were forced into lies by 'the false and ambiguous position in which the Party found itself at the conclusion of the civil war'. How is it, he asks, that party minorities were called upon not merely to submit to the majority but openly to deny their views? Kamenev protested when such pressures were applied to him, but he and the others had made similar demands when they were in the majority. This was part of the worship of party unity. Stalin always so manoeuvred that he represented the majority, and many who did not particularly like him accepted the majority view because it was the majority view. Lenin, too, had given priority to party unity over democracy. Klyamkin goes on to state that at the 17th party congress 292 delegates dared to cast a secret vote against Stalin, but this 'was the agony of inner-party democracy'. The vote cast against Stalin on that occasion has long been a subject of speculation, and some have denied that it happened at all (among them was Adam Ulam, no 'revisionist' he!). However, it is now accepted and cited by a number of Soviet authors.

The following general point seems valid: the de-moral-ization of the party was not Stalin's doing, but it was helpful to him during and after his rise to power. It helps to explain the behaviour pattern and lack of scruple of his associates in the thirties, whether they were dealing with the peasants, the intellectuals or with each other.

In my own work I have often used a military parallel. Sergeants have everywhere the reputation of bawling at and bullying their subordinates. And recently promoted men of the people often attach great value to their recently acquired privileges. Such considerations help us to understand some of the crude and rude ways of many of those who benefited from the opportunities for rapid upward mobility in the thirties.

Was There an Alternative? Was he Necessary?

This question has also a personal aspect. Volkogonov, in his *Triumph and Tragedy*, expresses the view that Stalin gained much from the fact that the potential alternatives lacked political competence and/or support within the party. Trotsky may or may not be correctly characterized as 'the Demon of the revolution' (the title of an article by the same Volkogonov), but he was well out of the running already in 1923. Zinoviev was a rather offensive loud-mouth of modest intelligence. Kamenev was widely respected as an honest and thoughtful man, but hardly of leadership quality. Bukharin, for all his charm and ability, was not a political heavyweight. Rykov was more of a statesman, but was notoriously given to the bottle (vodka became known as Rykovka). Such other future victims of Stalin as Rakovsky,

Krestinsky, Preobrazhensky, Pyatakov, Tomsky, despite possessing many qualities, could not be seriously considered as top leaders. Their actions during the years of Stalin's rise to power present a sad catalogue of political incompetence. One thinks, for instance, of Zinoviev and Kamenev, their role in defeating the left opposition, which they then joined to be easily defeated in their turn. Or Bukharin's truly amazing blindness, until much too late, concerning the character and policies of his erstwhile ally, Stalin.

However, the main problem concerns policies. Was it necessary to destroy NEP, forcibly collectivize the peasantry, launch hugely overambitious plans for crash-programme industrialization, imposing heavy sacrifices on the people, all this accompanied by a reign of terror? Needless to say, this is not a simple either–or. There were a number of less extreme policies, such as that represented by the first version of the first five-year plan, which during 1929–31 was replaced by ever higher and more unattainable growth targets, which naturally proved to be totally out of reach. It is necessary to remember, as several of the Soviet critics have been pointing out, that the industrialization resolution at the 15th party congress was proposed by Rykov with the full support of Bukharin. It is a legitimate but different question whether even these more modest targets were consistent with the continuance of NEP. In particular, the 'conversion' of Bukharin from '*obogashchaites*' ('get rich', addressed to the peasantry) in 1925 to 'a forceful offensive against the kulak' in 1927 seems to me to underline a fatal inconsistency, not just of Bukharin but of the whole attitude of the party to NEP. How could a successful and energetic peasant, who managed to produce efficiently for sale in the market, not become seen as a kulak, and so as a class enemy, against whom one must launch a forceful offensive? Yet there was a most urgent need for an increase in marketed produce. A poor peasant, by definition, does not produce enough even to support his family. Even a *serednyak*, middle peasant, is a moderately successful or moderately unsuccessful husbandman, with relatively little to sell.

There is a controversy among Soviet scholars, typified by the sharp exchange, in *Istoriya SSSR*, No. 3, 1989, between V. Tikhonov and V. Danilov. The former maintained that there were practically no kulaks in the twenties, there being little hired labour; the real kulaks had nearly all been eliminated in 1918. Danilov disagreed, emphasizing the prevalence of loans of horses, tools, grain, at high rates of interest. The debate continues.

Klyamkin, in *Novyi mir*, No. 11, 1987, comes closest to providing what could be called an anti-stalinist rationale for Stalinism. Despite his evident detestation of the man and what he did, he sees little alternative, given all the circumstances of the time, including external threat and isolation. Yes, Hitler was not a menace when Stalin turned ultra-left. However,

socialism in one country was a slogan of survival, of national defence. It combined the socialist idea with national independence. Yes, I know, I have often heard. It was wrong to eliminate NEP, it was a gigantic error for which we are still paying. . . . Yet once again: could NEP have been preserved? If you answer 'yes', please transfer yourself into that time and explain how you would resolve the problems that arose in the second half of the twenties. . . . Those who won then were the strongest, and only they could have won, and no project capable of competing with collectivization then existed.

In another article, in *Politicheskoye obrazovanie*, No. 10, 1988, he again attacks those who consider that there was an alternative to Stalinism in the situation of 1929; those who believe this 'could think and feel in the spirit of Lenin or Milyukov, Martov or Bukharin, slavophils or the "Vekhi" authors, and yet be unanimous in their belief in the possibility of an alternative. . . .' The minority view stresses the 'objective circumstances and logic of the post-October period, not to be explained by the personal qualities of Stalin and his supporters'. This minority in turn can be divided into two groups: those who see it all in heroic and thus morally justified terms, and those who see it as a tragedy. Klyamkin sees himself in the second of these groups. Events can be *zakonomerny* (following a historical law-like tendency) and none the less be immoral.

Could there have been an effective industrialization policy within the bounds of NEP, i.e. based upon a market-type relationship with an individual peasantry and a mixed economy? A number of Soviet authors give a positive answer to this question and criticize Klyamkin. Others (including such impeccably anti-stalinist authors as Gefter and Yuri Afanasyev) stress, in my view rightly, the basic political and economic contradictions of NEP. Was the bulk of the party prepared to accept the basic logic of NEP, prepared to tolerate the logic and consequences of a market economy when stresses and strains arose, as they did already in 1926? Even then the talented economist Novozhilov was writing of the 'goods famine'. Already in that year a whole number of measures inconsistent with NEP began to be taken. Of course we cannot assert that there was no alternative road that could have been taken. But could it have been taken by the Bolshevik party?

There was a logic within the notion of 'primitive socialist accumulation'. The use of this term, associated with the name of Preobrazhensky, does not imply the acceptance of the view that Stalin's policy was that of the Trotskyist 'left opposition'. I agree with Klyamkin that the 'left' policy was conceived as being within the confines of NEP, that Stalin went much further left in 1929–30. But it can certainly be argued that the requirements of rapid industrialization were inconsistent with a market-based relationship with the peasantry, that speed required economic centralization and coercion. Sacrifices had to be imposed. And then, to cite Klyamkin, 'by what means could one stimulate labour? Economic methods ended with the liquidation of NEP. In their place – orders, fear and enthusiasm'.

Klyamkin's analysis has also been sharply questioned by a number of Soviet critics from the standpoint of the non-conformity of the actions taken to Stalin's own aims (other than the achievement of supreme power by himself, or even including this aim). If collectivization had as its primary object an increase in the size of the surplus derived from agriculture, the damage done was so severe that in the end the surplus so extracted was modest (though writers as different as Ellman and Gordon and Klopov make the point that enough produce was forcibly extracted to maintain the high levels of investment in heavy industry). The imposition of absurdly high growth targets in the early thirties had disruptive effects, imposing quite unnecessary sacrifices and causing much waste (e.g. grain taken from starving peasants was used to buy machines which were smashed by untrained personnel). If engineers were acutely scarce, it was not exactly helpful to launch a campaign against 'bourgeois spetsy' and to arrest large numbers of them. In this last connection the point is sometimes made that ordinary workers regarded engineers with deep suspicion. No doubt this was so, but this is a totally inadequate explanation of the campaign against them; workers were deliberately set against them (the good Russian word for this is '*nauskivanie*'). A similar point will be made about the kulaks in a moment. And the terror clearly did a great deal of economic damage, and its scale surely went far beyond the practical requirements for the consolidation of Stalin's despotic power.

I had already attempted to discuss this theme in my 1961 article

('Was Stalin Really Necessary') by trying to distinguish between the rationality of a strategy, and specific acts and policies which were not as such necessary, even within this strategy. I also tried to coin the term 'excessive excesses'. By this I meant that certain strategies or methods are inherently associated with excesses, but these could go too far. To take a seventeenth-century example, the armies of the time made a practice of sacking and looting towns, but the massacre at Magdeburg could be seen as an excessive excess even by such standards. To return to the Stalin era, it would be reasonable to see a rational purpose in the deliberate fomenting of a sense of external and internal danger, to mobilize the people and to impose discipline and sacrifices upon them. There was a logic, too, in the creation and strengthening of what Gavriil Popov has called 'the sub-system of fear', and also in the imposition of compulsory delivery quotas on the peasants. But it is an impermissible logical leap to derive from this any sort of justification or rationality for the killing of millions of peasants in 1930–3, or the Great Terror. In other words, surely we must accept that there were alternatives even within the strategy which Stalin and the majority of the party had adopted in 1929. Indeed this may help to explain why the large majority of those who had supported Stalin in that year perished in the thirties. (I recall my late colleague Rudolf Schlesinger saying: 'It was not necessary to kill Bukharin, even though he was wrong. He could have been sent to teach in school in Omsk!' A fortiori this applies to the future victims within the Stalin faction.)

Before proceeding to discuss the number of victims, here is one quotation, from the well-known writer Fedor Abramov, from notes he wrote in 1973, published in *Novyi mir*, No. 5, 1989. Citing an estimate that, in all, some 20 million persons passed through Stalin's camps, and nine-tenths perished, he wrote: '20 millions, that is inaccurate. People are not counted in Russia. Pigs, horses, cubic metres of timber, yes, but not people.' He went on:

> Were there kulaks in Soviet times? No, how could there be? Were there really bloodsuckers who robbed the poor and the landless while the Soviet authorities stood aside? Hardly likely. . . . They dekulakized the most energetic, the most enterprising peasants. He built a grinding mill, a smokehouse, acquired a butter churn – then he is an enemy. Anyone showing initiative is an enemy, initiative in work, or in thought; how many were arrested for speaking. The desirable kind of citizen was seen as a lazy good-for-nothing. Economically effective peasants were extirpated, and

lumpen-proletarians were appointed to run agriculture. It all went wrong. We were left without bread. Millions died of hunger.

The point of the quotation is not the statistics, which can only be a rough guess and on which we will have more to say in a moment. It is to raise the question of sources. Getty, and some of the other 'revisionists', tend to pooh-pooh literary sources, as well as evidence from dissidents and émigrés, contrasting them with archives and documents. Probably we would all agree that one must treat all evidence with caution. But surely this applies also to archival materials and contemporary official reports. Why should we assume that local officials reported truthfully to their superiors, when they knew what it was that their superiors wished to hear? And at the centre they were not above statistical falsification, for example, as we shall shortly see, of demographic data. Thurston has asserted that 'general fear did not exist in the USSR' in the late thirties. The statements to the contrary by poets such as Akhmatova and Tvardovsky, plus a long list of memoirists of the most varied backgrounds and opinions, cut no ice with him. Extraordinary! Though doubtless fear was more intense among party officials and army officers, say, than among rank-and-file workers and soldiers, and, *pace* Akhmatova's 'Requiem', even the living occasionally smiled or even laughed, kicked a football, pursued girls and filled theatres.

The Scale of the Purges

Back to statistics. How many died? Here there are many statistical pitfalls, and I agree with Getty and others that some of the estimates made, in and out of Russia, are too high. It is also important to define what it is that one is measuring. The demographic data on the thirties is still somewhat fragmentary, but necessarily includes not only peasant deaths due to famine and deportations, but also a fall in the birth rate, and the victims of the terror, i.e. those who were shot or died in the camps and prisons. Then there is the question of the credibility of the published results of the 1939 census. And of course there follow the war and postwar years, with more deaths in Gulag, and some from hunger too. There is still an argument going on about the scale of war losses. One must also bear in mind that alongside those sent to Gulag were large numbers of so-called *spetspereselentsy*, deported or exiled, in conditions that varied from dreadful to tolerable, a category which included many alleged kulaks, but also such intellectuals as Ariadna

Efron, Tsvetayena's daughter (her correspondence with Pasternak was published in *Novyi mir*).

In the absence of any hard data, estimates of the number of victims varied widely, in and out of the Soviet Union. Some were plainly too high: thus such figures as '40 million' do not fit any of the demographic data and leave too few to serve (and die) in the war (though I have spoken to Soviet anti-stalinists who include war losses in the list of Stalin's victims, on the grounds of his dreadful misjudgement of events in June 1941; it is also possible to argue that, had he not killed so many senior officers in 1937–9, Hitler might not have attacked in 1941).

In the most recent years a great deal more evidence has come to light, as both Soviet and western scholars gain access to archives. The long-suppressed 1937 census data have been published, plus hitherto secret information relating to the 1939 census. Much more information has become available also on the death rates in the famine years, and Kazakh historians have published a devastating account of the tragic losses that accompanied collectivization, worse even than the catastrophe that befell the peasantry in the Ukraine, the North Caucasus and the Lower Volga. I have tried to set out the detailed evidence elsewhere.[7] There are interesting instances of falsehoods in the actual archive materials. Thus in his pioneering recomputation of surplus deaths in the 1930s, V. Tsaplin (in *Voprosy istorii*, No. 4, 1989) cites an unpublished contemporary report to the effect that 2 million (mostly Kazakhs) had 'fled' from the Soviet Union. Clearly its author did not dare admit that most of them had died.

After making some allowance for the overstatement of the population in the 1939 census, surplus deaths in the decade of the thirties would seem to be of the order of 10–11 million, the large majority of them being peasants. To these one must add the high wartime death-rate in Gulag, and those who did not survive the deportations (of Crimean Tartars, Kalmucks, Chechen-Ingush, etc., and also from the Baltic republics and the western Ukraine) carried out in 1944–6.

Figures have also been published of the total numbers arrested and executed for 'counter-revolutionary offences', i.e. under article 58 of the criminal code (3.78 million in the years 1931–53, of which 786,000 were shot, according to *Moskovskie novosti*, 4 March 1990). But plainly many were shot without having been charged under article 58, in mass executions at Kuropaty and elsewhere (not to mention the Polish officers). As for the numbers 'repressed', archival data for 1939 show

3.6 million in the 'care' of the NKVD, plus an unknown number of exiles not behind wire. For the postwar years we have figures from Zemskov (*Argumenty i fakty*, No. 35, 1990): citing archives, for 1950 he found there were over 2.8 million in labour camps and prisons, and nearly 2.7 million in exile, giving a total of 5.5 million (note that the 1939 figure of 3.6 million excluded many exiles).

Though significantly below the highest estimates of deaths and of prisoners, in my view the figures cited above will prove not too wide of the mark, though we certainly need more information. Surely such totals are grim, by any standards. Thus they are consistent with deaths directly and indirectly due to the famine of between 6 and 7 million peasants in the first half of the thirties. Stalin had much, very much, to answer for.

Most of the deaths in the thirties were of peasantry. How many perished in the purges? Here again there is wide disagreement about numbers. Gabor Rittersporn, for example, cannot get beyond the low hundred thousands. Others, referring to the party purge, point out (correctly) that in the year 1937 only 100,000 were expelled, which in fact was much less than in some previous years. Though, of course, one can arrest and shoot individuals who had been expelled from the party earlier. It is, of course, possible that the special notoriety of the years 1933–8 was due to the fact that the victims were mainly officials, officers, intellectuals. Some Soviet critics, for example Kozhinov, point out that the peasant victims of the previous years greatly outnumbered the number of purge victims, which may well be true.

Getty's book on the origins of the great purge seems to be 'guilty' of over-concentration on the Smolensk archives. No one doubts their value if one is trying to see the impact and purposes of the terror insofar as it related to the provincial party bureaucracy. One would have no difficulty in accepting the view that Moscow's control had been far from complete.

But is this not something of a worm's eye view? The purge swept up so many others, both at the centre and at the periphery. Commissars, planners, engineers, designers, theatre directors, diplomats, intelligence officers, the army, the navy, poets, journalists, the leadership in all the national republics, much of the Comintern, not to mention wives, relatives of 'enemies of the people', plus an unknown number of ordinary folk. Surely one is unlikely to illuminate the causes of so vast a bloodletting by a meticulous examination of the party archives of a minor province? No doubt there were rivalries and conflicts within the apparatus, and it is certainly useful to try to examine the relationships between elements of the apparatus and segments of society. But how can one avoid the conclusion that it was Stalin's decision to purge the party and society of what he regarded as suspect and unstable elements – even if one can accept that orders might have been distorted by their executants? One is struck by the number of references to arrest plans, which zealous locals sought to fulfil or overfulfil. However, the whole process was set in motion from the top, and we do have the known telegram sent by Stalin and Zhdanov demanding the appointment of Yezhov to replace the apparently too lenient Yagoda. Some recent statistics reflect the more vigorous activity of the NKVD under Yezhov. According to G.Kumanev (*Pravda*, 22 June 1989), political shootings by the orders of troikas, special councils (*osobykh soveshchanii* of the NKVD) and military tribunals were as follows:

in 1936: 1,118
in 1937: 353,074

The author adds: 'These figures seem too low, as they do not include those disposed of without any judgement or investigation, or those who died during deportation, of hunger, sufferings, sickness or torture during interrogations.' Many sources indicate that the use of torture was specifically authorized, indeed urged, by Stalin. It must be stressed that this in no way resembled what the last tsars did to their revolutionary opponents, as Stalin well knew. It is a throwback to Maliuta Skuratov, Ivan's chief torturer.

The same source goes on:

According to archival evidence, just between 27 February 1937 and 12 November 1938 the NKVD received from Stalin, Molotov and Kaganovich authorizations to shoot 38,679 military personnel. If we add to this over three thousand naval commanders, plus the fact that some were shot before and after the above dates, then the number of serving commanders alone must approach 50,000, and the total of those repressed in the army and navy undoubtedly exceeds even this number.

Stalin's personal responsibility is attested by much evidence. But in any case there is indirect proof in the fact that, from the time of his death, mass arrests ceased and so did 'political' executions, with the exception of Beria and his gang.

Of course there were mass denunciations from below. Kumanev, for example, speaks of 'mass repressions which engendered in society an atmosphere of total suspicion, extreme distrust, spy-mania. . . .' He cites a report written by General Voronov in 1940: 'In the Army there is such an atmosphere that a commander cannot act with confidence: any of his subordinates can for any reason make trouble concerning any of his measures through party, komsomol or special organs, or go to complain to the political officer or commissar. . . .' The same was doubtless happening among civilian institutions. As in Mao's cultural revolution, the lower ranks were encouraged to open fire on the staffs. Some did so out of sincere beliefs, others out of fear of the consequences of not showing sufficient 'vigilance', still others out of careerist considerations, or out of a desire to acquire the victim's housing space or girlfriend. It seems very far-fetched to regard this as a period of glasnost'. This might seem to be the equivalent of taking the so-called Stalin constitution of 1936 seriously.

This said, it is essential to recognize that a significant portion of the public did approve of Stalin. The fact that a large number of unpopular high officials were shot seems to have been a source of pleasure, especially to those predisposed to believe that the tsar does not know of the evil acts of his ministers and satraps. Otto Latsis, bitter critic of Stalin though he is, considers it quite wrong 'to regard the cult of Stalin as merely the result of terror and fear. . . . It drew its strength from the proletarian revolution. . . .' There was 'a favourable soil for the growth of the cult in the consciousness of an immature working class and of the youth generally. . . . Among the people, there was both hatred and reverence for the Leader and Teacher. . . . In real life there was both.'

The Revisionists and the Social Dimension

Sheila Fitzpatrick, in her 'New perspectives on stalinism' (p. 359), alleged that 'social processes unrelated to state intervention are virtually absent from the literature'. The implication is that the bulk of the authors of the period presented an image of an all-powerful state doing what it pleased with a passive society. Of course she does not deny that the state, and indeed Stalin, were extremely powerful. But society existed, and influenced decision-making, albeit passively. The thirties saw profound social changes, very substantial vertical mobility, worth studying as such, as are the conflicts among and within various strata.

She attributes to some unnamed thinkers the view that 'society is irrelevant to an understanding of stalinist political processes'. This surely is going too far. Even those who believe that Stalin was making war on society thereby consider it relevant: in a war, the enemy is not irrelevant to one's strategy!

In any case, were social processes ignored? They were present in early work by Dobb and Jack Miller, they figured prominently in that of Moshe Lewin, R. W. Davies, my own 'Economic history' is full of them. Needless to say, there is ample scope for more detailed work on the situation and attitudes of various strata during the Stalin years. Also it is clear that many of Stalin's policies were explicable by the emergence of real problems, of resistances by and in society. Thus excessive labour mobility in the first half of the thirties gave rise to a series of laws restricting freedom of movement. A falling birth rate (plus excessive deaths) led to the adoption of a law forbidding abortion. Poor labour productivity led to the initiation of and support for the Stakhanov movement, which has been the subject of some valuable research. One notes with approval some Soviet work, for instance in novels by Alexander Bek and by Fedor Belov, about the emergence of certain types of people as leaders in industry and in the villages in the thirties. Their presence and their nature had some influence on the course of events, for it is they that 'translated' orders from above into action or inaction on the ground. Even one who is totally slavish towards authority can affect the course of history. Thus good Soviet sources tell that the head of Soviet military intelligence in 1941, General Golikov, knowing what his boss wanted to hear, informed Stalin that the evidence concerning the imminent German attack was not to be believed.

One imagines that some of the policies actually adopted in the thirties were genuinely popular. I have in mind what could be called the cultural counter-revolution of those years: traditional schooling, the suppression of modern art, the rewriting of history along traditional lines, the elimination of literary and other zealots. All this reflected not only Stalin's taste and preferences. Bureaucrats, and ordinary folk, are usually much more conservative than is the radical intelligentsia.

Millions of people in the 1930s really did believe that they were building a new world, that they were besieged by internal and external enemies, that Stalin was their one and only leader. Many of the new men who rose in the thirties took a very active role in disposing of the older political leadership and of those in technical, managerial and academic positions who were blocking their promotion. As for ordinary workers and peasants, no doubt they used such opportunities as could be devised to avoid or evade whatever could be avoided or evaded. Hence the attempt to impose increasingly strict regulations.

While of course Stalin could not take all decisions himself, and had to rely on information, proposals and suggestions from subordinates, all the evidence points to an astonishing degree of personal dominance, in any matters to which he desired to give attention. These extend from arrest lists to the thickness of tanks' armour-plating, but also to 'Stalin' prizes in literature – he actually read the books! (Simonov's memoirs are informative on this point.) As for the influence of even such important satraps as Molotov and Zhdanov, the following extract from the memoirs of Admiral Kuznetsov, published in *Pravda* of 29 July 1988 is very much to the point:

> . . . Molotov was his closest assistant. A careful man, he took many decisions, but most matters of importance he always referred to Stalin. He and Zhdanov were appointed to supervize the Navy, and in some degree they did help me to decide, but most often they suggested that I write to comrade Stalin. The 'supervisors' even refused to 'push' (*protalkivat'*) such questions without knowing how the 'Boss' would react. . . . They sometimes promised to support me, but in Stalin's office would change their minds having determined which way the wind blows.

Collectivization and the Famine

There are several controversies. One, which I have dealt with elsewhere and which has only partial relevance in the present context, relates to the contribution, if any, of collectivization to capital accumulation in the thirties. I will confine myself to making two obvious points. One is that no one doubts that the motive (or the principal motive) of collectivization was to mobilize a larger agricultural surplus. The other is that the (obviously unplanned and unexpected) heavy losses which followed collectivization reduced the expected 'take'. The questions to be further examined here are: firstly, those connected with peasant attitudes and the degree of coercion, and, secondly, the scale of human losses. On both these points I have disagreements with some at least of the American 'revisionists', such as Roberta Manning and Lynn Viola.

Earlier the question was already raised: were there real 'kulaks', i.e.

genuine exploiters, in the villages, or were the bulk of those so considered simply successful and hard-working peasants? Related to this is another question: how much support was there from the poorer peasants for collectivization and the liquidation of the kulaks? Klyamkin, in several of his works, stressed the pre-bourgeois, patriarchal, communal traditions of the majority of the Russian peasantry, their negative attitudes to those among them who were successful. In his article in *Politicheskoye obrazovanie* he speaks of the emergence, in the place of 'communal collectivism', of a sort of non-bourgeois individualism, shedding obligations to others but without ambitions of personal betterment through enterprise. Gordon and Klopov (in their book *Chto eto bylo*) noted there was some support for collectivization from among the village poor, and went on to stress how

> the process of differentiation of the peasantry, which determined the nature of the poor in the twenties, . . . took place under Soviet power and free land utilization. In this situation differentiation meant that among the poor there was a high proportion of weak, incompetent or simply irresponsible persons. In the 10–15 years since the revolution the mass of more or less capable peasants had succeeded to at the least the status of a serednyak.

Some of the poor, jealous of their more successful fellow-villagers, and aware that they were being offered the chance to grab for themselves a part of the property of those that could be labelled kulaks, could well have gone along with dekulakization and joined collectives of their own free will. We also know of cases, notably in the Kuban and on the Don, where whole villages were deported. There is plenty of evidence from all over the country of pressure, threats, of deportations as '*podkulachniki*' (sub-kulaks?) of peasants who simply refused to join kolkhozy. In such circumstances it is surely not possible to identify the proportion of genuine volunteers, with or without the help of local archives. The point is sometimes made that there were few peasant revolts, but this is surely a far-fetched argument. There was no chance even to begin to mount in 1930 anything resembling Antonov's Tambov rising of 1921.

A whole number of Soviet sources assert, with reason, that deportations affected far more than the 'kulaks' on any definition of that word. Danilov (in *Pravda*, 16 September 1988) considers that a total of 1.1 million households were liquidated in the process of dekulakization, which together with families could be 7–8 million persons.

All sources agree that the fate of the so-called kulaks varied widely.

Some died in unheated cattle-trucks or of hardships in remote areas to which they were deported. Others were able to get jobs on construction sites. Only a minority were sent to prison or labour-camp. However, there were also many victims of the notorious 1932 decree which punished very severely any pilfering of kolkhoz grain or other foodstuffs.

Not even Stalin doubts that there were excesses of coercion during collectivization, since he said so himself in his 'Dizzy with success' speech. Consideration of this document at once raises problems. Was it, as I and many others believe, an example of Stalin's incredible barefaced effrontery? Junior executants were being blamed for carrying out orders. Surely Stalin knew perfectly well that full-scale collectivization was unthinkable without coercion. Yes, warnings against excesses were issued. But, in one case in the same document, local cadres were told not to use force, but to 'put themselves at the head of the spontaneous [*stikhiinyi*] growth of collectivization'. How could they lead a non-existent spontaneous movement? In the atmosphere of the time, as was noted by Ivnitsky, citing a contemporary report, 'excesses are to a considerable extent to be explained by the fact that regional and local organizations, fearful of being accused of right-wing deviation, preferred to overdo rather than underdo (*peregnut' chem nedognut'*).'

No one supposes that Stalin personally knew about any specific act of brutality. Local officials might declare specific individuals to be kulaks subject to deportation because of personal grudges, or of a desire to acquire a given peasant's house or wife. However, Vyltsan found solid evidence to the effect that commissar Yakovlev did try to allow the peasant family within the kolkhoz to retain small tools, small livestock, milch cows, and that it was due to Stalin's intervention that this did not figure in the decree of 5 January 1930. It is true that some years later Stalin favoured allowing the peasant household to cultivate an allotment and to keep a limited number of private animals. This was a necessary consequence of imposing on the farms high delivery quotas at very low prices. This fact was interpreted by Hough as showing that Stalin entered into negotiations with the peasants. Negotiations? By the mid thirties cows ceased to die of hunger, their numbers rose, in contrast with the situation through 1933. Did this mean that Stalin had entered into negotiations with the cows? Or might it not be better to see him making a necessary compromise with reality? Surely one does not have to be a 'revisionist' to recognize that policies in those years were affected by really *existing social and economic circumstances*?

On the famine there are two questions for us: Stalin's responsibility, and the numbers involved. On the first of these the evidence really is overwhelming. He knew. Zelenin cited archives, according to which Stalin said at a politburo meeting on 27 November 1932 that certain groups of kolkhozy and peasants had to be dealt 'a devastating blow'. Orders for ruthless enforcement of high procurement quotas came from Moscow. Signals about excess procurements and about hunger were deliberately disregarded, or disbelieved. On all this there is no difference between Conquest and a growing number of Soviet sources. It was a crime of unique dimensions against one's own fellow-citizens. Moscow imposed a news blackout, allowed or took no relief measures.

The severe damage done to agriculture was used to justify further systematic measures to force farms to deliver produce. Livestock losses were immense. Some of the 'revisionists' have played down the scale of coercion and human losses. Recently published information does indicate that Conquest's estimate of kulak deaths was too high. However, his figures on the famine stand up well: hunger and its consequences carried off up to 7 millions, in the Ukraine, Kazakhstan, the lower volga, the north Caucasus. Though I would question Conquest's interpretation of Stalin's motives: he starved to death those whom he believed to be recalcitrant peasants, many of whom were Ukrainian, rather than relcalcitrant Ukrainians, many of whom were peasants. But this in no way diminishes the scale of tragedy.

It is one thing to say that rapid industrialization involved an element of coercion in the villages. But quite another to assert the necessity of losses and brutalities on such a scale.

My conclusions about the stalinist system as a whole appear on pp. 204–6 below.

Notes

1 *Stalinism*, ed. Tucker (New York, 1977), p. 283.
2 See Lenin, *Sochineniya*, Vol. 4, pp. 195–6.
3 *The Challenge of the Left Opposition, 1923–25* (New York, 1975).
4 *Sochineniya*, Vol. 12 (Moscow, 1925).
5 These three were blamed for collectivization by another writer, Mozhayev, in the postface to his novel *Muzhiki i baby* (see *Don*, No. 3, 1987).
6 The episode is described in R. Medvedev's *Let History Judge*.
7 See, for instance, *Soviet Studies*, Nos. 2 and 4, 1990.

CHAPTER 2

Economic Aspects of Stalinism

R. W. Davies

This chapter discusses the nature of the Soviet economic system during the period of Stalin's personal rule, roughly from the breakdown of the New Economic Policy at the end of the 1920s to his death in 1953. In common with many other students of Soviet affairs, I take the view that the main features of the economic system established under Stalin, apart from his personal despotism and the brutal repressions associated with it, continued until it began to break down in 1987. I therefore seek to place the 'Stalinist' economic system in this wider context.

The main argument of this chapter is that this system cannot be described simply as what Gorbachev called an 'administrative-command system'. Economic and social pressures did not overturn the command economy as originally envisaged, but they did result in its considerable modification.

The Economic System of the 1930s: A Command Economy?

In 1929, the 'year of the great breakthrough', NEP was swept aside by the 'socialist offensive along the whole front'; and at the December 1930 plenum of the party central committee, 1931 was characterized as the year in which 'the construction of the foundations [*fundament*] of socialism' must be completed.[1]

What was the socialist economic system envisaged in the Soviet Union when Stalin and his supporters embarked on this precipitate change? First and foremost, it was a system in which all means of production were socialized, in agriculture as well as in industry.

Capitalist relations of production would be eliminated, bringing the exploitation of one human being by another to an end. Hiring of labour by individuals, even on a small scale, and the sale of goods by individuals, were seen as incompatible with socialism. So much is familiar ground, as is the proposition that under socialism (as distinct from the higher stage of communism) the social product would be distributed unequally on the basis of the quantity and quality of work. It is perhaps less generally realized that throughout the 1920s all Soviet Marxists agreed that socialism would involve the complete replacement of trade, the market and the money economy by direct planning and product exchange.

These principles of socialism did not formally contradict the concepts of classical Marxism. But Marx and Engels also saw socialism as a new form of social relations: 'society', wrote Engels, would 'reorganise production on the basis of a free and equal association of producers'. In 1914 Lenin quoted Engels' forecast with approval.[2] But during the Civil War this vision of socialism had already been undermined in the Soviet Union – or postponed to an indefinite future – by the stress on central planning by the state and on one-man management in state enterprises. In Lenin's time the view was still prevalent that the establishment of socialism would involve the withering away of the state. But after his death the withering away of the state was postponed to a remote future. In November 1928 Stalin argued that in Soviet conditions, in which the economy lagged far behind that of the capitalist states, 'we must use the dictatorship of the proletariat . . . in order to catch up and *overtake* the advanced capitalist countries *economically*'.[3] Then at the 16th Party Congress in June 1930 he announced that 'the higher development of state power in order to prepare the conditions *for* the withering away of state power – this is the Marxist formula.'[4]

The incorporation of a powerful state as a crucial feature in the design for socialism reinforced the argument advanced by many Marxist economists that an all-embracing centralized plan would be required not only for the construction of socialism in a single relatively backward country but also for the further transition to communism. Planning was universally seen by the Bolsheviks as the antithesis to the anarchy of the capitalist market, and its validity was demonstrated when the whole capitalist world began to suffer economic crisis and mass unemployment on an unprecedented scale in 1929–30. Addressing Gosplan (State

Planning Commission) specialists in December 1929, the senior party economic official Grin'ko proclaimed:

> We need to organise a social and political mechanism with which 150 million people will act, guided by a single plan, a single concept, a single will, a single effort to accomplish what is laid down by the plan.[5]

By this time the supporters of the 'great breakthrough' generally assumed that in the near future the socialist moneyless economy would be fully established, and product-exchange would replace trade. In December 1929, Krzhizhanovsky, chairman of Gosplan, drew attention to the declining role of monetary as against physical planning in the control figures for 1929–30. Many party economists believed at this time that money would soon be eliminated.[6] In February 1930 a government decree called for the 'gradual transition from the general planning of commodity turnover to planned socialist product-exchange'.[7] In June Stalin looked forward somewhat more cautiously to the abolition of the NEP, which would eliminate 'commodity turnover and the money economy'.[8] Unlike some of his enthusiastic associates, however, Stalin always seems to have taken the view that the currency should be kept stable until the time came to replace it.

In the socialist economy, the state and its unified plan would be responsible for directing all the resources of the country, including labour. '*The words "labour exchange" and "labour market" should be finally driven out of our vocabulary*,' the deputy commissar for labour told an all-Union conference in November 1930.[9]

Crucial features of this scheme for a socialist economic system remained intact during the storms and crises which followed in the early 1930s. In the system which actually emerged in 1930–4, public ownership – primarily state ownership – was predominant. Both the hire of labour by individuals and the re-sale of goods for profit were regarded as incompatible with socialism, and banned by law. The economy was managed from the centre primarily by plans in physical terms, by budgets in kind (material balances) and a priorities system. This was in major respects the 'administrative-command system of party-state management of the country' described by Gorbachev in November 1987, the Administrative System of Gavriil Popov:

> The basis of the system is the centralisation of decisions and the punctual, undeviating, over-riding fulfilment of directives from Above and particularly from Stalin – the Boss.

> This is a system of specific and detailed management in kind [*in natura*]. It is a system of continuous operational management of the course of production from the centre.[10]

Thus far the Stalinist economic system as we have described it closely resembles the Western model of 'planning under a dictator', later renamed the 'command economy', and also fits in with the Western 'totalitarian model' of the Soviet regime.

However, this is an incomplete description. In several important respects the Stalinist and post-Stalinist economic system departed from the 'command' or 'administrative' model. These modifications are no more than superficially acknowledged in the Western 'command economy' and 'totalitarian' models and they are incompletely dealt with in the Soviet analysis. I shall examine here several ways in which the Stalinist system differs from the model. I begin by discussing 'autonomous' or uncontrolled behaviour at various levels within the administrative system, from the Politburo to the factory floor. I then consider the market or quasi-market aspects of the Stalinist system.

'Autonomy' Near the Top

There are despotisms and despotisms. Did Stalin lead from the front or was he pushed from behind? Was he a ringmaster or a puppet? These are very difficult questions to answer in any political system, even when full access is available to records of the proceedings of the bodies which govern the state. Information available from those who had dealings with Stalin on economic affairs does, however, shed some light on this important question, by providing evidence on the role of other Politburo members, of senior economic officials, and of leading industrial managers, in Soviet policy-making.

The available evidence shows that we need to distinguish fairly sharply the early 1930s, when the system was still in process of formation, from the late 1930s and 1940s. In what follows I concentrate on two somewhat contrasting sub-periods of Stalin's rule.

(a) *1929–1933*

In these years the policies of forced industrialization and the collectivization of agriculture emerged triumphant. They were policies with which Stalin is closely identified. However, there is strong evidence that the Politburo did not automatically endorse Stalin's policies in these years.

Jonathan Haslam's work on Soviet foreign policy in the 1930s portrays a Stalin who in the early part of this decade often left the conduct of foreign affairs to Litvinov.[11] Several recent Soviet publications reveal a Politburo which sometimes questioned Stalin. Thus Mikoyan's son, citing the old Bolshevik A. V. Snegov, reported that at a 'Central Committee' (i.e. Politburo or Orgburo) session sometime in 1931, chaired by Kaganovich, several of those present, including Kartvelishvili, first secretary of the Trans-Caucasus regional party committee, strenuously objected to Stalin's proposal that Beriya should be appointed second secretary of the Transcaucassian committee, and the proposal found no support (Ordzhonikidze was said by Mikoyan to have deliberately absented himself from the meeting). Mikoyan's son comments:

> It is interesting [*lyubopytno*] that at that time, apparently, disagreement could still take place. So far opponents able to express and defend other points of view had not been removed.[12]

In my own work on the early 1930s, it has become increasingly clear that members of the Politburo argued with 'Koba' (Stalin), particularly on issues where they had a special competence. In economic affairs, there is strong evidence that opposition developed within the Politburo to the course of collectivization sanctioned by Stalin. At one meeting nearly all members may have opposed him.[13] In 1931–2 the protracted dispute about planned rates of industrial growth undoubtedly involved acrimonious discussions behind the scenes at the top level in the party, though the position of Stalin in this dispute is ambiguous. In 1932–3, the growing famine and the economic crisis led to a profound crisis of confidence within the party.

A more detailed examination of industrial planning in 1929–33 will help to assess the influence of the leading industrial administrators and the technical and economic specialists on the outcome. This exercise will also reveal the considerable difficulties involved in handling the inadequate sources at present available.

The course of events may be briefly summarized. The 'optimum' variant of the five-year plan adopted in the spring of 1929 was already extremely optimistic and had been strongly resisted by specialists in Gosplan and Vesenkha (the commissariat responsible for industry).

Between the spring of 1929 and the summer of 1930 every component of the plan was increased, largely as a result of pressure from Rabkrin (the Workers' and Peasants' Inspectorate). Thus the pig-iron plan for 1932–3, some seven or eight million tons on the proposal of the Vesenkha specialists, rose to ten million tons in the five-year plan of spring 1929. It was increased to seventeen million tons by the 16th Party Congress in June–July 1930. The 1931 annual plan, the most ambitious annual plan in Soviet history, assumed that the revised plans would be achieved in full. The 1932 plan was less extravagant but still extremely over- ambitious. In the midst of economic crisis and growing famine, the annual 1933 plan and the broad goals for the 1933–7 five-year plan announced at the January 1933 Central Committee plenum marked the return to more realistic planning.

There is ample evidence that many factory managers, industrial specialists and administrators resisted the unrealistic plans. This is not quite the whole story. Some specialists supported the upwards revision of the plans. Technologists on the staff of Vesenkha advocated reforms such as the continuous working week (*nepreryvka*) which were damaging to industrial plant in the long run, but in 1929–31 enabled production to be pushed up.[14] Rabkrin had its own specialists, including foreign specialists such as the notorious Dr Karner, director of a small German iron and steel works. He backed proposals for extremely high efficiency coefficients in the Southern iron and steel trust Yugostal', which were an essential element in the exaggerated five-year plan for the industry.[15] But Karner was an exception: nearly all foreign specialists who recorded their views opposed, perhaps a little too firmly, the notion that American or German levels of utilization could be achieved under Soviet conditions.[16]

Throughout the winter of 1929–30 complaints appeared in the press about the hostility of Soviet managers and specialists to increases in the plans and even to their existing level. In December 1929, Kuibyshev condemned those who criticized the high targets.[17] In March 1930, S. Kosior noted that 'in many factories and mines the management and technical personnel formed the firm opinion that the programmes are exaggerated and cannot be fulfilled'.[18] In May, *Izvestiya* claimed or admitted that 'some leaders of industrial enterprises, a certain part of the engineering-technical personnel and even in some places the voluntary organizations of the workers consider that the high rates of development of the economy, and particularly of industry, are a temporary transitory phenomenon'.[19] At the 16th Party Congress in June–July 1930, Mezhlauk claimed that both the 17-million-ton plan for pig-iron and the Ural-Kuznetsk project had been adopted by the party 'against the Soviet apparatus, which hesitated, doubted and did not know what to do'.[20] In his autobiography Bardin, chief engineer of the Kuznetsk part of the project, admitted that he had resisted the proposed increase in capacity of the plant at the end of 1929.[21]

It should be remembered that these objections were being voiced at a time when many specialists had been arrested for wrecking activities. The accusation of advocating low production targets was often prominent. Open opposition to the plans required considerable courage. Syrtsov, in his famous critical speech of 30 August 1930, remarked that factory directors believed the plans were unrealistic, but lacked the civil courage to oppose them.[22] Even so, during the autumn of 1930 the Soviet press published numerous reports that factory directors and industrial officials were resisting the 'counter-plans', which were a fashionable method of increasing factory and branch plans at that time. The industrial newspaper wrote of the counter-plan that 'as a rule it is not greeted with joy by economic officials, and it is sometimes even held off at bayonet point'.[23] It was in August that Kuibyshev, still chairman of Vesenkha, is reported to have come to the conclusion that capital investment in 1931 would be too low to enable the 17-million-ton pig-iron plan to be achieved in 1932–3.[24] It seems safe to assume that his view was based on the advice of Vesenkha officials.

The 1931 plan, with its proposed increase of industrial production by as much as 45 per cent in a single year, aroused fresh resistance. According to an émigré source, the chief assistant to the non-ferrous metals combine objected to the plan to produce 150,000 tons of copper and was dismissed.[25] A leading Vesenkha official reported that some senior managers and mine managers in the coal industry displayed 'lack of faith in the rates of growth approved by the party'.[26]

During the first few months of 1931 almost every industry fell badly behind the plan. In June, a report from the medium engineering combine to the Vesenkha presidium noted 'a certain perplexity of leading personnel at a number of factories'; 'in many instances energy was directed to a considerable extent to proving that the targets could not be fulfilled.'[27] After the results for the first six months became known, the financial journal noted that 'individual voices have been heard both in the Soviet administration and inside our party to the effect that the failures in the first half of 1931 will make it necessary to pose the question of re-examining the annual plan'.[28] In circumstances when open opposition to official policies was increasingly hazardous, a headline in the industrial newspaper drew attention to the disquiet behind the scenes: '*Do Not Whisper that the Plan is Unrealistic!*'[29]

Similar reports continued to appear intermittently in the course of 1932. Among the most striking was a thinly veiled criticism of the iron and steel plans published in the industrial newspaper by a senior metallurgist.[30] He pointed out that the 1932 plan proposed to install as many as twenty-four new blast-furnaces but only nine had been installed in the first eight months of the year. To achieve the plan, equipment to a value of 750 million rubles would be required but only 150 million rubles was available:

> In the capital investment plan for 1933 there is a very great deal to be said for the need *to place the main emphasis on completing projects carried over into 1933; preparation for new construction should begin only after the actual completion and start-up of projects already being built.*

While all these complaints were being voiced the Politburo gradually and painfully adjusted the plans downwards towards reality. The decisive change came at the beginning of 1933 and was encapsulated in Stalin's sensational announcement of the shape of future plans at the Central Committee plenum of January 1933:

> Even if we wanted to, we could not carry out . . . a policy of accelerating rates of growth to the maximum during the second five-year plan, especially in the first two or three years . . .
>
> During the first five-year plan the annual increment to industrial production was on average 22 per cent. I think that for the second five-year plan it is appropriate to take an average annual increment to industrial production of 13–14 per cent as a minimum.[31]

For Stalin, the 1931 plan, with its 45 per cent growth-rate, had already become a conveniently forgotten episode in the history of planning.

How far was the shift to more realistic planning at the beginning of 1933 a response to the open and muted pressure during the previous three years from the industrial specialists and administrators? Perhaps such pressure was hardly necessary. In 1931 and 1932, industry continuously failed to achieve its plans. Pig-iron production was 4.9

million tons in 1931 and 6.2 millions in 1932, and most of the new blast-furnaces were far from complete. It must have been increasingly obvious to the most enthusiastic Bolshevik that it was impossible to produce ten million tons in 1932–3, let alone seventeen million. But the change in the approach of the party leadership to planning was more fundamental than a mere recognition of failure. Stalin's speech of January 1933 heralded a more or less permanent shift to much more realistic planning.

Soviet publications by participants in these events provide tentative evidence about the influence of technical specialists and administrators on this change of approach.

According to these accounts, the realism of the annual and five-year plans for the iron and steel industry, which were at the heart of all Soviet planning, began to pre-occupy members of the Politburo in the course of 1931. Sometime during the summer, Ordzhonikidze, who as chairman of Rabkrin had led the campaign for the 17-million-ton plan, suggested to the metallurgical engineer A. S. Tochinskii, with whom he had been acquainted since 1918, that 'perhaps the plan is not realistic'. After some hesitation Tochinskii replied that there was a vague optimism in the plans received by factories because they were not based on specific conditions. He strongly criticized Rabkrin and Dr Karner: Karner had 'pedantically estimated' how much each furnace would yield on the basis that all necessary resources were available: 'A psychological situation is created; you won't reach the plan, and so you don't care whether you get 80 per cent or 60 per cent'.

Tochinskii also told Ordzhonikidze that many new leaders of the industry 'led with their vocal cords', but were afraid to reveal the real position. He then produced a notebook containing estimates of the possible production of each works in the Southern iron and steel industry, and bluntly told Ordzhonikidze that a realistic plan for 1931 would be a mere five million tons of pig-iron, less than in the previous year. His figures proved to be approximately correct.

Ordzhonikidze was evidently impressed by Tochinskii's evidence. A few months later, on 9 November 1931, he summoned him to a session of the central committee commission on metallurgy which was discussing the 1932 plan; the session was attended by two other Politburo members, Voroshilov and Rudzutak.[32]

In the summer of 1931 preparations for the second five-year plan (1933–7) were also under way. On 11 August Kuibyshev, who became chairman of Gosplan after Ordzhonikidze took over Vesenkha in November 1930, presented reports about the iron and steel industry to the Politburo and Sovnarkom (Council of People's Commissars). In these reports he proposed a reduction in the pig-iron target for 1937 from 60 to 45 million tons. In the same month a metallurgical conference meeting under the auspices of the Politburo and Sovnarkom concluded that this reduced figure was still too high. It therefore resolved to re- examine the plan 'taking into account the exchange of opinions' at the conference, on the basis of a 1937 target for pig-iron production of only 25–30 million tons. The conference also prudently decided to seek the opinions of Stalin and Molotov, who were not present. When it reassembled, it was informed of Stalin's counter-proposal that a 'precise figure' of 25 million tons should be approved for 1937, and duly accepted it.[33]

Both the 1932 annual plan for iron and steel and the revised target for 1937 were still a long way from realism. The Soviet source I have cited gives the impression that under Tochinskii's influence the 1932 plan for ferrous metals was realistic. But the pig-iron target adopted by the Politburo on 10 November 1931 was nine million tons, and a counter-plan of ten million tons later acquired more or less official status.[34] Only 6.2 million tons was actually produced in 1932. Stalin's 'precise figure' of 25 million tons for pig-iron production in 1937 also proved to be too high. In the course of 1932 and 1933 it was reduced first to 18 million tons; then, in accordance with a dramatic proposal by Ordzhonikidze at the 17th Party Congress, to just 16 million tons.[35] Realism was at last almost achieved: production in 1937 amounted to 14.5 million tons (though the plans for some other major industries were still too optimistic).

An even more interesting event occurred during the January 1933 Central Committee plenum: a consultation about planning between Stalin and Zavenyagin. According to a *Pravda* journalist, Zavenyagin told him:

> Just before the plenum Sergo [Ordzhonikidze] and I were with comrade Stalin. He asked what I thought was the main thing in industry. I answered: 'assimilation' [*osvoenie*]. He tried to push me in different directions, asked me about the importance of supply, transport and personnel, and like a *vas'ka-vstanka* [rocking doll] I kept coming back to my point of view, and insisted: 'assimilation'.[36]

No doubt Zavenyagin was not the only person consulted by Stalin; and this was in any case not as entirely new an idea for Stalin as Zavenyagin implied. In January 1932 the 17th party conference asserted that 'mastering technology' (*ovladenie tekhnikoi*) was an urgent necessity; this notion of 'mastering' was close to the notion of 'assimilation'. In the summer of 1932, in a letter to heavy industry, Stalin wrote that 'we have a passion for construction, and that's excellent, but we lack the passion for mastering [*ovladenie*] production'.[37] Nevertheless there was an important change of emphasis at this time. At the January plenum Stalin emphasized assimilation much more strongly, treating what had previously been a sub-theme of party policy as the main key to successful development.

Stalin closely linked assimilation with his call for a switch to a slower pace of industrialization. During the second five-year plan, with its slower rate of growth, he insisted, the passion for construction must be complemented by concentrating on 'enthusiasm and passion for *assimilation* of new factories and new technology, a serious improvement of labour productivity, a serious reduction in costs'.[38] A few days later, on 12 January, Yaroslavsky told the *Pravda* editorial team that this was 'a real change of direction in the policy of industrialization'.[39]

If this account is reliable, it provides a remarkable example of the way in which both Ordzhonikidze and Zavenyagin, a Soviet-trained and rapidly promoted engineer, modified their revolutionary enthusiasm. They did so by acquiring some of the professional realism of the older specialists; and then played an important part in winning Stalin over to this approach.[40] But it seems to me that the available evidence does not enable us to interpret these events as a straightforward battle between Ordzhonikidze backed by the 'technostructure', and Stalin and Molotov on behalf of the 'political structure'. Ordzhonikidze seems to have taken a long while to conclude that the Rabkrin plans could not be achieved. We have seen that at the end of 1931 he supported an exaggerated iron and steel plan for 1932. His cry from the heart at the October 1932 Central Committee plenum seems genuine: construction of the iron and steel industry 'is a huge task, we torment ourselves, we bang our heads against it, and we learn':

> We thought we could construct Magnitka [Magnitogorsk steel works] in 2 or 3 years. It didn't come off, we strained every nerve, but it didn't come off.[41]

On the other hand, Stalin, who had vigorously defended the higher targets in February 1931, on the available evidence appears (no doubt wrongly) to have accepted moderate plans ever since August 1931. The growth-rates for 1933–7 which he advocated at the January 1933 plenum were *lower* than those eventually accepted at the 17th Party Congress a year later.[42] Obviously much remains mysterious about the inter-relationship between industry and the Politburo in those years. What is clear is that there was some kind of one-sided dialogue, not a simple *diktat*.

(b) *1938–1941*

Following the extensive arrests and executions of economic officials at all levels during the 'great purge' of 1937–8 such Soviet-trained specialists as Zavenyagin, Tevosyan, Vannikov, Shakhurin, Yakovlev and Emel'yanov were promoted to very senior positions. Stalin's power was enormously enhanced. How did this affect the process of decision-taking and policy-making? The reminiscences and biographies of some of the leading actors provide useful material.

The evidence from both admirers and critics of Stalin confirms both his wilfulness and his uncontrollability. His colleagues and his advisers bent to his will. Vannikov describes how Zhdanov, in a discussion about the 107mm gun, 'unfortunately took Stalin's comments to indicate approval of G. I. Kulik's project, and this influenced his future attitude to this question'.[43] On another issue 'I was angered to hear military engineers express views contrary to their experience and knowledge, solely because Stalin had expressed liking for the discs the previous day'.[44] For his own part Vannikov frankly admits:

> The then leaders of the People's Commissariat for Armaments, including myself, while having a correct attitude, did not, however, display enough firmness and principle, and carried out orders which we considered harmful for the state. And we were influenced not only by a sense of discipline, but also by the desire to avoid repressions.[45]

This environment of fear and suspicion corrupted major and minor decisions about the defence industry. Leading designers were arrested and perished; senior industrial officials and factory management were persecuted by the NKVD for failures which were not their fault.[46] In the last couple of years before the war, Stalin pressed ahead with unwise plans for 'a fleet for seven seas and oceans', and gave orders that new armaments factories were to be constructed in the Ukraine, where they would be invulnerable only on the unrealistic assumption that an aggressor would not succeed in penetrating Soviet borders.

But debate at the top had not ceased. According to Vannikov, the draconian legislation enforcing tighter labour discipline in June 1940, which might be thought of as a typical Stalin measure, was approved reluctantly by Stalin after frequent requests from the commissariats.[47] Stalin often acted as arbiter between the commissariats, and (where his pet prejudices were not involved) struggled desperately to hear the rival points of view. At the Defence Committee the Commissariat for Foreign Trade nearly persuaded Stalin to stop importing an expensive machine-tool with the argument that it would cost a boat-load of wheat.[48]

Behind the clashes at the top, within the commissariats, the People's Commissars in their turn were subjected to pressure and persuasion from more junior industrial officials. Vannikov describes how his deputies insisted that he should phone Voznesensky to try to reverse the decision of a commission headed by Molotov. The commission had decided to switch the rifle factories to the production of self-loading rifles in 1941 and to cease producing ordinary rifles altogether. Voznesensky crudely told Vannikov to stop his 'sabotage and red tape'. Vannikov's deputies then insisted that he should appeal to Stalin. After four hours Stalin phoned back with the news that the Politburo agreed. Vannikov comments that without the pressure on him from his deputies the Soviet Union would have been left without a single operating rifle factory in the worst period of the war.[49]

In the command economy, technical innovations had to be endorsed from above. Soviet publications report many cases of 'false innovators' who succeeded in imposing their ideas on a Stalin and a Politburo desperately anxious to achieve technical primacy in their military race with Nazi Germany. Here are three examples.

(1) The wretched Kulik, then head of the Chief Artillery Administration, on the basis of a mis-reading of the technical level of German tanks, persuaded Stalin to cease production of 45 and 76mm guns, shifting all production to the 107mm gun; the decision was reversed, after much waste, a month after the German invasion.[50]

(2) In the summer of 1940, when Yakovlev was deputy commissar for aviation responsible for research and development, a designer complained to the Politburo that Yakovlev had blocked his design for a

new aircraft because he was afraid of competition. A full meeting of the Politburo allocated resources to the complainant; his aircraft crashed on its first flight.[51]

(3) An engineer persuaded the head of the relevant department of the Red Army to support his new type of tank armour-plating. He presented a good case in non-technical terms to a commission chaired by Molotov at which Stalin was present, describing his metal as 'armour which defends in being destroyed'. Stalin, commenting 'there you are, dialectics in action!', gave the project his support. The sceptical Emel'yanov, then in charge of research in the Armour-Plating Administration of the People's Commissariat for the Defence Industry, acquired a sample of the metal and submitted it to an official test without the military realizing that the new metal was involved. The metal was completely destroyed, and the project was dropped. Emel'yanov claims that, in order to protect the military from Stalin's wrath, he joined with them in persuading Stalin to concentrate on armour which would resist shells as well as bullets.[52]

This last example illustrates how a technologist was able to sidetrack one of Stalin's decisions. This is an example of a poor innovation being brought to a halt without Stalin being fully aware of what was going on. On another occasion a good innovation was pushed through by stealth. An enlightened military representative endorsed a scheme to cast tank turrets experimentally in whole units rather than forging and welding them. The prototypes were produced at a shipyard with the approval of Emel'yanov, who was then head of the metal administration of the People's Commissariat for Shipbuilding. When this type of turret was compared with the existing forged and welded turrets at the Committee of Defence, Voroshilov was astonished to find that they had undertaken this work on their own initiative. The experiment was endorsed by the Committee. At the subsequent meeting of the Politburo its advocates answered Stalin's questions incompetently and it looked as if the new type of turret would be blocked. But Savel'ev, who then worked in the Politburo secretariat, helped Emel'yanov to get the project approved by advising him that he should draft a resolution which gave permission for 'cast turrets to be produced *as well as* welded' (my italics – RWD). This was endorsed by Stalin.[53]

It is not always clear, of course, whether an innovation is 'poor' or 'good'. Marshal Voronov argues that the story of the 107mm gun was rather more complicated than Vannikov suggested.[54] And

Kudryavtsev, who was engaged in work on the 'poor' innovation, reluctantly supported by Tevosyan on Stalin's orders, points out that this did not seem such a bad mistake when considered in a comparative context. Soviet experiments with this technology for smelting iron were brought to an end by the decision of a government commission in 1954, the year after Stalin's death. But work on the same technology continued unsuccessfully in the United States until 1964, when the firm ceased to exist.[55]

Plenty of unambiguously 'good' innovations were taken up by the administrative system between 1939 and 1945; only this can explain the high quality of Soviet tanks and aircraft at the height of the Second World War. Some Soviet participants present their story as if these successes were achieved in spite of Stalin. But Yakovlev's Stalin on the whole encourages successful innovation. On one occasion, for example, blocked by bureaucracy, Yakovlev successfully appealed to Stalin to allow him to design a light-weight jet engine.[56] Others present Stalin as their principal supporter, notably the famous artillery designer V. G. Grabin, who describes how he received support from Stalin against Tukhachevsky when the latter was over-enamoured with a universal gun which he wrongly believed was becoming standard in the United States.[57]

This was a brutal and devious world. The People's Commissar for Armaments was arrested early in June 1941. After the German invasion, still in prison, he was ordered by Stalin to prepare an assessment of the armaments situation in the light of war-time developments of which he knew nothing.[58] Yakovlev describes in some detail the atmosphere of fear and provocation which surrounded him for several years before Stalin's death.[59] The leading armaments designer Shpital'nyi is said to have accused industrialists of sabotage when production went wrong because of defects in the designs. He also destroyed the designs of rivals who had been arrested.[60] From such accounts we get the impression that the repressive machine used so ruthlessly by Stalin during the Ezhovshchina had acquired a life of its own, weaving around him tales of plots and intrigues in which he was unable to distinguish fact from fantasy.

Nevertheless the political leaders and the technologists continued to work together in amity, rivalry and hatred. Designers, engineers and technicians appeared before Stalin, or before commissions headed by Molotov, Voroshilov, Zhdanov or Voznesensky. Technological and production decisions were thrashed out, sometimes after stormy debate. The senior managers of industry were subordinates in the achievements and failures of the Administrative System, but they were influential subordinates.

'Autonomy' of Managers and Workers

Two classic studies, by Joseph Berliner and David Granick, both published over 30 years ago, deal with the role of the factory managers.[61] Berliner's research, based on interviews with émigrés and on published material, disclosed a number of important regularities in the Soviet planning system. High targets from the centre, reinforced by the 'ratchet principle',[62] and coupled with supply uncertainty, lead factory managers to systematic irregular practices. Thus they seek to provide a safety factor, particularly by hoarding reserves. They simulate fulfilment, for instance by economising on quality. The irregular practices, and the rise of the *tolkachi* (pushers or chasers), eases the plans and helps managers to fulfil them.

Granick's study of factory managers in the 1930s also emphasizes their active and flexible role in the system. Comparing this with the Weberian model of bureaucracy as a hierarchical formalized rational structure, working by applying known rules, Granick iconoclastically argues that 'it is precisely in its antibureaucratic development that major strengths and weaknesses of Soviet industrial administration can be found'. In the Soviet Union rules are not fixed, criteria of success are not clear-cut. Officials at all levels are (in a sense) 'policy makers', and the successful factory manager has to exercise political as well as technical judgement, to be able to evaluate in his factory practice the political criteria of the leadership. He is an entrepreneur, but an entrepreneur whose activity is restricted to developing better methods for carrying out the existing party line. Granick's 1954 study points to the arbitrariness inherent in the Soviet system of planning, with its multiple criteria and its erratic priorities, but the main emphasis is on the dynamism of the system.[63]

Over twenty years after these pioneer studies, Nicholas Lampert re-examined the world of Soviet managers and technologists through the eyes of a sociologist, dealing with the technical specialists as a whole rather than specifically with the factory managers.[64] In Lampert's account the drive against the bourgeois specialists in 1929–31 forms the essential context in which the new generation of specialists acquires its position in society. The rise of the new specialists serves to break down professional solidarity. They rapidly achieve promotion and acquire privileges. But at the same time they are agents rather than actors in a new mode of state domination. Politics is in command and the state authorities seek the politicization of all social relations. Nevertheless (in contrast to China during the Cultural Revolution), the old social division of labour more or less remains. The new technical specialist is both a representative and victim of the state. The command system (as with Granick and Berliner) necessarily grants a certain autonomy both to managers and to engineers. But Lampert stresses that this autonomy is strictly circumscribed. The punishment for 'mistakes' is severe and unpredictable. In the case of engineers, both their authority and the rewards are very limited. They are accordingly unwilling to take risks and many of them escape from the factories to safer activities. Granick's dynamic factory managers are thus surrounded by an apathetic mass of ordinary specialists.

Kendall Bailes in an influential book reaches conclusions similar to Lampert's about the role of the technical specialist in production.[65] But he places this study of a social group in the context of a far-ranging analysis of the relationship between the 'technostructure' and the 'power structure', covering the whole inter-war period and beyond. According to Bailes, the members of the technical intelligentsia are 'in a continual interaction with the power structure and the rest of society, initiating and debating plans and projects among themselves and with the power structure'. In this context the terror against the old specialists in 1929–31 and the purges of 1937–8 both aimed to secure the 'dominance of the political machine in the planning process . . . over the economic and educational bureaucracies'.

Carefully piecing together the fragmentary evidence, Bailes seeks to show that, following the appointment of Ordzhonikidze as chairman of Vesenkha in 1930, he acted as spokesman for the industrial managers and specialists, together with some other members and candidate members of the Politburo (Kirov, possibly Kosior, Rudzutak and Chubar). Between 1931 and his suicide in 1937 he consistently called for realistic planning, and resisted acts and campaigns of repression against the specialists.

Sheila Fitzpatrick's article on Ordzhonikidze in 1930–1 confirms one part of this story. She shows that as early as the industrial conference of

January 1931 Ordzhonikidze 'treated wrecking by experts almost as a thing of the past', and henceforth sought to develop a 'corporate identity' in Vesenkha. She also briefly argues that later in the 1930s heads of bureaucratic institutions regularly defended their departmental interests in the Politburo; Stalin acted as an 'arbiter' as well as 'a destroyer of barons and baronies'.[66]

Two Western studies deal with the role of the working class in Stalinist society. In view of the fact that they have been published quite recently and are readily available, I will deal with them briefly in spite of their importance to the study of Stalinism.

Donald Filtzer's detailed analysis of Soviet industry in the 1930s concludes that, while the workers had been deprived of all collective power, they were able individually to resist the imposition of high targets and severe discipline, and in conditions of full employment to force factory managers to adapt their behaviour. This in turn limited the powers of the Politburo to control the system.[67] Vladimir Andrle, in a study covering the same period, concentrates rather on the extent to which a structure of labour relations emerged in the factories which was semi-autonomous from the power of control of the central authorities.[68] In spite of their different approaches, both these studies fit in with Lampert's finding that technical specialists and lower management are frustrated because they are expected to discipline the workers but have very little influence over them.

Market and Quasi-Market Aspects of the Economy

By the end of 1934, the main outlines had been established of the Soviet economic system as it operated throughout Stalin's lifetime, and has in important respects continued until the present day. The command economy remained central. Industry was nationalized and agriculture collectivized. Most retail trade was conducted by the state or the state-managed consumer 'cooperatives'. Capital construction and industrial production were centrally planned, and a large part of agricultural production was compulsorily acquired by the state. All producer goods, both materials and capital equipment, were physically allocated by the central authorities. Prices within industry, and those of agricultural products compulsorily acquired by the state, were fixed. Consumer goods produced by state industry and taken from the peasants were sold at fixed prices. Internal passports controlled the movement of labour from the countryside and to some extent between towns.

But in several important respects this was not the moneyless product-exchange economy envisaged in 1930.

First, most collective-farm and state-farm peasant households worked their own personal plot and could own a cow and poultry. After obligations to the state had been met, both the household and the collective farm to which it belonged were permitted to sell their produce on the 'collective-farm market', which was in effect a free market, because prices were regulated by supply and demand.

Secondly, outside the large forced labour sector, with certain restrictions employees of the state were free to change their job. A very imperfect labour market existed during and after Stalin. Wages and other material inducements played an important role in persuading people to work in priority sectors. These arrangements are in sharp contrast to the Chinese economic system, where even today workers in the state sector have very limited rights to change their jobs.

Thirdly, from the end of 1934 the rationing of food and consumer goods in the state and cooperative retail trade was abolished (it was resumed during the Second World War until 1947, and on a local basis in the 1970s). Consumers were able to choose among such products as were available. This was, however, a very limited 'market', because prices were fixed by the state.

Stalin and his entourage did not make any systematic attempt to describe the general nature of this system. The personal plot and the collective farm market, though grudgingly classified as part of the socialist sector of the economy, were always regarded as temporary transitional phenomena. No acknowledgement was made of the existence of any kind of labour market. But Stalin did recognize that both money and 'Soviet trade', rather than product-exchange, were essential attributes of socialism. At the 17th Party Congress in January 1934, characteristically failing to admit that he had changed his own mind, Stalin vigorously condemned 'leftist chatter circulating among one section of our officials to the effect that Soviet trade is a past stage, that we need to establish direct product exchange, that money will soon be abolished, since it has turned into simple accounting units':

These people, who are as far from Marxism as the sky is from the earth, evidently do not understand that money will still remain with us for a long time, until the completion of the first stage of communism – the socialist stage of development. They do not understand that money is an instrument of bourgeois economy which Soviet power has taken into its own hands and adapted to the interests of socialism so as to develop Soviet trade to the utmost, and thus prepare conditions for direct product exchange.[69]

At this time the boundaries of the market within the centrally-planned economy were by no means firmly established. In the summer of 1932, M. I. Birbraer, a prominent economist working on the industrial newspaper, advocated far-reaching moves in the direction of a socialist market, including the adoption of a price system which would enable the abolition of the rationing of both consumer and producer goods. The party was committed to the ultimate abolition of consumer rationing. At the end of 1932 Ordzhonikidze, head of Narkomtyazhprom (the commissariat for heavy industry), tried unsuccessfully to abolish rationing ('funding') of some producer goods. But in 1933 *Pravda* authoritatively condemned Birbraer's 'attempt to give a theoretical basis to speculative policy'. It bitterly attacked another economist for his proposal that the iron and steel prices should be increased so as to eliminate subsidies.[70]

But this was not the end of the story. In the course of 1934–6 a series of reforms were discussed, and partly carried through, in the retail trade and within industry.

Retail trade reforms. In the course of 1934 the prospects for a radical price reform which would lead to the abolition of consumer rationing were vigorously discussed behind the scenes. In May, Bukharin, now editor of *Izvestiya*, published an article on the prospects for the economy in which he defended the role of the market in the socialist economy in guarded terms. He argued that owing to the advance of the economy '*the problematics of the market* have changed fundamentally'. He assured his readers that the market was now to a very great extent 'a relationship of organized state, semi-state and cooperative units, behind which stands a unified organized centralized will'.

According to Bukharin, the market could not be abolished in spite of this advance of state control, for two reasons. First, because of the existence of individual farms and the individual economy of the collective farmers '*which must not be despised in any case*' (my italics – RWD). Secondly, because the relation between agriculture and industry was not yet sufficiently well organized. Bukharin also sketched out what seemed to be a more permanent future for the market in retail trade:

> This is in no way the development of the anarchic market of the past, it is the creation of a material base for the distribution of growing production and the correct regulation of its movements through the utilisation of the market form, including in this the mass-retail links of Soviet trade, with sales at prices controlled by the organised forces of the proletarian dictatorship.[71]

Bukharin's article aroused the indignation of Stalin who circulated a criticism of it to the Politburo. This rejected Bukharin's statement that in past years the level of investment had been 'extremely high', and had been achieved in part at the expense of agriculture. Stalin apparently did not, however, comment on Bukharin's defence of the market.[72]

Later in 1934 the Politburo decided to proceed immediately to the abolition of consumer rationing, achieving this by substantial increases in the fixed state prices of bread and other foodstuffs. This was a reversal of previous policy, which had assumed that the abolition of rationing would not take place until supplies would equal demand without a large rise in state retail prices.

The decision to abolish rationing led to a wider discussion about the future of retail trade. The archives of Narkomtorg (the People's Commissariat for Trade) contain draft materials prepared for the plenum of the Party Central Committee in November 1934 which are very far-reaching in their implications. The authors slightingly describe the past phase as a 'period of distribution' (as distinct from a period of trade), and insist that its concepts, such as 'getting hold of' (*dostat*) goods, must pass into history. (*Dostat* was still a very active word in 1991.) They further argue that to develop trade in bread, the old merchant bakers must be collected together and their shops re-opened, so that the customer has the ability to choose to buy bread where it is best and freshest, and the shop will lose its customers if the bread is poor. Commissariats and their sales agencies must 'quickly react to all the changes and shifts taking place on the market'. While prices are unified, trade systems 'must engage in a broad competition between themselves in a struggle for the consumer', so that the best system wins. Moreover, the collective farm market must also be involved. State prices must be differentiated on the basis of a close scrutiny of 'bazaar' (free-market) prices and the state of local supplies.[73] These proposals are a striking departure from past principle and practice. Even under the NEP in the mid-1920s it was usually assumed that competition between state trading agencies was wastefully inefficient.

Following the murder of Kirov in December 1934, an article by Bukharin argued that the assassin's aim was to put a stop to the recent internal improvements. Bukharin referred to the political reforms of 1934, including the reorganization of the OGPU, the call for revolutionary legality and the reorganization of the political departments of the Machine-Tractor Stations. He linked them with economic reforms including the abolition of rationing and the provision of conditions for developed Soviet trade, which had provided a 'stable and real basis for *correct khozraschet* [economic accounting]'.[74]

In fact, the efforts to extend the role of the market did not cease in the grimmer political atmosphere of 1935 and 1936. The abolition of consumer rationing was on the whole successfully carried through at the beginning of 1935. And in August of that year the People's Commissar for Trade called in an internal document for contracts between state enterprises to be treated as 'holy', even if Sovnarkom ruled against them, and coupled this bold proposal with the suggestion that planning should be narrowed so that 50 per cent of the production of various consumer goods was simply sold direct on the market.[75]

Industrial reforms. Simultaneously with the reform of retail trade, in industry the effort continued to find ways of replacing allocation of producer goods by trade between the producer and the industrial customer. In December 1935, Kaganovich, addressing a Builders' Conference, went so far as to declare that 'in view of the growth of our economy we shall abolish the "ration-card system" for building materials, as we abolished it successfully for bread, meat, sugar, iron and other products'.[76] The following year an authoritative study of the industrial supply system published by Narkomtyazhprom praised the abolition of restrictions on the purchase of pig-iron in 1935. It claimed that in general 'from funding [central allocation] . . . and closed distribution of the most important kinds of output used in production we are going over to developed Soviet trade'.[77] Another Narkomtyazhprom economist claimed that 'the time is not far distant when the volume of production will be determined by the requirements of the economy, and we will produce as much as is needed, where it is needed and what is needed.'[78]

Some important practical changes were achieved within industry in 1934–6. Side by side with the abolition of consumer rationing in 1935 there was a determined effort to abolish subsidies in heavy industry as a stride towards rational pricing of producer goods. A campaign to reduce costs and renounce subsidies, launched in the 'Serp i Molot' factory in January 1933, was taken up by the Makeevka iron and steel works in September 1934. Its manager, Gvakhariya, linked the campaign directly with the need to increase the role of economic incentives in the Soviet economy, declaring in August 1935 that 'today it is no longer possible to manage by administrative methods'.[79] In spite of the campaign, subsidies in such industries as coal and iron and steel still remained substantial. On 1 April 1936, the authorities, adopting the solution that they had indignantly repudiated three years before, greatly increased the transfer prices of coal and steel, abolishing subsidies simultaneously.

Following the reforms and the far-reaching discussions in 1934–6, in October 1936 Prokopovich's émigré research institute in Prague, inspired by intensive reading of contemporary Soviet economic literature (and perhaps by Bukharin's famous visit in 1936 to Paris, Prague and elsewhere), wrote about Soviet policy in terms which seem to anticipate Gorbachev's 'radical economic reform' half a century later:

> The Soviet government at present is seeking in the new conditions, and with a different arrangement of the participants [*kontragenty*] on the internal market, to return in the organization of sales to the same commercial principles which were the foundation of the work of industry in the years of high NEP. These are the basing of production on profitability and on the functional interdependence of the cost and the price of a product. Belief in the might of the plan, in the possibility of organizing and distributing everything by rational planning, is as it were beginning finally to fade away. An attempt is being made to organize production and exchange between state enterprises on the principles of a competitive economy, on the basis of personal interest and of profitability. The near future will show the outcome of this attempt to combine the principles of a competitive economy with the state management of the whole national economy.[80]

The outcome was negative. Just at this time the impact of the 'great purge', followed by the inflationary pressures of rearmament and partial mobilization, brought all attempts to increase the role of prices and the market to an end. A limited discussion about the rights of enterprise directors in the summer of 1940 seems to have been the only other venture in this direction before the German invasion in 1941.[81]

The economic system which had emerged by the summer of 1936 was still a long way from a rational system of cost-pricing. The prices of consumer goods incorporated a greater tax on profits than those of producer goods, as well as high rates of turnover tax. And while consumer goods' prices, however imperfectly, took demand into account, the prices of producer goods, even at their most rational, were based on costs. This was certainly not a radical reform. Nevertheless the original concept and practice of the command economy had been modified in a number of directions. The collective-farm market at free prices was responsible for a substantial part of the food sales. There was a quasi-market for labour. Workers had limited freedom to move and their movement was influenced by the level of wages in different industries and areas. In the state and co-operative retail market, rationing had been abolished; state prices were fixed, but were influenced by the level of demand.

Conclusions

Thus important attributes of the Stalinist system were not present in the original Soviet model of a socialist economy, in the Western analysis of Stalinism as a variant of totalitarianism, or in Gorbachev's 'administrative-command system'. First, at the top level, economic decisions were actively influenced by senior economic administrators and even by leading factory directors. In the early 1930s, their objections to the over-optimistic hopes for rapid economic growth which dominated the Politburo played an important part, together with the crisis in the economy, in changing the approach to planning of Stalin and the party leadership. From 1933 onwards, plans, though taut, were relatively realistic, and henceforth much greater care was taken, by Stalin personally and by his entourage, to consult senior administrators and specialists before approving the plans. After the Ezhovshchina (the Great Purges of 1936–8), Stalin's power had greatly increased. But even then Stalin and his entourage in the Politburo directly discussed crucial production plans and decisions about new products with the senior staff of the commissariats and key factory directors. On occasion (we do not know how often) these subordinates initiated quite wide policy changes, and got them accepted.

Secondly, in their routine behaviour managers and specialists – and this certainly also applies to other groups in the Soviet elite – were not simply *vintiki*, cogs in the machine. If they were to carry out their duties to the state and the plan, factory managers, supported by the factory administration and the specialists, had to be quasi-entrepreneurial. They systematically broke the official rules, assisted by a vigorous stratum of 'pushers' (*tolkachi*). On the other hand the system also inhibited enthusiasm and conscientiousness. The penalties incurred for failing to carry out orders from above led many specialists and officials to avoid risk and innovation.

Thirdly, the mass of ordinary citizens influenced the operation of the system by their reaction to the policies of an apparently all-powerful state. In industry, the shortages of labour, endemic since 1931, together with the prestige attached to the working class, enabled workers to exercise a certain independence. In consequence work often proceeded at a leisurely pace. Managers found that, if they cut the rate for the job too much, or sought to impose a more exacting discipline, their workers would depart for another job. In the countryside, collective farmers – following the bitter experience of the famine of 1932–3 – produced the grain required by the state. But to secure most of the other food requirements the state had to permit collective farmers to grow a substantial amount of food on their household plots.

This brings us, fourthly, to the economic system as a whole. We have seen that the concept of socialism prevailing at the beginning of the 1930s was substantially modified. The household plot and the free market were grudgingly recognized to be long-lasting features of the socialist economy. There were also quasi-markets for labour and consumer goods. Wages and prices were fixed by the state but labour was free to move and consumers free to choose between different goods. This was a command economy in which money and the market retained important if limited functions.

Thus the Stalinist system was not simply a tyranny or oligarchy in which Stalin and his entourage controlled all economic and political power, confronting a passive and atomized population. In its social structure it was a kind of class society; a substantial ruling group, or class, hierarchically divided, had to deal with an increasingly complex articulation of social groups. The rival concepts of Soviet society which have been fiercely debated in Western literature over many decades turn on the nature of the ruling group, and on its relation with the rest of society. I agree with Alec Nove that the dominant group in Stalinist society can be established reasonably precisely, and corresponded broadly to the members of the 'nomenclature', the list of posts appointed with the approval of the party.[82] While this group did not own the means of production, it was responsible collectively for decisions about the allocation of resources analogous with those taken by private owners and their agents in a capitalist economy. The members of the ruling group and their families were afforded special privileges in housing, education, medical services, and in the use of special shops. They used their power over economic resources to allocate substantial personal incomes to their own group.

Their position in relation to Stalin was paradoxical. They were, especially after 1938, obedient and often devoted executors of his will. But at the same time, their corporate identity and corporate inertia limited the changes which could be made in the system by Stalin and by the political leadership which succeeded him. General secretaries could acquiesce in the power of the bureaucracy, as was the case with Brezhnev, but the price would be the growing influence of conservative trends within the system. Alternatively they could follow the difficult road of trying to overcome the inertia of the bureaucracy in order to innovate from above: the path of Stalin, Khrushchev and Gorbachev. By the mid-1930s the political system and social structure had already acquired their own laws of behaviour, and even the most powerful dictator found it difficult to manoeuvre them.

These are all significant modifications to the 'administrative-command' and 'totalitarian' models of the Soviet system. This is not at all to deny the importance of commands from above; this has certainly been the crucial feature of the Soviet economic system from the late 1920s until the present day. Moreover, from the late 1930s until the death of Stalin in 1953 the command system was combined with personal despotism. The Soviet economy – like the rest of Soviet society – was ultimately subject to the personal orders of Stalin. If Stalin regarded it as necessary, he could order the arrest or even the execution of any of his subordinates.

Yet Stalin also always took care to insist on the popular basis of the Soviet system. Even his notorious statement about the role of ordinary people as *vintiki* ('nuts and bolts') was made in the context of a homily addressed to the leading members of the Soviet hierarchy, stressing that they could not manage without the 'vintiki'. Stalin also saw himself as a great innovator on behalf of the people in face of the inertia of bureaucracy. Stalin's 'populism', while in a fundamental sense hypocritical, was significant, because it influenced both his own behaviour and the operation of the system. Yet ultimately the passive resistance of the peasants and the technological conservatism of the system proved more powerful than Stalin. These important aspects of the Stalinist system – the 'populist' aspects of Stalinism, and the autonomous power of social forces – are rightly strongly emphasized by such historians as Rittersporn and Getty.

However, Stalin's personal despotism, and the administrative system which outlived him, were central to the system. The state which Stalin headed was weak in the sense that it was not able to impose its will on the peasants. But it was strong in the sense that it possessed very harsh powers, which enabled it to manipulate its servants, although with major unintended consequences. Stalin's despotism had to work within a certain social, political, economic and ideological framework. But it was despotism.

Stalin and Stalinism: Some Comments

None of the contributors to this volume endorses the 'totalitarian' concept of Stalinism. As Professor Fitzpatrick points out, the essential feature of the 'totalitarian' concept was that the politics of the centre were the only important determinant of the behaviour of the system. It was usually associated with the belief that Stalin's personal power was decisive. In a classic expression of this approach Professor Leonard Schapiro wrote about the industrialization drive of the 1930s:

> I see no valid reason for assuming that it had to take place at the time and in the manner which Stalin determined, other than the reason that Stalin so determined it and was able to put his determination into effect.[83]

None of the contributors to this work takes the opposite view: the extreme 'revisionist' position that the decisions of Stalin and the state are of little significance as compared with the underlying economic and social forces that determined the shape of the regime. Professor Getty, in his study of the Great Purges of 1936–8, came near to this extreme view when he concluded (somewhat ambiguously) that 'the question of Stalin's role as planner was – or should have been – a secondary one in this analysis'.[84] But his present approach is far less one-sided.

The departure from extreme positions is part of a general trend, at least among Western historians of the Soviet period. It is pleasant to see that in the second volume of his monumental biography of Stalin,

Robert Tucker carefully considers the part played in the triumph of Stalinism not only by 'the decisive trifle' of Stalin's personality, but also by the influence of pre-revolutionary history and Russian political culture.[85] Our abandonment of simple models of Stalinism reflects perhaps the great expansion of our knowledge of the system in the past thirty or forty years.

However, I do not agree with Professor Fitzpatrick's lively account of the Western historiography of Stalinism in one important respect. She claims that the totalitarian model was overwhelmingly predominant in the West in the years of the Cold War and not seriously criticized until the work of Stephen Cohen and Moshe Lewin in the 1960s. In fact both Cohen and Lewin formed part of a long-established trend (Cohen's biography of Bukharin was actually published in 1974). The debates about 'totalitarianism' versus 'social forces' – involving well-informed writers from Trotsky to Kautsky – began in the 1930s, and even in the 1920s. Then soon after the war Isaac Deutscher and Rudolf Schlesinger published major works about the Stalin period which rejected the totalitarian hypothesis. Re-reading Schlesinger's *Spirit of Post-war Russia*, I am tempted to describe him as the Arch Getty of 1946 . . . And the first volume of Carr's *History of Soviet Russia* appeared as early as 1950, three years before Stalin's death. While this volume dealt with the Lenin period, its theme was the historical background to the Soviet system as it emerged in the ensuing decades. Carr's general message was clearly stated. *Both* society *and* the Soviet state contributed to the emergence of Stalinism:

> Politically, the [Bolshevik] programme involved an attempt to bridge the gap between autocracy and socialist democracy without the long experience and training which bourgeois democracy, with all its faults, had afforded in the west. Economically, it meant the creation of a socialist economy in a country which had never possessed the resources in capital equipment and trained workers proper to a developed capitalist order. These grave handicaps the victorious October revolution had still to overcome. Its history is the record of its successes and failures in this enterprise.[86]

When I took up my first academic job in Glasgow in 1954, I found that the small sub-department of Soviet Studies was rocking with ferocious debates about the nature of Stalinism. The main protagonists were Jacob Miller and Schlesinger, occasionally visited by Alec Nove, whose stimulating publications were already beginning to appear at that time. We all took it for granted that the totalitarian hypothesis was a crude over-simplification. The articles and reports published in *Soviet Studies* about late Stalinism and the interregnum of 1953–5 reflect these debates, and are still worth reading.

Nor was this counter-movement to the totalitarian hypothesis confined to liberal Britain. In the United States, life for heretics was tougher. Nevertheless the pioneering and profoundly 'non-totalitarian' studies of Stalinist industrial management by Granick and Berliner (see my chapter above) were both undertaken in the early 1950s. Even in the USA this counter-movement was not confined to the economy. In my view Professor Fitzpatrick underestimates, for example, the profound change brought about in Fainsod's approach to the political history of Stalinism by his unsurpassed study of the Smolensk archives. It is true that he described Stalinism as 'inefficient totalitarianism'. But he also referred to 'the totalitarian facade' which 'concealed a host of inner contradictions' and concluded that the consolidation of the Bolshevik revolution had brought about profound social changes:

> It tapped fresh talent from the lower depths of society and harnessed it to the revolutionary chariot. It gradually welded together a new governing apparatus, drawn substantially from social elements that had previously been political ciphers. It built its own network of revolutionary beneficiaries with vested interests in the perpetuation of the new order.[87]

These conclusions – in a book completed in 1957, many years before the publications of the 'revisionists' – are probably common ground for all the contributors to the present volume. But important differences of interpretation still remain. I strongly agree with Professor Getty's view that what he calls 'Russian plebeian attitudes' were an important factor in the emergence of the Soviet system, and are ignored by most historians. Nevertheless, in my view he places too much emphasis on the inexorability of the historical, economic and social factors which led to Stalinism. He underestimates the importance of ideology and personality. Thus he argues that 'routine killing of opponents' and other inhumane aspects of Stalinism were 'in fact [!] the products of the long and short term history of Russian society', and were not 'defined and created by Stalin's personality'. But his view of Russian history is one-sided. It highlights autocracy, class war, world war and civil war. It ignores or underestimates the powerful trend towards greater democracy and the rule of law, from which even the Tsar was not exempt. There was no 'routine killing of opponents' under Nicolas II. The murder of Stolypin, for example, may have been sinister, but it was hardly routine. Professor Getty also underestimates the operation of the same trends after the Civil War in the first years of the NEP. And surely he also somewhat oversimplifies plebeian and peasant attitudes? During collectivization, an important element in the disturbances was the view widespread among the peasants that their 'kulak' neighbours had been unjustly treated. Belief in solidarity of the whole village community was also a peasant attitude.

I would also place somewhat greater emphasis than Professor Getty does on the role and the power of both Stalin and the Soviet state. He presents Stalin as 'moderator or referee, choosing from among numerous policy possibilities'. We know more about Stalin's personality and political outlook than Getty suggests. Even Stalin's published writings for the 1930s show a political actor who was usually pressing for harsh innovative actions – though also ready to retreat and present himself as a moderate if he had let things go too far. I write 'if *he* had let things go too far' deliberately. Take the collectivization drive of 1929–30 as an example. It was Stalin who gave the go-ahead to mass dekulakization by his speech to the agrarian Marxists in December 1929. Then Stalin and Molotov pressed for more rapid collectivization in January and early February 1930. Stalin's call as late as 10 February to 'strengthen the work on collectivization in districts which do not have comprehensive collectivization' was a very strong encouragement to the local cadres. This is the context in which Stalin (apparently responding to criticism from most of the Politburo) then presented himself as a moderate in 'Dizzy from Success' on 2 March. The collectivization drive illustrates the paradox of the Stalinist state. As I argue in my chapter, it was not weak, as Professor Getty believes. It was powerful in some major respects and weak in others.

On the other hand, I find that Dr Mikoyan, in his stimulating chapter, underestimates the economic and social obstacles to his enticing alternatives to Stalinism. Western historians and economists are sharply divided in their assessment of the results of the New Economic Policy. But I think most of us would agree that the NEP achieved economic stability only for very short periods. Only two harvests, those of 1922 and 1926, were not followed by serious economic crisis. The NEP could, I believe, have maintained a respectable rate of industrial growth. But this would have required the Soviet Politburo to handle price and fiscal policy with an understanding and subtlety greater than that displayed by politicians in Western countries in the inter-war years. Even then, would industrial growth have been sufficient to meet the requirements of an isolated Soviet Union, faced during the next decade with world economic crisis and the triumph of Hitler? Even in economic terms, it seems to me that the serious alternative to Stalinism was Dr Mikoyan's 'Trotsky' variant, a more flexible and less inhumane version of the 'command-administrative system', rather than his 'Rudzutak' or 'Bukharin' NEP-type alternatives. In the 'Trotsky' alternative the market could have played a much greater part than in the Stalinist alternative. And it could have been headed not by Trotsky but by Kirov or Kuibyshev, or even by a Rudzutak pressed by circumstances to increase the role of central state management of the economy.

On the role of Stalin in Stalinism, Dr Mikoyan argues that 'the system and the structure were just like the dictator wanted them to be' and resists my conclusion that 'even the most powerful dictator found it difficult to manoeuvre' the political system and the social structure. He also claims Stalin could 'move them in any desirable direction'. Yet elsewhere in his chapter Dr Mikoyan accepts that Stalin had to tolerate the peasant household plots and offers us other examples of the system failing to respond satisfactorily (from Stalin's point of view) to orders from the centre. As I see it, Stalin wanted a system in which the economy and the people were obedient but were also innovative and creative. This was unachievable. Stalin was unable to move the system and the structure in the direction he desired. On the eve of his death, he hoped for an agriculture so prosperous that trade could be replaced by product exchange. But he also tried to impose ridiculously high taxes on the peasants. This was completely unworkable. Some compromise would have had to be found. In important respects, Stalin was a prisoner of the system.

Finally, the problem of sources. In my view Professor Getty underestimates the value of memoirs. He does not mention, for example, the large number of memoirs by senior officers. These need to be used with great caution, but shed a great deal of light on central decision-making and on Stalin. On the other hand, Professor Getty is rather too closely wedded to the importance of documents. He readily accepts the authenticity of the 'Politburo documents' discovered by Dr Reiman in the German archives. I would be more cautious. But all the contributors to this volume would applaud his statement that the absence of archival material greatly weakens our understanding of Stalin's role in Stalinism. The Politburo and associated party archives have been made available even in part only to a small group of Soviet scholars and no Western historians have been able to use them. The archives of Sovnarkom, the Ministry of Foreign Affairs and the NKVD/MVD/KGB are similarly restricted. From what has already been published, it is certain that these materials would greatly enhance our knowledge. They would, incidentally, enable us to achieve a far greater understanding of the scale of the repressions. The statement made by Anastas Mikoyan – usually a reliable witness – to our colleague Sergo that as many as seven million people were shot between 1 January 1935 and 22 June 1941 is completely at variance with the data so far released from NKVD archives and simply cannot be reconciled with the demographic data from the 1937 and 1939 censuses. Who is right? Soviet and Western historians should be given the access to archives which is normal in all modern countries and then we would get closer to the truth.

March 1991

Notes

Note. The party and Sovnarkom archives – through not the NKVD and foreign affairs archives – are now much more accessible to both Russian and foreign historians (October 1992).

1 See Kuibyshev's report to the plenum in *Planovoe khozyaistvo*, no. 12, 1930.
2 Lenin, *Sochineniya*, 4th edn, vol. xxi (1948), pp. 57–8.
3 Stalin, *Sochineniya*, vol. ix (1949), pp. 250–1.
4 *Sochineniya*, vol. xiii (1951), pp. 369–70.
5 *Ekonomicheskaya zhizn'*, 26 December 1929.
6 See R. W. Davies, *The Soviet Economy in Turmoil, 1929–1930* (1989), pp. 174–6.
7 *Sobranie zakonov*, 1930, art. 181.
8 *XVI s''ezd VKP(b): stenograficheskii otchet* (1931), p. 37; in his *Sochineniya*, vol. xii, pp. 306–7, published in 1949, he replaced the phrase 'commodity turnover and the money economy' by ' "free" commodity turnover', reflecting his changed view of the nature of the socialist economic system.
9 *Za industrializatsiyu*, 17 November 1930.
10 See his review of A. Bek, *Novoe naznachenie*, in *Nauka i zhizn'*, no. 4, 1987.
11 J. Haslam, *Soviet Foreign Policy, 1930–33: the Impact of the Depression* (1983), and *The Soviet Union and the Struggle for Collective Security in Europe, 1933–39* (1984).
12 *Komsomol'skaya pravda*, 21 February 1988. He added, however, that 'the "democratic discussion" was immediately broken off', and the posts were

reshuffled a few months later without referring the matter to the Politburo; Beriya got the job and Kartvelishvili was posted elsewhere.

13 See Haslam (1983), pp. 121–2, citing the Italian archives; the meeting was held at the end of February 1930.

14 Engineers Shauer and Rappoport are named as the initiators of the *nepreryvka* proposals (see *Ekonomicheskaya zhizn'*, 4, 5, 6 June, 5 July 1929).

15 *Promyshlennost': sbornik statei*, ed. A. P. Rozengol'ts (1930), p. 25; *Byli industrial'nye* (1970), pp. 186–7; and see *Soviet Studies*, vol. xxxvii (1985), pp. 158–60 (Fitzpatrick).

16 There are many examples of this assessment in the files of American engineers in Russia, held at the Hoover Institution, and many complaints about this attitude of foreign specialists appeared in the Soviet press at the time (see for example the report about Yugostal' in *Za industrializatsiyu*, 1 January 1930).

17 *Torgovo-promyshlennaya gazeta*, 15 December 1929.

18 *Pravda*, 9 March 1930.

19 *Izvestiya*, 20 May 1930.

20 *XVI s"ezd:stenograficheskii otchet* (1931), pp. 330–1.

21 I. P. Bardin, *Rozhdenie zavoda: vospominaniya inzhenera* (Novosibirsk, 1936), p. 7.

22 S. Syrtsov, *K novomu khozyaistvennomu godu* (1930).

23 See for example *Pravda*, 26 August 1930, *Za industrializatsiyu*, 21 October 1930, *Bol'shevik*, no. 15–6, 31 August 1930, p. 4.

24 See A. Khavin, *U rulya industrii (dokumental'nye ocherki)* (1968), p. 78.

25 A. Barmine, *Memoirs of a Soviet Diplomat* (1938), pp. 234–5; Barmine claimed that Serebrovsky, head of the industry, while publicly defending this plan, knew perfectly well that it could not be achieved. Production did not exceed 150,000 tons until 1940 . . .

26 *Za industrializatsiyu*, 4 January 1931 (S. Lobov).

27 TsGANKh, 3429/1/5242, pp. 45–6 (report to sitting of 28 June 1931).

28 *Finansovye problemy*, no. 3–4, 1931, p. 21. See also V. V. Kuibyshev, *Stat'i i rechi*, vol. v, *1930–1935* (1937), pp. 118, 122–3.

29 *Za industrializatsiyu*, 3 July 1930.

30 *Za industrializatsiyu*, 1 September 1932 (S. Abramov). The article was strongly criticized in subsequent discussion (see, for example, *Za industrializatsiyu*, 3 November 1932 – P. Zhigalko).

31 I. V. Stalin, *Sochineniya*, vol. xiii (1951), pp. 185–6.

32 *Byli industrial'nye: ocherki i vospominaniya* (1970), pp. 186–8; this chapter, by the journalist A. Peshkin, was apparently based on a talk given by Tochinskii in 1967, on the occasion of the 80th anniversary of Ordzhonikidze's birth. This incident was first described in English in Bailes (1978), pp. 272–3.

33 V. I. Kuz'min, *V bor'be za sotsialisticheskuyu rekonstruktsiyu, 1926–1937* (1976), p. 188, citing party archives.

34 *Industrializatsiya SSSR, 1929–1932gg.: dokumenty i materialy* (1970), p. 606; for the 10-million-ton target, see for example A. Gurevich, *Zadachi chernoi metallurgii v 1932 g.* (1932).

35 See Bailes (1978), p. 278 (for this work see note 65 below).

36 S. Gershberg, *Rabota u nas takaya* (1971), pp. 199–200.

37 Cited in indirect speech by Ordzhonikidze in September 1932 (S. Ordzhonikidze, *Stat'i i rechi*, vol. ii (1957), p. 427).
38 Stalin, *Sochineniya*, vol. xiii (1951), pp. 185–6.
39 Gershberg (1971), p. 197.
40 Other influences were certainly also present. In November 1932 Trotsky published his article 'The Soviet Economy in Danger', in which he argued that 1933 should be a 'buffer year' between five-year plans, in which resources in industry should be concentrated on first-priority investment, on putting factories into order, and on supplying food, clothes and housing to the workers; inflation should be halted, and capital investment should be boldly reduced (*Byulleten' oppozitsii* (Berlin), no. 31 (November 1932), pp. 3–13). At the January plenum Trotsky was bitterly criticized, but industrial policy in 1933 to a considerable extent conformed to this approach.
41 Ordzhonikidze, *Stat'i i rechi*, vol. ii (1957), pp. 417–19; this report was published for the first time in 1957.
42 See E. Zaleski, *Stalinist Planning for Economic Growth, 1933–1952* (1980), pp. 129–33; little is known about the adoption of higher growth-rates for industry in the course of preparing the second five-year plan in 1933.
43 *Znamya*, no. 1, 1988, p. 140.
44 *Znamya*, no. 2, 1988, p. 136.
45 *Znamya*, no. 1, 1988, p. 149.
46 *Ibid.*, pp. 144, 149.
47 *Znamya*, no. 2, 1988, pp. 148–9.
48 *Ibid.*, pp. 154–5. After a pause, Stalin said: 'grain is gold – we must think again', but Vannikov convinced him that no gold would be able to buy them if they weren't acquired before war broke out.
49 *Znamya*, no. 1, 1988, pp. 159–60.
50 *Znamya*, no. 1, 1988, pp. 137–9.
51 A. Yakovlev, *Tsel' zhizni* (1967), pp. 198–200.
52 Emel'yanov's memoirs, in *Novyi mir*, no. 2, 1967, pp. 87–94.
53 *Ibid.*, pp. 103–7.
54 *Znamya*, no. 1, 1988, pp. 131–2.
55 *Nauka i zhizn'*, no. 12, 1987, pp. 28–32.
56 Yakovlev (1967), pp. 452–4.
57 His detailed account appears in *Oktyabr'*, nos. 10, 11 and 12, 1973. It is distinguished by the care with which it establishes that the technologically most advanced weapon is not necessarily the best in terms of military need or industrial possibilities. These reminiscences appeared at a time when criticism of Stalin in the press was muted, and frank references to repression had almost ceased; perhaps we shall soon get a new version?
58 *Znamya*, no. 1, 1988, p. 133.
59 Yakovlev (1967), pp. 447–57.
60 *Znamya*, no. 1, 1988, pp. 143–9.
61 D. Granick, *Management of the Industrial Firm in the USSR* (1954); J. S. Berliner, *Factory and Manager in the USSR* (1957).
62 The ratchet principle is that 'once a new high level of performance has been

achieved, the next plan target may not be reduced below that level but must usually be raised above it' (Berliner (1957), p. 78).

63 See especially Granick (1954), pp. 262–85.

64 N. Lampert, *The Technical Intelligentsia and the Soviet State: a Study of Soviet Managers and Technicians, 1928–1935* (1979).

65 K. E. Bailes, *Technology and Society under Lenin and Stalin: Origins of the Soviet Technical Intelligentsia, 1917–1941* (1978). For a careful examination of the rise of the new technocracy, and of the political power acquired by certain members of it in the wake of the Ezhovshchina, see S. Fitzpatrick, *Education and Social Mobility in the Soviet Union, 1921–1934* (1979), especially pp. 235–54.

66 See *Soviet Studies*, vol. xxxvii (1985), pp. 153–72, especially pp. 164–7.

67 D. A. Filtzer, *Soviet Workers and Stalinist Industrialization: the Formation of Modern Soviet Production Relations, 1928–1941* (1986).

68 V. Andrle, *Workers in Stalin's Russia: Industrialization and Social Change in a Planned Economy* (1988).

69 *Sochineniya*, vol. xiii, pp. 342–3.

70 See my article in *Slavic Review*, vol. 42 (1984), pp. 201–23; the *Pravda* editorials appeared on 21 April 1933 (versus Birbraer) and 19 March 1933 (versus N. Dol'nikov).

71 'Ekonomika Sovetskoi strany', *Izvestiya*, 12 May 1934.

72 Stalin's note is summarized in *Kommunist*, no. 13, 1988, pp. 106–7, by G. Bordyugov and V. Kozlov, but unfortunately its text has not been published.

73 TsGANKh, 7971/2/8, LL. 16–17, 24, 45, 159, 165, 174.

74 *Izvestiya*, 22 December 1934.

75 TsGANKh, 7971/2/36, L. 185, dated 26 August 1935 (Veitser).

76 *Za industrializatsiyu*, 20 December 1935 (speech of 20 December).

77 Yu. I. Moshinskii, *Ekonomika i organizatsiya obrashcheniya sredstv proizvodtsva v SSSR* (1936), pp. 178–9; this book was sent to press on 10 April and signed for the press on 23 May.

78 N. S. Burmistrov, *Ocherki tekhniko-ekonomicheskogo planirovaniya promyshlennosti* (1936), p. 15.

79 See F. Benvenuti, *Fuoco sui sabotatori!* (1988), summarized in English as Benvenuti, 'Stakhanovism and Stalinism, 1934–8', unpublished *CREES Discussion Papers*, SIPS No. 30, Centre for Russian and East European Studies, University of Birmingham (1989).

80 *Byulleten' Ekonomicheskogo Kabineta prof. Prokopovicha*, no. 131 (October 1936), p. 108.

81 On this 1940 debate, see *Kommunist*, no. 1, 1988 (O. Khlevnyuk).

82 See his 'Is there a Ruling Class in the USSR?', *Soviet Studies*, vol. xxvii (1975), 615–38.

83 L. Schapiro, *The Communist Party of the Soviet Union* (1960), p. x.

84 J. A. Getty, *Origins of the Great Purges: the Soviet Communist Party Reconsidered, 1933–1938* (1985), p. 220.

85 R. Tucker, *Stalin in Power: the Revolution from Above, 1928–1941* (1990), pp. 1–43.

86 E. H. Carr, *The Bolshevik Revolution, 1917–1923*, vol. 1 (1950), pp. 100–1. In

numerous articles and reviews published between 1931 and 1940 Carr was already struggling with the problem of the role of 'totalitarianism', 'social forces' and the Russian past in the emergence of Stalinism.

87 M. Fainsod, *Smolensk under Soviet Rule* (1958), pp. 454, 451–2.

CHAPTER 3

Constructing Stalinism: Reflections on Changing Western and Soviet Perspectives on the Stalin Era

Sheila Fitzpatrick

What is Stalinism? This is an apparently simple question to which there is no simple or single answer. Interpretative constructs like Stalinism are invented – not once but many times, by many different people, in response to a variety of circumstances, observations and experiences. In the first instance, Stalinism – as a construct associated with a specific political regime and socio-economic system – was invented by that regime's ideologists and political leaders (who called it 'socialism'). But it was also simultaneously being invented by Soviet society and by different groups within the society. Not surprisingly, the regime's notion of Stalinism ('socialism') and the society's experience of it were not identical.

Moreover, the intellectual construction of Stalinism was not just the work of one generation. The task was continued in the post-Stalin period by new generations of political leaders and ideologists, by scholars and by Soviet society itself. Stalinism has meant something different each time the question 'What is Stalinism?' has been addressed. The number of possible Stalinisms is not infinite, because the construct has to be linked with a concrete set of historical data. But that set is extremely large and complex. No single Stalinism embraces the whole set of relevant data. Each Stalinism, on the other hand, incorporates some of it – the particular subset of data that is cast into relief from one particular angle of vision.

At present, Stalinism and the historical significance of the Stalin period are being dramatically re-evaluated in the Soviet Union in connection with Gorbachev's new era of perestroika. This re-evaluation proceeds on several different levels. At one level, it involves deconstruction – repudiation of the old Stalinist concept of Stalinism, revelation of what was concealed about Soviet history and society under the old Stalinist rules, correction of what was distorted or falsified. At another level, it involves intellectual reconstruction – the formulation of a new answer (or answers) to the question 'What is Stalinism?'

The purpose of this chapter is to provide a framework for understanding the present Soviet re-evaluation of Stalinism. The first part is an examination of the past to see what Stalinism meant to different interpreters and in different contexts. The main interpretations that will be discussed are the old Soviet (Stalinist) concept of Stalinism, formulated in the 1930s; the Western totalitarian model, dominant in American Sovietology during the Cold War; the Soviet 'de-Stalinization' interpretation of the late 1950s and early 1960s; and Western 'revisionist' reinterpretations of the Stalin era of the 1970s and 1980s. The second part of this chapter deals with the current[1] Soviet reinterpretations of Stalinism.

While there have been many different interpretations of Stalinism, the majority have one trait in common, namely the assumption that only one interpretation is legitimate. The most vehement and sinister insistence on a 'single-truth' approach came from the Soviet Union during the Stalin period. But Western Sovietology has also tended to be intolerant of differences of interpretation; and a similar characteristic may be found in Soviet 'de-Stalinizing' episodes as well. For Soviet radical intellectuals, as for their nineteenth-century predecessors, challenging state-approved orthodoxies does not necessarily mean challenging the assumption that truth is monolithic. On the contrary, it may even reinforce the belief that historical interpretation is an arena of Manichean struggle between truth (*pravda*) and falsehood (*nepravda*).

Thus, reinterpretation of Stalinism in the Soviet Union is often conceived as a simple process of substituting 'the real truth' (news of the outrages, scandals and disasters of the Stalin period that could previously be discussed only in whispers) for the old official cover-ups and lies. When Soviet perspectives on history shift, as they frequently have done in connection with leadership and ideological changes, it is always said that the old 'incorrect' view has been replaced by the 'correct' interpretation. This is not just the way dogmatic Stalinist minds work in the Soviet Union. It is the way the minds of many 'new thinkers' of the present era of glasnost – and their precursors in the de-Stalinization movement of the 1960s and dissident movement of the 1970s – work as well.

Yet Gorbachevian glasnost contains, at least in embryo, the notion that intellectual pluralism is a necessary part of democratization. One of the most interesting questions about the present period of Soviet historical re-interpretation is whether Soviet new thinkers are finally ready to abandon the old 'single-truth' approach to history. If they are not, Glasnost and democratization may have no real future in the Soviet Union.

The Stalinist Picture: 'Building Socialism'

In the classic Soviet version of Soviet history (that is, the official Stalinist version prevailing from the mid-1930s to the mid-1950s), the phenomenon which we now call 'Stalinism' was identified as the 'building of socialism' (*stroitel'stvo sotsializma*) in the Soviet Union. Discussion of the phenomenon was much constrained by Soviet censorship and concern for ideological orthodoxy. Interpretation was vulgarized because of propaganda needs. Nevertheless, there was a real intellectual core to the classic Stalinist version. Its roots lay in Marxism and the assumption that it is the economic basis, especially ownership of the means of production, that determines the superstructure of political, social and cultural institutions.

This means that the key to understanding Soviet society in the 1930s was state ownership of the means of production. This was partially established after the October Revolution and greatly extended at the end of the 1920s, with the elimination of the urban private sector, the adoption of the First Five-Year Plan and centralized state planning of economic growth. The collectivization of peasant agriculture, conducted at great speed and cost in the first half of the 1930s, eliminated capitalism in the countryside. According to Marxist premises, these were the basic prerequisites of socialism.

From the Soviet point of view, therefore, all other phenomena had only secondary importance in defining the essence of the epoch. Even the political system was secondary, despite the great importance attached to Communist Party leadership and the inspirational role of the Leader (*vozhd'*) himself, comrade Stalin. There were some theoretical problems associated with the continued existence of a strong central state power, since in the Marxist understanding of socialism the state must ultimately whither away. These were overcome by reference to the continuing threat from 'capitalist encirclement', which for the time being obliged the Soviet state to remain strong and vigilant, as well as the internal threat from residual class enemies (that is, representatives of the formerly privileged 'feudal' and 'bourgeois' classes overthrown by the Revolution, and of the lesser capitalist groups, Nepmen and kulaks, eliminated at the end of the 1920s by state and party action).

The latter threat constituted the chief justification for the existence of a powerful security police, the NKVD (previously known as the GPU and OGPU and, in the Civil War period at the beginning of the 1920s, the Cheka). From the official Stalinist point of view, however, this was not a systemic feature of prime importance. In systemic terms, the most important index of Soviet progress in 'building socialism' was the promulgation in 1936 of a new Soviet Constitution which announced that 'enemy classes' had essentially been liquidated, and it was therefore possible, as it had not been in the first decades after the Revolution, to give full political rights to all citizens regardless of class.

In reality, the task of 'building socialism' meant industrializing at breakneck speed, forcing collectivization on the peasantry and at the same time pursuing more modest goals in the field of literacy and education. It may be easier for contemporary Western readers to conceptualize this as a modernization drive, fuelled by a consciousness of Russian economic backwardness and its dangers for national survival, than in 'building of socialism' terms. The Soviet press of the 1930s hailed the economic achievements of the Five-Year Plans (the writer Maxim Gorky, turned publicist for the regime, even started a journal called *Our Achievements*) and the exploits of Soviet aviators and Polar explorers. By comparison, Soviet leadership of the world revolutionary movement, though a source of pride, was of lesser importance.

The Classic Western Paradigm: Totalitarianism

The totalitarian model provided the framework for most Western Sovietology in the decades after the Second World War.[2] In contrast to the classic Soviet paradigm just described, the totalitarian model emphasized the primacy of politics and treated economic and social structures as derivative. Totalitarianism was defined as a political system which maximized state and party control over society and its individual members, enforced by police repression and terror, depending on mobilization of the population to achieve the regime's goals. The goals of the Soviet totalitarian regime, justified in terms of Marxist-Leninist ideology, were economic and social transformation. A charismatic leader provided inspiration to the population; a powerful mass party (the only political party allowed) acted as transmission belt for the regime's commands to the population. Popular participation was minimal in this political system but brain-washing by propaganda was ubiquitous. Societal and even family bonds were weakened because the regime perceived all associations outside the direct purview of the state and party as a potential challenge to its total control.

The model was developed on the basis of observed similarities between the Soviet Union and Nazi Germany. It represented the antithesis of the Western-democratic values of the theorists who formulated it; and it carried with it overtones of extraordinary evil and deviation from a 'normal' historical path. Although the totalitarian model scholarship of the 1950s, unlike its contemporary Soviet counterpart, was not constrained by political censorship, Cold War pressures nevertheless produced a high degree of politicization, especially in American Sovietology. Two popular literary works drawing on the totalitarian framework highlighted the dominant images associated with the totalitarian model: terror and lack of individual freedom and privacy. These were Arthur Koestler's *Darkness at Noon*, based on the Great Purges and the fate of Old Bolsheviks like Bukharin, and George Orwell's *1984*, the classic imaginative representation of a society held in the grip of a totalitarian regime, whose citizens were watched over by Big Brother.

From the standpoint of the totalitarian model, it was important that the regime had transformational aspirations but less important exactly how it sought to transform the economy, society and culture. (The Nazi regime in Germany, of course, had different transformational aspirations from those of the Communist regime in the Soviet Union.) Thus, the economic-modernization thrust of Stalinist policy was not in the forefront of Western consideration in the heyday of the totalitarian model. Indeed, modernization theory was often ill-regarded by the totalitarian-theory scholars, both as a potentially competing paradigm and because of its implication that the Soviet case might not be extraordinary.

In the totalitarian model (as in the classic Soviet paradigm) it was assumed that Stalinism was a direct outgrowth of Leninism and the Bolshevik Revolution. Totalitarian theorists seeking to explain the origins of Soviet totalitarianism found them in Marxist-Leninist ideology, particularly the Leninist theory of party organization. For this reason, scholarship of the period paid particular attention to questions of Soviet ideology, propaganda, and (as a derivative of the above) culture. There was little study of Soviet society or social history. This was, in the first place, because the society was not seen as having a dynamics independent of the totalitarian regime. It was simply the passive object of regime manipulation.

In the second place, detailed scholarly study of the society in either past or present by Westerners was discouraged at this time because of the problem of access to Soviet libraries and archives, and even the Soviet Union itself. It was not easy for foreigners to make research trips to the Soviet Union in the 1950s, and some of the weaknesses of the totalitarian-model scholarship must be explained by the scholars' actual as well as emotional distance from their subject.

Soviet Revisionism after 1956: De-Stalinization

The classic Soviet interpretation of the Stalin period began to come apart in 1956 after Khrushchev's Secret Speech to the 20th Party Congress in which he denounced Stalin's 'cult of personality' and abuse of power. Historians and other members of the intelligentsia (notably writers) leaped at the chance to investigate hitherto unmentionable historical episodes such as the deportation of kulaks at the beginning of the 1930s, the Great Purges of 1937–8 and the existence of a labour camp system (brought into public view for the first time in Solzhenitsyn's *One Day in the Life of Ivan Denisovich*). Writers and other members of the intelligentsia also registered their protests against the limitations on creative freedom of the past decades in works like Dudintsev's novel *Not by Bread Alone*.

In the thaw following Stalin's death, censorship and ideological rigor had been considerably relaxed. Still, the de-Stalinizing historians and writers found that not everything they wrote could be published, even in the post-Stalin era.[3] The historians had a particular problem, since what they were seeking to revise was virtually contemporary history. It turned out that there was still considerable resistance within Soviet society to any basic reappraisal of Stalin's rule. This was presumably because too many senior members of the bureaucracy were personally involved and because the population still associated Stalin with the nation's greatest achievement, victory in the Second World War.

As a result, the critique of Stalinism in the late 1950s and early 1960s (even before the dampening down of criticism under Brezhnev) was largely limited to specific 'mistakes' and 'excesses' committed by Stalin. (These did not include the 1932–3 famine; and with regard to the purges, they included only the victimization of loyal Communists – not even extending to Communists from the Oppositions of the 1920s.) By implication, therefore, the key to the phenomenon of Stalinism was Stalin himself – a leader whose pathological traits were abetted by an 'unhealthy' situation in the Communist Party and a security police operating without the necessary restraints. The major thrust of the de-Stalinization campaign was to demythologize the person of Stalin without demythologizing the rule of the Communist Party. It was Stalin personally who was made responsible for Soviet disasters and failures, just as he had once been held personally responsible for Soviet achievements.

Around the middle of the 1960s, with Khrushchev's fall from power, there was a move away from active de-Stalinization, though no outright repudiation of the previous policy. Publication of a number of major de-Stalinizing historical and literary works was blocked, and their authors were obliged to keep them 'in the drawer'. In a number of cases they circulated them surreptitiously at home or allowed their publication abroad. There was a large volume of *samizdat* and *tamizdat* publications[4] in the late 1960s and 1970s, when the Western press was giving extensive coverage to Soviet dissidents and their efforts to continue the exposure of Stalin's crimes. Works like Roy Medvedev's *Let History Judge: The Origins and Consequences of Stalinism*, Solzhenitsyn's *Gulag Archipelago*, Nadezhda Mandelshtam's *Hope against Hope*, Evgeniia Ginzburg's *Into the Whirlwind*, and Antonov-Ovseenko's *The Time of Stalin: Portrait of a Tyranny* were widely read in the West and created a vivid and immediate sense of the realities of Stalinist repression. As time passed, *samizdat* and *tamizdat* editions of these works achieved broad dissemination within the Soviet intelligentsia.

The official Soviet line on Stalinism in the 1970s was that 'Leninist norms' had been violated during the period of 'cult of personality', but the basic system was nevertheless sound. Rapid Stalinist industrialization, despite the enormous costs and sacrifices imposed on the population, was both necessary and 'socialist'. Without it, the country could not have emerged from backwardness to the pre-eminent position in the world that it held after World War II (much emphasized under Khrushchev). It could not have won the war against Germany. Collectivization was also a necessary and basically correct socialist policy, even though there were many 'excesses' in the treatment of peasants ('middle peasants' being classified as 'kulaks' etc.). For the generation that had lived through the Stalin period and had some real feeling of identification with the Bolshevik revolution and the Communist Party, it was an important psychological crutch to dissociate Lenin from Stalin and think wistfully 'If Lenin had lived . . .'.

Western 'Revisionist' History of the 1970s and 1980s

The starting point for Western 'revisionism' scholarship was rejection of the totalitarian model. This was part of a broader reaction of younger scholars in the US against the politicized 'Cold War scholarship' of the older generation, exemplified in the field of Sovietology by the totalitarian model.[5] It was also a response to the waning explanatory power of the totalitarian model in the face of contemporary (post-Stalin) political realities in the Soviet Union. The model had implied that totalitarian regimes were endlessly self-perpetuating unless overthrown by external force. Yet under Khrushchev and Brezhnev, the Soviet Union was clearly changing, and the regime seemed to be losing many of its totalitarian characteristics.

At the same time, Western Sovietology was undergoing its own internal changes. Political scientists had set the tone in the postwar decades, but by the 1970s historians were beginning to enter the field in significant numbers. The historians tended to dislike models in general, and the totalitarian model in particular. Their disciplinary bias was empirical. Once they started working on the Stalin period, they were much less likely to be impressed by systems, planning and regime controls than to notice evidence of improvisation, spontaneity and accident. The political scientist Merle Fainsod, who made similar observations after working on the Smolensk Archives relatively late in his scholarly career, tried to square the circle by describing the Soviet system of the 1930s as 'inefficient totalitarianism'. But historians like Arch Getty thought that after a certain degree, inefficient totalitarianism ceased to be totalitarianism at all.[6]

There have been several currents in revisionist scholarship. One was criticism of the totalitarian model.[7] Another was essentially a Western continuation of the Soviet 'de-Stalinizing' work of the 1960s, associated primarily with Stephen Cohen and Moshe Lewin.[8] Following Soviet 'de-Stalinizers' like Roy Medvedev, Cohen wrote sympathetically of Bolshevism and the Revolution, saw a basic discontinuity in Soviet history between Lenin and Stalin, and regarded Stalinism as an aberration. He and Lewin, however, went further than the Soviet revisionists had done, at least in their published work, by postulating a genuine 'Bukharin alternative' to Stalinism.[9] They were, in effect, advocates of Bukharin's position, which they saw as compatible with Lenin's in his last years. In their interpretation of Stalinism, they followed the basic critique of Western anti-Stalinist Marxism whose classic statements are Trotsky's *The Revolution Betrayed* and Djilas' *The New Class*.

A third trend in Western Sovietological revisionism was the turn towards social history. Most of the younger scholars entering the Soviet field were, or wished to become, social historians. This partly reflected current trends in the historical profession as a whole. But it also implied a conviction that the dynamics of Soviet historical development were not purely political and ideological, as assumed in the totalitarian model. The revisionists wanted to shift the emphasis to social forces and processes.[10] Some thought it particularly important to study the Soviet working class.[11] Others emphasized the theme of social mobility, suggesting that the opportunity for working-class and peasant upward mobility into the new elite played a role in legitimizing the regime in the Stalin period.[12] A shared assumption of revisionist historians was that Soviet society was more than a passive object of regime manipulation and that scholars should investigate Stalinism 'from below' as well as (or, in some cases, rather than) 'from above'.[13]

Glasnost and 'New Thinking' in the Soviet Union

The present Soviet revisionism started off as a continuation of the interrupted revisionism of the 1960s. This time, however, the historians were initially slower to react to the winds of change and at first left the initiative largely to writers and journalists. Novels like Rybakov's *Deti Arbata*, Trifonov's *Ischeznovenie*, Mikhail Alekseev's *Drachuny* and Mozhaev's *Muzhiki i baby*, as well as the film *Pokaianie* (*Repentance*), began a reappraisal of many controversial episodes of the 1930s including the Great Purges, collectivization, the famine and Kirov's murder. The writers attacked the historians for perpetuating *nepravda* – outmoded official lies – about the Stalin period. The historians, clearly disoriented and demoralized, failed to defend themselves or their discipline and even admitted that they had been perpetrators of *nepravda*.[14]

The most daring and informative re-evaluations of Soviet history in the early years of *glasnost* appeared in the mass media – weeklies like the illustrated *Ogonek*, *Literaturnaia gazeta* and *Moskovskie novosti* (*Moscow News*), 'thick' journals like the ideological monthly *Kommunist* and the literary *Druzhba narodov*, even daily newspapers – rather than the specialized historical journals. Journalists, flinging themselves enthusiastically into the campaign against Stalinism, quickly produced a startlingly wide selection of exposé material in the print media: for example, memoirs of purge victims and their families, information on the discovery of mass graves dating from the late 1930s, data on closing of churches and repression of religion, discussion of the famine and abuses against the peasantry during collectivization, speculation on Stalin's role in Kirov's murder, information on the privileged life-style of the political elite, case studies of Stalinist repression in culture.

The early forays into historical revisionism by professional Soviet historians also appeared in the mass media. *Pravda*, for example, initiated a 'Friday' series[15] in which progressive historians tried to give the public the 'real truth' about major historical episodes like the political faction fights of the 1920s, collectivization and the forced-pace industrialization drive of the 1930s. For the most part, these 'truth-telling' historians were veterans of the aborted de-Stalinization trend of the 1960s,[16] though a few new names[17] appeared in *Pravda* and *Kommunist* in the 1980s. Not surprisingly, the 'truth-telling' view presented in *Pravda*'s 'Fridays' was essentially a summation and recapitulation of conclusions from the de-Stalinizing scholarship of the 1960s. It exposed Stalin's 'mistakes' and 'excesses', but treated them as deviations from Leninism and socialism rather than as evidence of basic systemic weaknesses. From a specialist point of view, there was relatively little new hard data in these articles, since the historians had not had time for major archival investigations under perestroika conditions. From the standpoint of perestroika radicals like Iu. N. Afanasev, Rector of the Moscow Historical-Archival Institute, the historical profession was still lagging behind.

In 1988–9, however, it became increasingly clear that the revaluation of the Stalin period in the mass media was going far beyond that of the 1960s. Television joined the print media in publicizing the evils of Stalinism. Some writers in the 'thick' journals began questioning not only the value of Soviet objectives and priorities in the Stalin period but also the basic soundness of the Soviet system itself. This affected the tenor of the professional historians' debates, conducted largely in a series of roundtable discussions of central historical questions like collectivization, Soviet labour history and the Second World War. By 1989, the historical journal *Voprosy istorii* was publishing scholarly material almost as sensational as anything in the mass media.

Stalin's Crimes

The trend of Soviet 'new thinking' in history at the end of the 1980s is exemplified by the common use of a new term for Stalinism, the pejorative '*stalinshchina*'. This is sometimes used with specific reference to Stalinist repression, but at other times it sounds more like a blanket condemnation of everything associated with the 1930s and the postwar Stalin period. The current Soviet discussions of Stalinism are qualitatively different from those of the 1960s. Their dominant tone is one of unqualified rejection and denunciation. This is closer in spirit to the *samizdat* and *tamizdat* publications of Soviet dissidents in the 1970s than to the 'in-system' critiques of Tvardovskii's *Novyi mir* or the narrower de-Stalinization objectives of historical journals like *Voprosy istorii*, *Istoriia SSSR* and the military *Voenno-istoricheskii zhurnal* in the 1960s. Soviet journal publications of previously arch-heretical works like Solzhenitsyn's *Gulag Archipelago*[18] or Trotsky's *Stalinist School of Falsification*[19] are beginning to seem almost routine.

For many Soviet intellectuals, it is clear that Stalin has become an outright villain rather than just a flawed leader. In the present intellectual climate, a discussion of Stalin that portrayed any of his actions in an unambiguously favourable light would be almost as surprising to the reader as the opposite would have been in the heyday of Stalinism. Of the two major works on Stalin serialized in Soviet journals in 1988–9, the more sensational and uncompromising in its denunciation of him was a memoir-based history by the son of a prominent Bolshevik Oppositionist of the 1920s and victim of Stalin's purges. It was published a decade earlier in the West with the subtitle *Portrait of a Tyranny*[20] and probably accords more closely with the current maximalist mood of the Soviet intelligentsia. The other work, the impressive and weighty biography of Stalin by Volkogonov, approaches its subject in a more even handed way, as is indicated by its title, *Triumph and Tragedy*. Although Volkogonov's book scarcely looks like a justification of Stalin, judging by the excerpts that have appeared in a Soviet journal,[21] it is symptomatic of the temper of the time that some Soviet readers have criticized it for choosing a balanced tone rather than a prosecutorial approach and stopping short of casting Stalin as the 'demon' of the revolution.

Along with the indictment of Stalin goes rehabilitation of former leaders who were Stalin's rivals and ultimately victims. The Right Oppositionist Bukharin, convicted of treason in the 1938 Moscow show trial and rehabilitated in February 1988, is the prime example of a Communist leader whose rehabilitation was sought unsuccessfully under Khrushchev and achieved only under Gorbachev's perestroika. But there are many other cases[22] and the Politburo's Commission on Stalinist repression and rehabilitations continues its work.[23] Even Trotsky has been rescued from unmentionability, if not formally rehabilitated. There have been dramatic accounts of Trotsky's assassination by a Soviet agent in Mexico in 1941 drawn from Western sources, not to mention a remarkable story in *Moscow News* about the assassin's own later life, after release from a Mexican prison, as a Soviet personal pensioner.[24] Stephen F. Cohen's biography of Bukharin[25] is being translated and published in the Soviet Union. A shorter Soviet biography and devoted recollections of Bukharin by his widow have already appeared.[26]

New information is regularly emerging on a wide range of disasters and crimes of the Stalin era. Prominent among these are collectivization, which some though not all Soviet scholars are ready to treat as an almost total mistake causing the deportation of kulaks and the famine of 1933–4. The Great Purges of 1937–8 and the Gulag labour-camp system are a central theme. Many personal Purge memoirs have been published, along with some very interesting data from local NKVD files[27] and the first statistics from the central archives on the size of the Gulag population in the 1930s and 1940s.[28] A new theme in the press, starting in the late summer of 1988, has been that of purge-related executions, suggested by the discovery of mass graves in Kuropaty in Belorussia and sites in the Ukraine and Siberia.[29]

Some discreditable aspects of Stalin's foreign policy came under close critical scrutiny in 1989. These include the Nazi-Soviet Pact of 1939 and its notorious Secret Protocols,[30] the Winter War of 1939–40 against Finland and the Katyn massacre of Polish officers.[31] The post-war period has also come under scrutiny, with publications on the 'Leningrad affair' of the late 1940s[32] and the Doctors' Plot of 1952.[33] There has been a recent upsurge of attention to nationality questions, with harsh criticism of repressive Stalinist policies including the wholesale deportation of certain small national groups like the Crimean Tatars in the 1940s, mass arrests and further deportations in the newly-incorporated Baltic states.[34]

Openness to Western Concepts and Methodologies

For Western scholars, perhaps the most breathtaking aspect of Gorbachevian 'new thinking' is the current Soviet enthusiasm for Western Sovietology. Western scholarship on Soviet history was routinely dismissed as 'bourgeois falsification'. Indeed, 'bourgeois historiography' was virtually a separate sub-discipline in Soviet historical research institutes. It was this specialized and ideologically-vigilant branch of the profession that produced at least one of the leading New Thinkers of perestroika, Iurii Afanasev. He has been particularly critical of his colleagues in Soviet history, as well as a number of lesser-known figures who have emerged as perestroika activists in history and advocates of closer intellectual contacts between the Soviet Union and the West. This is perhaps less strange than it seems at first glance. In the Khrushchev and Brezhnev periods, critical reviews of the work of Western 'bourgeois falsifiers' often functioned in practice as a medium for introducing and publicizing Western ideas that would otherwise have been inaccessible to most Soviet scholars.[35]

The present enthusiasm for Western Sovietology is eclectic, embracing such disparate figures as Robert Conquest[36] – author of *The Great Terror*, *Harvest of Sorrow* on the famine of the early 1930s, and a number of less scholarly works including the 1983 'survivor's guide', *What to Do When the Russians Come* – and the revisionist Stephen Cohen. The concept of totalitarianism, long anathematized by Soviet commentators, has now acquired an aura of radical chic in the Soviet intelligentsia and is frequently invoked in discussions. Orwell's *1984* has been published in the Soviet Union; and even works published in the West by Stalin-period defectors such as Kravchenko and Orlov have been cited as evidence of Stalin's crimes. Trotsky's classic indictment of Stalinism, *The Revolution Betrayed* (1937) – the key interpretation of the Soviet system for Western anti-Stalinist and anti-Soviet Marxists, as well as for many 'revisionist' Sovietologists in recent years – has not yet (as of December 1989) been published in the Soviet Union but copies are in great demand among Soviet intellectuals, and some of the recent discussion of Stalinist bureaucratization seems to draw on Trotsky's analysis.

Soviet historians and social scientists are now showing great interest in Western methodologies as well as Western ideas. In the field of history, the most popular 'new' methods are those of quantitative history, on the one hand, and oral history, on the other. Quantitative methods appeal to Soviet historians for various reasons. One is that they represent a way of objectifying the data base underlying historical work and assumptions. Another is their association with personal computers. These are much coveted but not yet widely possessed by Soviet scholars, who often make the mistake of thinking Western historians use their PCs for computing rather than word-processing. In practice, quantitative techniques involving computerization are still only at an early stage, although a group of historians led by the late V. Z. Drobizhev has done pioneering work on the creation of computerized biographical data bases.[37]

Quantitative methods have been applied mainly in the rising field of demographic history (which is quantitative, but does not generally involve computer processing of data). Demographic history is now widely perceived as an essential tool in addressing some of the most controversial questions of the history of the Stalin period. These include the deportation of kulaks, the 1932–3 famine, the Great Purges, the development of Gulag, forced population resettlements, and the Soviet military and civilian losses of World War II.[38]

One of the most striking manifestations of historical perestroika so far is the Soviet entry into a bitter and long-running Western argument about the impact of 'excess deaths' during the Stalin period related to collectivization, famine and so on. The director of the State Archive of the Soviet Economy has recently offered a calculation, based on hitherto unavailable archival materials, of 8 million 'excess deaths' in the pre-war Stalin period.[39] But the Soviet press has also published much more sensational and less scientific estimates like Roy Medvedev's 40 million 'victims of Stalinism'.[40]

The new interest in quantitative methods and demographic history is equalled by a new interest in another previously neglected Western historical methodology, oral history. Until quite recently, oral history was not a recognized genre in Soviet historiography. Indeed, Soviet historians tended to look askance at any kind of individual personal testimony: there were also comparatively few personal memoirs published, they were difficult to access through Soviet bibliographical aids, and there were even theoretical doubts expressed about their value as historical data.[41]

The first large-scale oral history projects, started in the early 1980s, focused on 'safe' groups such as World War II veterans and 'leading workers'. Now the focus seems to be shifting to groups such as victims of the Great Purge and Ukrainian famine and on the collection of individual testimonies from all persons who experienced the dark side of the Stalin era. At the Moscow Historical-Archival Institute, whose rector is the radical Iurii Afanasiev, students are now required to conduct as part of their studies an oral-history project: for example, interviewing their grandparents in depth about their experiences in the Stalin era.

Was Stalinism Really Necessary?

The questions 'What is Stalinism?' and 'What were its origins?' have become a central preoccupation of Soviet intellectuals in the past few years. Many different answers have been offered, and a fair number of them will already be familiar to the reader because they come from the 'de-Stalinization' discussions of the 1960s, the *samizdat* and *tamizdat* works of the 1970s, or from various schools of Western Sovietological scholarship. The intellectual range is remarkable in comparison with the past. Among the competing theories jostling for space in Soviet periodicals and newspapers today are the totalitarian model, Trotsky's *Revolution Betrayed* hypothesis, the theory of a 'Bukharin alternative' to Stalinism, Slavophile and neo-Populist arguments about the course of Russian history, and the 'barracks socialism' view of Stalinism. As always in Russian and Soviet argument, the question 'Who is to blame?' is well to the fore. Suggested scapegoats include a psychologically-disturbed Stalin, Russia's backward peasantry, Russia's partially-peasant working class, the Russian intelligentsia (because of its utopianism and impractical idealism), the Bolsheviks of the early Soviet period (because of their cult of party unity), Bolsheviks of the Civil War cohort (because of their cult of *machismo*), the Stalinist bureaucracy (or, alternatively, the contingent of ill-educated, upwardly-mobile workers and peasants in the Stalinist bureaucracy), international Marxism, and the Jews. Some writers even suggest that Lenin – particularly the Lenin of 'War Communism' as distinct from the 'NEP' Lenin – and the October Revolution should share the blame.[42]

Two types of general explanation of Stalinism are emerging as dominant. The first finds the origin of Stalinism in the political system of one-party with a ban on internal factions established after the Revolution. This implies that the core characteristic of Stalinism was repressive dictatorship not limited by rule of law, and that Stalinism was essentially an outgrowth of Leninism. It is similar to one of the standard Western interpretations related to the totalitarian paradigm, for example Schapiro's *Origins of Communist Autocracy*.

The other type of explanation focusses on social forces. In the most popular argument of this type, it is bureaucratization and the emergence of a new bureaucratic ruling class that are the quintessence of Stalinism.[43] This view is similar to that of many European Marxists and some 'revisionist' Western historians such as Moshe Lewin. It implies a judgement that Stalinism had no social support except from the new bureaucratic elite. But there is also some cautious discussion of the possibility that Stalinism did in fact have some social support from outside the elite. This includes the theory that Stalin's 'revolution from above' at the beginning of the 1930s had support from urban workers and rank-and-file members of the Communist Party and Komsomol.[44] Such ideas are broached cautiously because many Soviet intellectuals feel that they are not appropriate to the Perestroika objective of discrediting and rooting out *stalinshchina*, or that they may be incorrectly interpreted as a justification of Stalinism.

Discussion of the phenomenon of Stalinism leads inexorably – especially for Soviet intellectuals – to the question of historical necessity: was Stalinism an inevitable development in Soviet history, or could it have been avoided? Soviet historians have been conditioned to take a much more determinist view of history than is normal in the West. Their Marxist training leads them to think in terms of underlying historical regularities or laws (*zakonomernost'*); and in past Soviet historiographical usage these laws were often invoked as justification of Bolshevik and Soviet actions and policies (for example the 'necessity' of the October Revolution or Stalinist collectivization).

However, Soviet historians are now trying to escape from this intellectual heritage of determinism and particularly from its misuse as a justification of Stalinist policies. One way of doing this is to develop a concept of 'alternatives' within the basic Marxist framework of historical laws. Historians of the older generation such as Volobuev,[45] who want to retain the Marxist framework but who avoid the old dogmatic stereotypes, have been initiators of a new theory of historical alternatives. As currently applied to the 1920s and 1930s, this allows historians to conceptualize Soviet history in terms of a series of crucial choices and moments of decision. Examples include the crucial choice facing the party in 1921, which resulted in the abandonment of War Communism and introduction of the NEP, and the crucial choice of the late 1920s when Stalin's program of forced-pace industrialization and collectivization prevailed over the 'Bukharin alternative'. To Western historians, such cut-and-dried, either-or frameworks may not seem very sophisticated, but they probably serve a useful function by expanding the sense of the possible as well as legitimizing Bolshevik Opposition platforms that were formerly condemned. One suspects, however, that with the passage of time the concept of alternatives may become less appealing, as younger Soviet historians find they can solve the problem of historical laws simply by ignoring it.

What Next?

It is too soon to say what new dominant interpretations of Stalinism will emerge in the Soviet Union out of the intellectual upheaval of perestroika. We can, however, draw some conclusions from the present situation about the likely course of development in the next few years.

In the first place, the new access to archival and other data ensures that much more detailed knowledge of Soviet high politics and workings of government in the Stalin period will be available, as well as more reliable information on economic and demographic questions. Some of this will reinforce the present strongly negative attitude to Stalin and Stalinism, since more information means more discoveries of the regime's dirty secrets, scandals and stupidity. After a time, however, other results of the historians' new access to Stalinist archives are likely to show up in the scholarly literature. Once party and government archives are open, historians tend, after a while, to lose interest in the great imponderables like Stalinism, exhaust the archives' supply of dirty secrets and sensational discoveries, and start writing 'ordinary' history. This was the case with German historiography after the post-war opening of Germany's Nazi-period archives. This 'ordinary' history will include a large component of bureaucratic and interest-group politics (as is the case with recent historiography of Nazi Germany), because that is a subject on which bureaucratic archives are invariably informative. For better or worse, the Stalinist regime will lose some of its aura of sinister mystery and monolithic purpose as historians find out more about it.

Whether the outside pressures on historians – from the Soviet political leadership and the public – will tend to encourage a more positive or more negative view of the Stalin era is anyone's guess. From the leadership's standpoint, there are obvious problems with root-and-branch denunciation of Stalinism, which implicitly puts in question the whole leading role of the party, Lenin and the Revolution. It seems clear that the anti-*stalinshchina* campaign has gone further than Gorbachev and his men originally desired. Nations cannot wholly repudiate their past and need the myths of the founding fathers. While episodes of repudiation do occur, as in the US during the Vietnam era, they are generally followed by a strong popular backlash and a subsequent reassertion of national pride. One would expect the Gorbachev leadership to be conscious of this.

As for public sentiments on the question of Stalinism, we simply do not have enough information about the state of Soviet public opinion to be sure what kind of pressure to expect. There must be sections of the Soviet (especially Russian) public that are offended by the current media attacks on Stalinism, construing them as unpatriotic, a slander on the victory in World War II, moral capitulation to the West, and so on. The pro-Stalinist attitudes expressed in Nina Andreeva's famous letter[46] may be more widespread than Soviet intellectuals like to think. There are indications that some Soviet citizens feel the same kind of suspicion of 'the liberal media' and 'radical intellectuals' as citizens of Middle America. But ultimately the resolution of this question may rest on the outcome of a broader one, namely whether the present Soviet regime – which, when all is said and done, is a direct descendant of the October Revolution, Lenin and Stalin – will retain the legitimacy to survive.

In the second place, we can expect an upsurge of nationalism in historical writing, together with the kind of nostalgic identity-seeking sentiment exemplified by *Roots* or *The World We Have Lost*. Signs of this have already appeared in Russian society, especially among the young – for example, a neo-Slavophile interest in Russian peasant life, folk customs, and the rituals and festivals of the Orthodox Church – and these are already reflected in literary and historical works. Perhaps even more importantly, the same is true, only to a greater degree, for all the non-Russian peoples and republics. They will be writing their own nationalist (quasi-separatist) histories, distinct from the Russian-dominated 'official Soviet' version given in the old history books. National heroes and martyrs (many of the latter being victims of Stalin's regime) will appear, along with hitherto unmentionable episodes of inter-ethnic conflict and oppression by Moscow.

This means that, for the first time, real diversity of historical interpretation will arise out of the ethnic diversity of the multi-national and multi-ethnic Soviet state. This point can be appreciated if one considers the recent territorial dispute between the Armenians and Azerbaidzhanians over Nagorno-Karabakh, an issue which was unknown to the outside world before perestroika. There is a legitimate Armenian historical perspective on this issue and an equally legitimate Azerbaidzhanian one. Future historians will no doubt also find a third perspective in the central archives, namely that of Imperial Russian and Soviet administrators trying to cope with the long standing ethnic conflicts of the region.

In the third place, we can expect to see a new emphasis on individual lives and fates in future writing on Soviet history. This has already begun for the individual victims of Stalinist repression, whose names and histories are being collected by the voluntary society 'Memorial'. But it is likely to go much further, judging by the recent enthusiasm of scholars for compiling biographical dictionaries and data bases and the general awakening of interest in family histories and genealogies. Memoir publication is likely to flourish, going beyond the present spate of publication of intelligentsia memoirs and those of Purge victims. Ordinary people's reminiscences, letters and personal diaries will probably also be gathered and fed into the data pool.

In the long run, these developments must contribute to the acceptance of diversity in historical interpretation. The more individual histories are available, the more historians and their readers are likely to acquire a sense of the multiplicity of human experience and individual trajectories, leading to a more complex understanding of the past. If, for example, the oral history project of Moscow history students mentioned above (p. 89) were applied broadly to the over-sixties population, a variety of characteristic 'Stalinist' experiences would undoubtedly emerge, with a corresponding variety of perspectives and assessments of Stalinism.

Some respondents in the oral history project would have experienced repression in the Stalin period: for example, victims of the Great Purges, veterans of Gulag, and their family members; members of the cultural intelligentsia who suffered from the *zhdanovshchina* of the late 1940s; Jews and members of other non-Russian ethnic groups that suffered various tribulations under Stalin; children of deported kulaks or of peasants who suffered in the famine of the early 1930s, and so on. But there would be others whose experiences and life histories were different. These include World War II veterans taking pride in the great patriotic victory, erstwhile Pioneers and Komsomols of the prewar decade, for whom the 1930s remains a time of youth, optimism and heroic national exploits; peasants who left the village as youths during collectivization and prospered in the towns; sons of peasants and workers who were chosen for advancement and sent to technical schools and universities, and so on. In addition, there would be memories of everyday life, often tinged with nostalgia for simpler times: how wedding rings and New Year trees came back in the mid 1930s; that food was abundant in 1937; when vodka was cheap and available and when not; when ice-cream first appeared in Moscow kiosks; how under Stalin there was discipline in the schools and no crime on the streets; and also of jazz bands and tea-dancing in the 1930s, and sad and sentimental wartime songs ('Wait for Me', 'No, the Soldier Won't Forget').

If glasnost is here to stay, diversity in the writing of history is not only a predictable consequence, it is also a necessary one. There are no single truths about a complex entity like the Soviet Union, with its diversity of regions and populations and multi-ethnic character. For historians, indeed, there are no single, indisputable truths about any era. The illusion that truth is monolithic belongs to regimes with monolithic aspirations, their political opponents, and – for a finite period – their triumphant challengers and successors. Once the process of political perestroika is fully launched, however, the justification for rewriting history in the dialectical manner (that is, turning old received truths on their heads) falls away. The ultimate de-Stalinization of Soviet history writing will come when the historians finally decide that there is more than one 'right' answer to historical problems and more than one legitimate interpretation of Stalinism.

Austin, Texas
December 1989

Afterword

A lot has happened in the Soviet Union in the fifteen months since this article was written. For most Soviet citizens, Stalinism is no longer a burning preoccupation. This is not just because the public has become jaded with sensational revelations about the past, or because the acute economic problems of the present have overshadowed all other concerns. The issue of Stalinism was incredibly important for Soviet society as long as the basic framework of a Soviet nation founded in the October Revolution of 1917 and led by the Communist Party seemed immutable. But now the old certainties have shattered. For many of the younger generation, it seems, Stalinism has become almost an irrelevant issue. Undoubtedly it was bad, they will agree, but then so were the Revolution, Leninism, the Communist Party, and the entire seventy years of Soviet history.

In the present situation, remembering and denouncing Stalinism (*stalinshchina*) is fast becoming the prerogative of middle-aged liberals; and middle-aged liberalism – or any other! – seems to be going rapidly out of fashion. The great political issues of the day are the national question (whether or in what form to preserve the Union), the economy, and the breakdown of public order. The turbulent national republics and ethnic groups have their own different perspectives on the Stalin era, based on specific historical experiences and their current political agendas.

In the context of Russian politics, and probably that of other republics, the decline of liberal intellectuals as a political force has been paralleled by the rise of what might be called a Communist New Right, which is clearly going to make patriotism, national pride, and public order its key issues. *Pace* Mikoyan, that means rejecting much of the liberals' blanket indictment of the Stalin period – a process that is already evident in journals like the once-liberal journal of military history, *Voenno-istoricheskii zhurnal*, which has recently become a New Right organ.

Chicago
March 1991

Notes

1 This article was written in December 1989, but the volume as a whole was not ready for the publisher until the spring of 1991. With the exception of the afterword, which refers to the developments of the 15–16 months between those two dates, the article's present tense should be understood to refer to late 1989.

2 On the origins of the concept of totalitarianism and its application in Sovietology, see Abbott Gleason, ' "Totalitarianism" in 1984,' *Russian Review*, vol. 43 (1984), pp. 146–51. Gleason identifies Carl Friedrich and Zbigniew Brzezinski's *Totalitarian Dictatorship and Autocracy* (Cambridge, Mass., 1956) as the most influential theoretical treatment, and Merle Fainsod's *How Russia is Ruled* (Cambridge, Mass., 1953) as the most widely-read study incorporating the vision of the Soviet Union as a totalitarian state.

3 For discussion of some of the major Soviet historical controversies of this period, see Nancy Whittier Heer, *Politics and History in the Soviet Union* (Cambridge, Mass., 1971).

4 The term 'samizdat' was coined for dissident works illicitly reproduced in the Soviet Union and circulated among Soviet intellectuals. The term 'tamizdat' refers to similar works smuggled out of the Soviet Union for publication in Russian in the West.

5 For an analytical account, see Gleason, *op cit.*, pp. 152–8; for a participant's account and revisionist manifesto, see Stephen F. Cohen, 'Sovietology as a Vocation', in his *Rethinking the Soviet Experience: Politics and History Since 1917* (New York, 1985).

6 J. Arch Getty, *Origins of the Great Purges: The Soviet Communist Party Reconsidered, 1933–1938* (Cambridge and New York, 1985), p. 198 and *passim*.

7 See Jerry F. Hough, *The Soviet Union and Social Science Theory* (Cambridge, Mass., 1977), and Jerry F. Hough and Merle Fainsod, *How the Soviet Union is Governed* (Cambridge, Mass., 1979).

8 Stephen F. Cohen, *Bukharin and the Bolshevik Revolution* (New York, 1973) and *Rethinking the Soviet Experience* (New York, 1986); M. Lewin, *Lenin's Last Struggle* (New York, 1968) and *Political Undercurrents in Soviet Economic Development: Bukharin and the Modern Reformers* (Princeton, 1974).

9 This interpretation was not shared by all Western 'revisionist' scholars. For an influential statement of another point of view, see Alec Nove, *Economic Rationality and Soviet Politics, or Was Stalin Really Necessary?* (New York, 1964).

10 For an interesting discussion of this trend, see the review article by Louis Menashe in *International Labor and Working-Class History*, vol. 35 (Spring 1989).

11 See, for example, Lynne Viola, *The Best Sons of the Fatherland: Workers in the Vanguard of Soviet Collectivization* (New York, 1986); H. Kuromiya, *Stalin's Industrial Revolution: Politics and Workers, 1928–1932* (Cambridge, 1988); Lewis H. Siegelbaum, *Stakhanovism and the Politics of Productivity in the USSR, 1935–1941* (Cambridge, 1988); Donald Filtzer, *Soviet Workers and Stalinist Industrialization* (Armonk, NY, 1986).

12 See Sheila Fitzpatrick, *Education and Social Mobility in the Soviet Union, 1921–1934* (New York, 1979) and id., 'Stalin and the Making of a New Elite, 1928–1939', *Slavic Review*, September 1979.

13 See Sheila Fitzpatrick (ed.), *Cultural Revolution in Russia, 1928–1931* (Bloomington, Ind., 1978), especially the Introduction. For argument among revisionists on the relationship of state and society in the Stalin period and the question of initiative 'from below', see Sheila Fitzpatrick, 'New Perspectives on Stalinism', *Russian Review*, October 1986, and comments by Stephen Cohen and Geoff Eley in *ibid.*, and J. Arch Getty, Roberta Manning and others in *Russian Review*, October 1987.

14 See conference of historians and writers, 27–8 April 1988, *Voprosy istorii*, 1988, no. 6.

15 The 'Friday' series ('*Pravdinskie piatnitsy*') was edited by Academician G. L. Smirnov, Director of the Institute of Marxism-Leninism of the Central Committee of the CPSU. The series began in *Pravda*, 26 February 1988, p. 3, with a discussion of 'Lenin's Testament' by V. P. Naumov, and continued for about eight months.

16 e.g. V. P. Danilov, Iu. A. Poliakov and V. S. Lelchuk. The best-known 'truth-teller' in this group was probably Danilov, whose bold scholarly writing on collectivization in the 1960s and subsequent tribulations had earned him the respect of perestroika supporters, as well as a considerable international reputation as a scholar.

17 Notably those of V. A. Kozlov and G. Bordiugov, both in their thirties and working at the Institute of Marxism-Leninism.

18 Excerpts from *Gulag* appeared in *Novyi mir*, 1989, no. 8, pp. 7–94.

19 Published in *Voprosy istorii*, 1989, nos. 7–9.

20 A. V. Antonov-Ovseenko, *The Time of Stalin: Portrait of a Tyranny* (New York, 1981). The Soviet version, little changed from the US publication, appeared in *Voprosy istorii*, 1989, nos. 1–4 and 6–9, under the title 'Stalin and his Time'.

21 D. Volkogonov, 'Triumf i tragediia. Politicheskii portret I. V. Stalina,' *Oktiabr'*, 1988, nos. 10, 11 and 12. The full biography, recently published in Moscow in

book form, was not available to the author at the time of writing.

22 For a chronology of major political rehabilitations up to November 1988, see Stephen G. Wheatcroft, '*Glasnost*' and Rehabilitations', in Takayuki Ito (ed.), *Facing up to the Past: Soviet Historiography under Perestroika* (Sapporo, Japan, 1989), pp. 211–14.

23 See, for example, the commission's conclusions rehabilitating former Workers' Oppositionists arrested early in 1935 in the wake of Kirov's assassination, *Izvestiia TsK*, 1989, no. 10 (October), pp. 56–79.

24 Juan Cobo, 'Trotsky's Assassin: Executioner or Victim?', *Moscow News*, 1989, no. 12, pp. 15–16.

25 Stephen F. Cohen, *Bukharin and the Bolshevik Revolution: A Political Biography, 1888–1938* (New York, 1973). The first extract appeared as 'Duumvirat: Bukharin i Stalin' in *Ogonek*, 1988, no. 45, pp. 29–30.

26 I. E. Gorelov, *Nikolai Bukharin* (Moscow, 1988); A. M. Larina, 'On khotel peredelat' zhizn', potomu chto ee liubil', *Ogonek*, 1987, no. 48, and *id.*, 'Nezabyvaemye', *Znamia*, 1988, nos. 10–12.

27 G. Izhbuldin (Cheliabinsk), 'Nazvat' vse imena', *Ogonek*, 1989, no. 7 (February), p. 30.

28 See V. V. Tsaplin (director of the Central Archive of the National Economy of the USSR), 'Statistika zhertv Stalinizma v 30-e gody', *Voprosy istorii*, 1989, no. 4, p. 176. Volkogonov also cites figures on Gulag from the Beria archive in an interview published in *Moscow News*, 19–26 February 1989, p. 9.

29 In Kuropaty, the first and largest site, it seems likely that only a minority of the bodies belong to Great Purge victims, since others can be identified by their clothing as citizens of the territory of Eastern Poland (now Western Belorussia), occupied and incorporated into the Soviet Union after the Nazi-Soviet Non-Aggression Pact of 1939.

30 On the Nazi-Soviet pact, see historians' round table in *Voprosy istorii*, 1989, no. 6. The text of the Secret Protocols is given on p. 20.

31 *Moscow News*, no. 21, 1989 (21 May), p. 16: A. Akulichev and A. Pamiatnykh produce some evidence suggesting Soviet guilt and imply that this is a possible conclusion (although the Polish-Soviet commission has yet to report). For a valuable survey of the situation up to spring 1989, see Takayuki Ito, ' "Blank Spots" in Polish-Soviet History: Pandora's Box or Catharsis?', in Ito (ed.), *Facing up to the Past*.

32 e.g. article by A. Afanasev on one of the victims of the Leningrad affair, A. A. Kuznetsov, in *Komsomol'skaia pravda*, 15 January 1988, p. 2.

33 Ia. Rapoport, 'Vospominaniia o "dele vrachei" ', *Druzhba narodov*, 1988, no. 4. See also *Moscow News*, 7 February 1988 (no. 26), p. 16.

34 'Natsional'nyi vopros i mezhnatsional'nye otnosheniia v SSSR: Istoriia i sovremennost' (Materialy 'kruglogo stola'), *Voprosy istorii*, nos. 5 and 6.

35 See, for example, the well-researched and fairminded work by N. Gushchin (a collectivization expert) and V. A. Zhdanov (an expert on Western historiography), *Kritika burzhuaznykh kontseptsii istorii sovetskoi sibirskoi derevni* (Novosibirsk, 1987).

36 *Voprosy istorii*, 1989, no. 3, published a letter from Conquest on famine casualties.

In no. 10 (p. 186), the same journal reported a meeting of its editors with Conquest and agreement to publish chapters from his book *Harvest of Sorrow* in the journal.

37 See description of V. Z. Drobizhev, E. I. Pivovar and A. K. Sokolov, '*Perestroika* and the Study of Sources on Soviet Social History. Appendix: Soviet Computerized Data Bases', in Sheila Fitzpatrick and Lynne Viola (eds.), *A Researcher's Guide to Sources on Soviet Social History in the 1930s* (Armonk, NY: M. E. Sharpe, 1990).

38 It is interesting to note that the widely-cited figure of 20 million total World War II casualties, offered by Khrushchev in place of the 7 million losses admitted in the late Stalin period, appears to have been little more than a guess, not a serious demographic estimate. Soviet total direct population losses were recently estimated by a Soviet historical demographer to be close to 40 million: that is, twice Khrushchev's figure, not including an additional 10 million indirect losses. See V. I. Kozlov, 'O liudskikh poteriakh Sovetskogo Soiuza v Velikoi Otechestvennoi voine 1941–45 gg.', *Istoriia SSSR*, 1989, no. 2.

39 V. V. Tsaplin, 'Statistika zhertv Stalinizma v 30-e gody', *Voprosy istorii*, 1989, no. 4, pp. 175–81. In addition to the 8 million deaths, Tsaplin estimates that perhaps 2 million Kazakhs fled across the border in the aftermath of collectivization. (Detailed archival data on the size of the Gulag convict population in the 1930s and 1940s have been steadily emerging over the past year in the Soviet press. For a convenient summary, see articles by Vera Tolz in Radio Liberty, *Report on the USSR*, 10 August 1990 and 7 September 1990.)

40 Roy Medvedev, answer to a reader's question, in *Argumenty i fakty*, 1989, no. 5. Medvedev's category of victims includes all those who suffered repression (imprisonment, deportation, exile and so on) under Stalin, not only those who died. It also relates to the whole Stalin period up to 1953, not just the 1930s, like Tsaplin's figure.

41 For a valuable discussion of Soviet memoirs, see the article by Hiroaki Kuromiya in Fitzpatrick and Viola (ed.), *A Researcher's Guide to Sources on Soviet Social History of the 1930s*.

42 For more detailed discussions, see the article by Alec Nove in this volume, as well as articles by Wada, Shiokawa, Okuda, Shimotomai and Wheatcroft in Ito (ed.), *Facing up to the Past*.

43 See particularly G. Popov's review article on the novel *Novoe Naznachenie* by Aleksandr Bek, published in *Nauka i zhizn'*, 1987, no. 4.

44 See, for example, the articles by G. Bordiugov and V. Kozlov in *Pravda*, 3 October 1988, p. 3 (especially the section headed 'Whose class interests did Stalin express?') and *Literaturnaia gazeta*, 12 October 1988, p. 11; and Iu. A. Poliakov, '20-e gody: nastroeniya partiinogo avangarda', *Voprosy istorii KPSS*, 1989, no. 10.

45 See P. V. Volobuev, *Vybor putei obshchestvennogo razvitiya: teoriia, istoriia, sovremennost'* (Moscow, 1987). There were some interesting exchanges on the question of historical alternatives at the roundtable of Soviet and American historians held in Moscow in January 1989: see contributions by Volobuev, Fitzpatrick, Kozlov, Danilov and Afanasev in *Voprosy istorii*, 1989, no. 4, pp. 97–8, 111–15. (Addendum, March 1991: Proceedings of the roundtable have now been published in English in *Journal of Modern History* 62:4 (1990).)

46 *Sovetskaia Rossiia*, 13 March 1988.

CHAPTER 4

The Politics of Stalinism

J. Arch Getty

Stalin ruled the largest country on earth for a quarter of the twentieth century and was perhaps the dominant personality of his era. His accomplishments are monumental in scope and his misdeeds are the crimes of the century. He continues to fascinate us: books about him sell well year after year and specialists endeavour to understand him and his deeds. Yet we know practically nothing about him.

His childhood is a blank and solid information about his parents comprises less than a paragraph. His adolescence is equally shadowy, as is his early political career. Only the occasional witness – his or her testimony inevitably clouded or scripted according to political needs – briefly enlightens Stalin's youth. His early writings are unrevealing, and the first focussed impression one gets comes only in 1917. Even then, his ideas, plans, conversations, and even role as a significant actor are hardly known and hotly disputed.

We know little more about the rest of Stalin's personal life. None of his intimates later came forward with truly revealing pictures; the memoirs of his daughter Svetlana Allilueva and his servant Nikita Khrushchev are the closest things one has to such testimony and although they tell us a lot, they provide only episodic snapshots of the master. Remembrances of other Soviets who had dealings with Stalin similarly consist of specific impressions at brief meetings.[1] Some of them describe an open-minded and intelligent administrator who valued the advice of experts; others portray him as narrow, stubborn, and arbitrary.

Stalin's published writings and conversations were inevitably official statements, dealing entirely with public issues and never with personal or private matters. His rare interviews and contacts with both his own countrymen and with foreigners were laconic and impersonal. He opened his heart to no one we know, and outlived or killed almost all of his early or close friends. We have no diary, no private or personal letters, no office log or appointment calendar, no words from the women in his life, and a scant collection of his writings.

Frustrating to historians and journalists, this strange situation has inevitably spawned a heterogeneous collection of purportedly serious writings on Stalin. In the absence of reliable first-hand testimony or revealing written evidence, and in their desperation to understand the man, writers on Stalin and his period have offered the specialized and general public a diverse but sometimes troubling bill of fare.

Although there have been some outright forgeries, the more common tradition has been to infer the details of his personal life and actions. Novelists (and novelists pretending to be historians) have presented fictitious dialogues and purported soliloquies by the dictator.[2] Others have made dubious claims of having known him closely and many memorists have reported scenes with Stalin that they did not witness.[3] We also now have published collections of myths about Stalin.[4]

Before and even after 1917, Russian historical scholarship was imbued with the traditions and methods of *istochnikovedenie*, the critical study of sources. Western students of Russian history are initially surprised at the detailed technical attention that masters of Russian historical writing such as Kliuchevskii and Platonov devoted to analysing documents. Many articles in Russian historical journals, especially those on early periods, consist of detailed investigation of a single charter, letter, or other document. Although it suffered mightily during the Stalin period, the tradition of source criticism was and still is comparatively well developed in Russia.[5]

It is a sad commentary that, as Patricia Grimsted recently observed, *istochnikovedenie* can be translated into no satisfactory single term in English.[6] Western graduate training in Soviet studies ignores the systematic appraisal of sources almost completely and there is practically no methodological literature on the subject in English. Accordingly, we have accepted almost anything the paper would hold as a valid source. In other fields of history, texts such as novels, plays, and poems are treated as evidence only for intellectual history or literary investigation. In our discipline, they have been somehow transformed into the primary documents and sources of political history, and some scholars even prefer poems to archives.[7]

If we did concern ourselves with *istochnikovedenie*, we would have to follow the strict rules of that discipline and worry about the degree to which a given text might reflect reality. We would be sceptical about the veracity, accuracy, and dependability of poems and plays as historical records. We would wonder about the testimony of memoirists when they report events and activities they remember hearing from others.[8] We would try to discriminate between facts and rumours, and we would not mistake the repetition of the latter for confirmation of the former. We would have to take bias seriously when we read the works of pro or anti-Stalin writers, and would not completely and uncritically accept the testimony of those who write *post factum* in order to magnify or justify their own roles. Of course, if we did apply the usual rules of source verification and criticism, our job as interpreters of Stalin would be much harder than it is. We would find that much of what we think we know is based on weak foundations.

Consider for example the famous 'Letter of an Old Bolshevik'. First published in a Menshevik journal in 1936, the text purports to be the record of a conversation between Nikolai Bukharin and Boris Nicolaevsky in Paris and is the original source for several key points about Stalin. Internal inconsistencies and other problems cast grave doubt on its accuracy and even its authenticity. Nevertheless, scholars continue to cite it as evidence.[9] Similarly, Alexander Orlov's *Secret History of Stalin's Crimes* has provided the bedrock evidence for another set of historical assertions. We learn here the 'insider's' account of Stalin's relations with the NKVD chief Nikolai Ezhov and other nefarious personalities. Yet, it turns out that Orlov was abroad during the 1930s and picked up his tantalizing titbits as second and third hand corridor gossip.[10]

It may well be that some of what Nicolaevsky and Orlov report is true. But the dubious origins of the works must cast doubt on their claims. How does one know what is true and what is not? Does one accept what one likes and believes and reject the rest?[11] In most other fields of historical research, such flimsy tales would be rejected as sources out of hand. Were we to do this here, we would discover that we no longer have evidence of Kirov's moderation or of Stalin's conspiracy to kill him.

There is, however, a considerable number of apparently dependable memoirs, many of which were published in the Soviet Union during the liberal period of Khrushchev's reforms. They describe the life events of their authors in graphic and gripping fashion and are indispensable sources for social and intellectual history. Unfortunately, almost none of these memoirists were highly enough placed in the Stalinist bureaucracy to report much about central decision-making or Stalin's intentions.[12]

In addition to suspicious memoirs and pretended letters, there is a large corpus of historical fiction and fictional history. The problems with such literary sources have been analysed in print.[13] They tend toward fictionalization, are tailored to produce emotional responses, and try to make moral points. Despite apparent similarities between historical and literary works as texts, they are different genres. Historians conduct research and handle data differently than do creative writers. Hypotheses are tested, discrete interpretations are discussed and documented, and evidence is carefully weighed. For example, Rybakov's *Children of the Arbat*, which has played a key role in anti-Stalin shock work and is even hailed as a historical source, contains numerous factual errors and flights of literary fancy.[14] Even Dmitri Volkogonov's more scholarly *Triumf i tragediia* contains invented dialogue between Stalin and his clique.

Unlike historians, literateurs are generally unconcerned about verifying their sources. Consider two recent examples. First, Mikhail Shatrov in his play *Dal'she, dal'she, dal'she* tells the story of Zinoviev and Kamenev being brought from prison to the Kremlin in order to be persuaded to confess. His account of this alleged event in fact closely paraphrases the first account of this tale in the spurious *Secret History of Stalin's Crimes*, published in the West decades after the event.[15] It is also noteworthy that no evidence to support this tale was found in the Party Central Committee's recent exhaustive archival examination and documentary publication on the interrogation and trial of Zinoviev and Kamenev.

Second, there is the currently popular story that Lenin's Testament was never discussed at a party congress and that, if it had been, Stalinism could have been prevented. In fact, the document was considered by the Party Central Committee shortly after Lenin's death and again in closed session at the congress in 1927. At that time, *Pravda* published a Stalin speech which included excerpts from it, including the part in which Lenin criticized Stalin's rudeness and called for his removal from the post of General Secretary. It was (like Khrushchev's 'Secret Speech' to the 20th Party Congress in 1956) not published until recently. But the congress delegates who heard the Testament consisted of virtually all key party leaders and even a scattering of common folk from across the country. Because, as Sergo Mikoyan notes, democracy and the ability to influence the leadership existed at that time only in the party leadership – the very group that heard the Testament – the idea that the Testament was a secret in the party and that its promulgation could have 'prevented' Stalinism is both inaccurate and absurd.[16]

Following strict rules of evidence exposes one to certain danger. If one insists on strictly adhering to credible sources, one runs the risk of being accused of trying to exonerate Stalin or being associated with the group of cranks that claims Hitler did not order the holocaust because we have no documents suggesting that he did. The parallel is not at all appropriate. We have plenty of evidence implicating Stalin in the most monstrous crimes. Certainly three-quarters of the Party Central Committee was arrested with his knowledge or on his direct order. Khrushchev has described documents bearing Stalin's signature which condemned thousands to death or imprisonment.[17] Whatever the actual number of innocents perishing at his hands, the moral question is settled. Stalin was a killer and it would be silly to pretend otherwise.

Yet the key problems remain unsolved. Why did the terror happen? How can one explain its scale? Who or what was to blame: Stalin's personality? Leninism? Socialism? Russian history? Trying to answer these questions has rightly been the business of commentators, politicians, and scholars interested in the Stalin period.

Old Ideas and Agendas

The results of historical investigations into the Stalin period have in many cases been coloured by two factors inherent in the subject itself. First, as we have seen, the paucity of reliable and creditable sources on the man (and even on the basic functioning of the system) has given rise to a most diverse and free-wheeling literature that often bears weak allegiance to basic rules of historical investigation. Secondly, nearly all studies have reflected the moral and political agendas of the authors. We have sometimes seen the eclipse of detailed scholarship by didactic preaching and political advocacy.

Because of the nature of the subject and the personal horrors involved, every Western writer has felt obliged to make his or her moral stance clear. Although no serious writer outside the former Soviet Union has sympathized with or defended Stalin in more than thirty years, every scholar feels the need to more than once disassociate him or herself from the phenomenon. In the United States, this urge was reinforced by the McCarthyism of the 1950s. Communism became so disreputable as to make it necessary ritually to denounce it in order to avoid the slightest suggestion that one might have subversive sympathies.[18]

Stalin was an evil person. At the same time, though, there is always the danger that our scholarship could become subservient to the urge to denounce. Indeed, some scholars and many publicists judge scholarly writing on the basis of the strength of its moral condemnation. They rate authors according to the perceived depth of their indignation and even according to the number of times the author denounces the devil.[19] The tail wags the dog: the critical use of sources, validity of scientific deduction, and strength of argument – the traditional measures of scholarly worth – take second place to the perceived values of the author. Reviewers worry more about the intentions of the author than about the sources or methodology involved and scholarship is transformed into a rite of exorcism. As we shall see below, this attitude is as prevalent in the former Soviet Union as it is in the West.

The parallels between this tendency and Stalinist practice are at least ironic. In the Stalinist scholarly milieu (if one can call it that), one's apparent loyalties were the test of one's writing and those who failed the mark were denounced or worse. Stalin-era scholarly writing took on a formulaic, almost liturgical, structure: invocations of the moral authority (Stalin or his writings) began and ended each piece and were sprinkled throughout. Western writers feel similarly obliged to sandwich their research between different moral incantations.

Politically, writing about Stalinism has meant taking a stance. Alec Nove has clearly shown how attitudes toward Stalin flow from the political agendas of the authors. The overarching importance of the Soviet Union and socialism to twentieth century political history, the strong communist, anti-communist, and patriotic passions they have inspired, and the tendency of revolutions to create camps of winners and losers have guaranteed a partisan field of study from the beginning. Especially for early non-Stalinist writers, many of whom were participants in the events of early Soviet history, the ultimate goal of studying Stalinism was deciding who or what was to blame. The task was to decide when Russia went wrong and where to draw the line between 'good' and 'bad' periods.

Those on the right of the political spectrum professed no surprise at the unfolding of Stalinist dictatorship. For them, Stalinism flowed from Leninism, which flowed from 1917 and ultimately from the Enlightenment. The problem was the contamination of traditional, happy, paternalist Muscovite traditions with Western rationalism. This slavophile position is encountered most clearly today in the works of Alexander Solzhenitsyn, who draws his good/bad line in the eighteenth century.

Liberals and conservatives draw their lines in different places. For some of them, the February Revolution of 1917 and fall of the Tsar were historical accidents. In their opinion, Russia after 1905 was proceeding in the right direction: the evolution of civil rights and constitutional thinking. If only World War I (an accidental factor) had not intervened and led to the surprise breakdown of society, Russia would be happy today. For others, the line should be drawn between February and October 1917. This group ranges from liberal Kadets through part of the Mensheviks and moderate socialists, and its adherents believe in the legitimacy and positive democratic potential of the Provisional Government. In this view, the Bolshevik Revolution of October was an illegitimate disaster which, via Leninism, led to Stalinism.

We next find the Trotskyists and 'leftist' Bolsheviks, for whom the October Revolution was positive and necessary. Trotskyists worshipped it (and Lenin) as much as Stalinists did. For Trotsky's adherents, Stalinism perverted the leftist heritage of Leninism with 'centrist', Thermidorean, or Bonapartist policies. An entrenched post-revolutionary bureaucracy produced Stalin, perverted Leninism, and dug the grave of the revolution.[20] Trotsky and his followers drew their line around 1923.

Similarly, the champions of Nikolai Bukharin and the 'rightist' Bolsheviks accepted and supported the Bolshevik Revolution. But unlike the Trotskyists (whom they helped Stalin destroy), the Bukharinists point to 1928–9 as the watershed and draw their line there. Idealizing the mixed capitalist/socialist system of the New Economic Policy, they condemn Stalin's abandonment of gradualism in the late 1920s as the important deviation from Leninism.[21] Agricultural collectivization and voluntarist industrial planning weie at the roots of the disaster. This still influential school of thought includes not only professed followers of Bukharin but also many scholars in the West and in the former Soviet Union today.

About five years later, in the early 1930s we find another line drawn by Nikita Khrushchev. Khrushchev praised Stalin's defeat of both 'left' and 'right' oppositions in the 1920s, approved of collectivization and rapid industrialization, and gave him credit for preserving the unity of the party in the first decade after the Revolution. His 'Secret Speech' of 1956 found few faults in Soviet history until about 1934, when Stalin's 'willful personality' and 'sickly suspicion' asserted themselves and things started to go wrong. Stalin was right to repress the kulaks, in this view, but later, when the 'class struggle' was over, he propounded the 'incorrect' theory that the closer one approaches to socialism, the sharper the class struggle becomes. The 'repression of honest Party cadres' of the 1930s, Stalin's mishandling of diplomacy and war, and the full-blown pathology of the late 1940s were the results both of Stalin's personality and of this erroneous formulation. But through it all, somehow, 'The Party' maintained its existence, preserving Leninist norms and traditions against the onslaught of the 'cult of personality'.[22]

Despite their differences and mutual hostility, the Trotsky, Bukharin, and Khrushchev views have much in common. All three measure Stalinism against the yardstick of Leninism and see major discontinuities between the two.[23] Stalin was not the heir to Leninism in this view: Lenin was good and Stalin was bad. Theirs is essentially a scholastic tradition concerned with fidelity to and continuity with original dogma: the 'great books' of Lenin are searched for writings and quotations to support Trotsky's, Bukharin's, or Khrushchev's claims of legitimacy.[24] All three are also anxious to save socialism and the October Revolution from Stalin.

By focussing the discussion on specific bad policy choices Stalin made (his 'mistakes'), they go to great lengths to prove that the system produced by the 1917 revolution was basically sound: socialism is not to blame; nothing about it inherently leads to terror. Just as the liberals and conservatives bemoaned the 'accident' of World War I, the Trotskyist, Bukharinist, and Khrushchevist partisans often blame the 'accidental' factor of Stalin's personality for derailing the revolution.

The Trotsky, Bukharin, and Khrushchev positions, as well as those of their traditionalist, liberal, and conservative predecessors, are those of participants and adherents. These people lived through (or feel connected to) the historical events surrounding Stalinism and have something to prove. Advocacy and blame are their goals. It is not surprising that they should be so partisan in their attempts to justify or exculpate their own politics and eulogize lost alternatives. Although their reasonable sentiments are accepted today by many scholars, they do beg a question or two. Is the Marxist social class approach to historical causality really compatible with 'Great Man' and other accidental theories of history?[25] How could it have happened that so heinous a usurper could rise to total power and so misdirect such a strong movement? As we shall see below, many of the proffered answers (among them trickery, mass hypnosis, and a general decline in democratic practices) are unsatisfactory and unconvincing. The question of the origins of Stalinism is a complex one that does not lend itself to simple answers.

While it is understandable for participants to do so, why is it necessary for scholars to draw lines between what we wish to protect and what we wish to denounce? Cancer researchers and scientists in other fields cannot afford to let their possible repulsion for their subject become the vehicle for their research. Is it possible to seek objectivity and detachment in social science?

New Ideas?

Since Mikhail Gorbachev became First Secretary of the CPSU in 1985, published historical evaluations of Stalin and Stalinism exploded in the USSR.[26] Beginning in 1985 and 1986 with a few tentative articles on the positive sides of the New Economic Policy of the 1920s, Soviet discourse advanced from 1987 toward an all-round condemnation of Stalin and Stalinism. Stalin and his lieutenants have been denounced harshly and directly and the major defendants at the show trials of 1936–8 have been mostly rehabilitated. The press has produced a flood of dramatic revelations of individual persecutions.

At first, Gorbachev avoided any discussion of the issue, denied there was any such thing as 'Stalinism', and even defended collectivization of agriculture.[27] In the course of 1987 and 1988, though, there was a dramatic shift. Official voices said that 'one must know everything' about the past in order to build the future. Special commissions and bodies were working on the problem of rehabilitations of victims, a monument commemorating Stalin's victims, and new textbooks about Soviet history. *Pravda* demanded 'The Truth' about the darker side of Soviet history.[28] Things seem to be moving in the direction of more open access to information (*glasnost*), honest appraisals of the early Soviet experience, and a humane reconsideration for those who suffered. Unofficial voices in the most popular Soviet weekly called for Stalin's posthumous expulsion from the Communist Party, the removal of his body from the area of Lenin's mausoleum, and the de-memorialization of his birthplace.[29]

Broadly speaking, one can recognize several currents in the Soviet press about Stalin. And, as might be expected, the currents replicate their Soviet and Western predecessors discussed above.

First, we find commentators whose views are analogous to those of the liberals and conservatives in previous decades who saw the October (and even February) revolutions as a mistake. From a traditional-conservative wing, Vadim Kozhinov and others ridiculed the notion that the cult of personality and the general phenomenon of Stalinism were the conspiratorial work of one man or even a small circle.[30] He has tried to place the rise of Stalinism in what he calls a more universal framework and believes that the system and ideology of socialism – stemming from the Russian Revolution – are at fault. Kozhinov's Great Russian nationalism and anti-semitism (he cites mostly Jews as Stalin's henchmen) are evident, as is his 'historical fatalism': he believes that Stalinism was the inevitable product of the Bolshevik revolution.[31] Similar to Kozhinov's conservatism is the Christian approach of mathematician Igor Shafarevich who, like Kozhinov, is anti-Stalinist.[32] Shafarevich finds fault with socialism from a Christian point of view but like Kozhinov (and the liberals and conservatives of 1917) he draws the good/bad line in that year. This anti-socialist conservative discourse has now been supplemented by elements of the radical-democratic 'left' who now reject socialism and Leninism. We might place in this category the philosophical writings of A. Tsipko, who locates the problem in the doctrinal history of the Russian revolutionary intelligentsia and 'left-wing radicalism'.[33]

There are also those who, not unlike Trotsky and Bukharin, see Stalin as an illegitimate counter-revolutionary and usurper: a wrecker of sorts, who left no positive heritage and nearly destroyed the country.[34] For these commentators, the positive Leninist legacy was betrayed by Stalin and his clique, and the lines are to be drawn somewhere in the 1920s.

Another point of view values Lenin's socialist program. It sees Stalin as a leader who committed serious crimes but who also made some positive contributions in building socialism and strengthening the Soviet state. 'We must see both Stalin's indisputable contribution to the struggle for socialism and the defence of our achievements and the gross political blunders and arbitrariness committed by him and his close associates'.[35] This neo-Khrushchevian position redraws the line in the early 1930s and makes a somewhat more positive evaluation of Stalin, while admitting certain 'mistakes'. This view has received 'official' sanction in Gorbachev's speeches and in *Pravda*.[36]

Within this camp of pro-Lenin anti-Stalinists there is disagreement about the roots of the problem. For some, the 'personal factor' of Stalin explains the sabotage of Soviet socialism and the terror which followed. This was the view enunciated by Khrushchev and his supporters from 1956 to 1964. Others rather suggest that Stalin's personality was less important than the 'administrative system' of centralized command that took shape from the 1920s.[37] For them, the Stalinist command system as a whole perverted Leninism, ruined the economy and provided the machinery for the terror.

Finally, even the old Soviet and Western communist defence of Stalin has received a contemporary echo. Some have even publicly defended him in the press.[38]

The appearance of a genuine spectrum of opinion in the former Soviet Union is in itself a sensational and fresh change. At the same time, from a scholarly point of view, all may not be as rosy as it appears.

Up to now, most of the sensational revelations about the Stalin period have come from publicists and literary figures; historians have not taken the lead. Soviet historians complained in pro-perestroika journals both about the hesitancy of others and about the tendency of journalists to sensationalize for the sake of popularity.[39] Several reasons have been given for historians' slowness: inadequate access to documents and archives; continuing influence of conservative senior historians; and the professional's natural coolness about sensational journalism. Some say that the present generation of Soviet-trained historians is methodologically and psychologically incapable of writing scientific, objective history.

But without the participation of professional historians, the process of glasnost will remain dangerously inchoate. Unevaluated and undocumented rumours, contradictory claims and false information will continue to cloud the historical and literary air in the former USSR as they have in the West for decades.[40] There are positive signs in re-staffed editorial boards, new publications, changes in the leadership of academic and archival bodies, and the expression of a fresh spirit among historians.[41] But at the present stage, journalists and creative writers have been leading the way and it is significant that presses are hurrying to publish Western scholarly (and non-scholarly) writings rather than those by Russian scholars.[42]

Although the 'shock work' of publicists is important, it does not generally represent serious historical research. Professional historians in the former Soviet Union privately express dismay at the ability of journalists and publicists to monopolize the discourse, and many of them are appalled at statements emphasizing the primacy of political utility over objective research. Such unfortunately utilitarian approaches to scholarship sometimes even come from leading scholars. For example, a leading writer on Stalin recently made the case for fighting Stalinism 'not with curses addressed to Stalin *and not even with objective exposure of its root causes*, but by perestroika, glasnost, democratization, and radical economic reform. That is what we are doing today.'[43]

But what, then, of Stalin? One of the general thrusts of traditional scholarship has been to equate Stalin and Stalinism; in most of the established literature, the terms denoted the same thing. It is enough to note that many of the classic works on the Stalin period have been biographies, and for years one assumed that Soviet reality was the simple reflection of Stalin's wishes. Huge political watersheds, titanic social processes, and economic revolutions were nothing more than the realization of his omnipotent will and omniscient plans. For some, Stalin's psyche (or rather sketchy, hypothetical suppositions about it) became the key to understanding decades of the history of the largest country on earth. Ironically, this approach represents acceptance of Stalin's own projection of his 'cult of personality'.

Some recent scholarship has seen Stalin and Stalinism as separate subjects of analysis.[44] None of these writers have argued for the autonomy of social process and none have tried to factor Stalin out of the equation. There is abundant evidence of Stalin's power, despotism, and influence on events. He had the power to kill anyone he wanted and he personally ordered the death or imprisonment of Central Committee members, military officers, officials at all levels, and even wives of 'enemies of the people'. More generally, he was responsible for the deaths of countless peasants and common folk. His decisions were catalysts which set processes in motion that would eventually result in the repression of millions.

To understand his guilt is not to comprehend 'Stalinism' or to explain Soviet history. Of course, Stalin's influence is a proper subject for serious study, but Khrushchev's explanation of the illegality and repression solely as a function of Stalin's personality surely is not only too simplistic but also ridiculous.

It is, after all, relatively easy to understand (if not explain) one man's insanity. But how much does such an appreciation tell us about the phenomena of violence or mass repression? To know that Hitler was deranged does not explain much about the origins of World War II or even about the invasion of Poland; it explains nothing of how the horror of Auschwitz could have happened. Similarly, to know that Stalin was malicious and deranged does not explain why so many volunteered to denounce, persecute, and torture 'enemies of the people'. His attitudes tell us nothing about the motivations of those who pulled the triggers at the NKVD's mass executions in Belorussia. Knowing about Stalin's psychosis does not help us understand some key questions: why the persecutors thought they were doing the right thing, why so many thought the victims deserved to die or why so many more thought it reasonable at the time.

To discuss the forms of the popular support Stalin enjoyed (as we shall below) is only one way to put the question. Stalin's ideas, however sinister and malicious, found clear resonance 'below' in the Party and in society, and not just from fearful or careerist 'little Stalins'. Alec Nove pointed out that the qualities of rulers 'fit the given situation', but the real point is more than that. Stalin's policies and initiatives reflected popular attitudes and vice-versa. As H. R. Trevor-Roper wrote,

> [N]o ruler has ever carried out a policy of wholesale expulsion or destruction without the cooperation of society. . . . Great massacres may be commanded by tyrants, but they are imposed by peoples. . . . The social resentment of the Spanish pueblo, not the bigotry of Spanish kings, lay behind the foundation of the Spanish Inquisition. . . . Afterwards, when the mood has changed, or when the social pressure, thanks to the blood-letting, no longer exists, the anonymous people slinks away, leaving public responsibility to the preachers, the theorists, and the rulers who demanded, justified and ordered the act. But the historian must present to it too its share of the account. Individually that share may be infinitesimal but collectively it is the largest of all. Without the

tribunes of the people, social persecution cannot be organized. Without the people, it cannot be conceived.[45]

Stalin may have given formal orders, but one still needs to explain how they were received, implemented, ignored or distorted on the ground. Is it realistic to believe that Stalin, or even a bureaucracy of 'little Stalins', managed to carry out huge social transformations of an unwilling population solely through cunning, mass hypnosis, concealed testaments, or even brute force? To explain Stalin's role and psyche (which are, of course, still poorly understood) is not to explain how an evil breeze so easily became a whirlwind. An understanding of the person is necessary but not sufficient to understand the phenomenon.

Attempts to explain Stalin's popularity have often foundered on the obstacle of partisanship. Everyone admits that, in some way or another, he enjoyed mass support: 'Although its nature and extent varied over the years, it is clear that there was substantial popular support for Stalinism from the beginning and through the very worst.'[46] But when it comes to specifying its forms, depth, and effect, some students have remained silent, recoiled in fear and confusion, or have posed rather unconvincing explanations.

Some Soviet and Western scholars have difficulty reconciling their idealized, virtuous Soviet workers with the undoubted fact that, as a class, they formed one of Stalin's bases of popular support. How could 'our' workers, who behaved in ways we like (democratic and egalitarian) in 1917 so easily give up these qualities in the twenties and thirties and support Stalin's faction? How could they betray these positive values (and us – the intelligentsia) after the revolution? Perhaps the proletariat of the 1920s was not the same 'genuine' or 'authentic' working class of 1917? Perhaps they were duped, confused, or terrorized into supporting Stalin?[47]

These days the Russian press offers a variety of explanations for Stalin's social support. The more crude suggestions are that those who followed Stalin were all either dupes or henchmen.[48] Others go so far as to elaborate explanations based on 'social hypnosis' or group psychosis.[49] In reaction to the simplistic Khrushchevian 'cult of personality' trend, other recent discourse locates the origins of Stalinism in social and cultural forces of Russian history. Some have seen a traditional 'Asiatic' servility of the Russian people, bred into them during the Tatar Yoke of medieval times and nurtured over centuries of autocratic repression and tsar-worship, as the real cause of Stalinist dictatorship. Adherents of this cultural view argue that the 'low' cultural and political level of the peasant population led to a servile and passive acceptance of dictatorship.[50] The people were not sophisticated enough to detect Stalin's cunning plan to seize power and 'were backward enough to be deceived'.[51] Those with 'high political culture' and political awareness (including the old Bolsheviks) were unable to stop Stalin because they were too few, too divided, and too embued with a fatal Bolshevik moral relativism. On a more sophisticated level, others conclude that the times generally led to political 'deformities' and created a climate in which cults of strong personalities and heroes could flourish.[52]

It is interesting to note that these views, like the other recent Soviet positions we have discussed, have a long history in the traditions of the Russian intelligentsia. Peter Chaadaev, as long ago as the 1830s, also complained about the ravages of the Tatar Yoke, about Russia being cut off from 'civilized' Europe, and about the cultural backwardness of his non-western country. Current Soviet writers from the intelligentsia, like Chaadaev, contrast 'low' Russian culture with the 'high' culture of European civilization they admire.[53]

But quite aside from the question of its origins in the world-view of the westernized Russian intelligentsia (to which we shall return) this particular cultural approach has other weaknesses. One could first wonder whether the Mongol influence of the 13th century was really such a determining factor in the 20th. More importantly, though, Russian workers and peasants have been anything but servile in this century. Their strikes of the 1890s, spontaneous uprising in 1905 and 1917, and their tenacity – on both sides – during the 1918–20 Civil War were anything but docile. The violent resistance of many peasants to collectivization in 1929–31 also does not point to servility.

To the intelligentsia, the Russian people were (and are) the *temnye liudi*, the dark, uncultured, politically undeveloped masses who blindly follow tsars and dictators. Today's westernizers ignore class conflict and social history in general, writing society off as the passive, stupid victim of the political regime. But when their vital interests were at stake, as in 1905, 1917, 1918–21, and 1929–31, the Russian masses have often been politically aware, astute, and willing to resist. There was indeed another side to the *temnye liudi*: an assertive, violent side of conscious class struggle and social conflict.

This Westernizing approach discourages locating historical problems or evils lower down in the apparatus and will have little interest in emphasizing unseemly social problems like class conflict, specialist baiting, populist hostility toward the intelligentsia, or wage and status conflicts. The leadership's brand of perestroika (and the intelligentsia that supports it) are ill served by pointing out the historical conflicts and hatreds between rank and file party members and leaders; among workers, peasants, and the intelligentsia; and between regional leaders and Moscow. In a period when workers are being disciplined to work harder and run the risk of dismissal, official historians will not be much encouraged to focus on grass-roots defiance of authority and mistrust of leadership.

Members of today's intelligentsia who seek social sources of Stalinism frequently note that the pre-revolutionary Russian intelligentsia (bearers of 'high' culture) were killed or dispersed by the Civil War, leaving in Russia only the common folk and their 'lower' culture. In this view, culture, attitudes, and 'patterns of thought and behaviour' are categorical: Stalinism thus resulted in part from a lack of culture and civilization.

In my view this analysis suffers from several problems, apart from the paternalism and condescension it exhibits toward 'lower' orders. First of all, the presence of an educated elite and higher culture have historically provided no guarantees against barbarism. Nazi Germany and Mandarin China are two ready examples and history is full of cases in which educated elites organized, tolerated and participated in social violence against their own populations.

Secondly, the contemporary version of this cultural approach ignores the *qualitative* dimension of Russian plebeian attitudes. Specifically, the social-cultural outlook of Russian mass society included a strong component of resentment and even hatred of the upper-class representatives of 'high' culture. The problem was not just a lack of culture, but the presence of a hostile one.

There is a risk of missing the obvious here. The element that every worker and peasant understood, the strand that the Bolsheviks recognized and used, the most obvious and basic aspect of virtually all printed discourse at the time was class struggle and conflict. Contemporaneous friends and foes, Whites and Reds, Bukharinists and Stalinists clearly understood that the motor of political change and violence was based on class attitudes.

It is often the case that members of the elite fail to recognize or understand the resentment that those at the bottom of society feel towards them. Educated, comfortable people often naively assume that everyone is as happy as they are. White American intellectuals, even those who sympathize intellectually with the 'masses', are often blind to the deep hostility of the black poor until it explodes in violence. Russian nobles convinced themselves that their peasants liked their condition and we can easily imagine their Soviet bureaucratic successors believing the same thing. Although such caricatures are always dangerous, the point is that intellectuals, including historians, do not automatically understand a resentment we have never had to experience. With our education and understanding of 'social theory', we often understand society less well than those at the bottom of it. When confronted by the reality of class hatred, we recoil in confusion and retreat to comfortable explanations like 'deviant behaviour' or 'low culture'. Others seek explanations in 'outside agitators' or the insidious effects of 'alien ideologies'. In general, we who write on these matters from our ivory towers are particularly ill-equipped to understand the most important social cause of the phenomenon we study.

From this point of view, writers like Shafarevich, Solzhenitsyn, Kozhinov, and Tsipko are looking in the wrong places when they search for Stalinism's intellectual origins, 'alien' (read Jewish) influences, or fatal flaws in the Russian revolutionary movement. That Stalinism was itself anti-intellectual and anti-Semitic and that it destroyed many of the members and traditions of the revolutionary movement should give us pause about such explanations. The additional fact that the plebeian masses and party activists who propelled and supported Stalinism were ignorant of the 'intellectual origins' that supposedly guided them raises further questions.

Emphasis on the intellectual origins of revolutions and dictatorships might make some explanatory sense in countries with a broad intelligentsia that participated in the process. Revolutionary England, America, France and even Nazi Germany lend themselves to analysis of ideological precedents. Actually, it is quite astonishing that one should ever have looked for the origins of Bolshevik transformation, which took place in a country with a backward, semi-literate rural population, in the sphere of ideological and intellectual precursors.

Explanations of Stalinism based on such notions as the premature nature of the Bolshevik takeover, Russian national character, the pressure from the West, or the 'inherent evils' of socialism are, in themselves, no more convincing than the 'evil prince' formula. The general problem is that few of the traditional approaches have delivered what virtually every other field of history has: a non-partisan sociology of Stalinism.

Toward a Political Sociology of Stalinism

One of the surprising things about the study of Soviet history is the lack of political sociology. Given the fact that many writers on the Soviet Union (both from within and from the West) have been Marxists, it is surprising that Trotskyist, non-communist Marxist, or other commentators have not to date produced a satisfactory one. Their attempts have mostly involved huge social categories, grand generalizations, and predictably partisan conclusions.

Political sociology's cousin, social history (which in the United States is more reputable) is alive and well for the Stalin period. Moshe Lewin, Sheila Fitzpatrick, E. H. Carr, R. W. Davies, Kendall Bailes, Alec Nove, and others have laid the foundations. They have elucidated the complexity of Soviet society and its components, 'rehabilitating' it from the obscurity it suffered during the reign of exclusively political studies. We now know that Soviet society does not lend itself to the simplistic categorization used by both Stalinists and earlier Western writers. We also know that social groups, forces, and relationships established the milieu and the parameters within which political actors necessarily functioned: political events had social roots and a social context. We are now willing to look at the political agendas of social classes and wonder about their influence and effects on the state.

More often than not, social historians concluded that although society was an important variable in the Stalinist system, ultimately the state called the tune. Society was usually a relatively passive component in the equation. One recalls Robert Tucker's classic exposition of 'revolution from above'[54] and Moshe Lewin's felicitous metaphor about the superstructure outrunning society.[55]

Recent Western revisionist scholarship doubts that the relationship between state and society was one in which influence always ran from the top down. This is not to say that Stalin's revolution originated from below, but rather that the lines of demarcation between state and society were blurred after 1917 and that regardless of the origins of the initiative, the resulting process was characterized by a dynamic interplay between elements of the state and elements of society.

Lines of social stress were drawn vertically as well as horizontally, and the result looked as much like civil war as simple repression from above. Some parts of the state allied with or represented parts of society against others, conflict and informal social negotiation took place, and it was not always clear which coalition was on top at any given time.[56] Both state and society were stratified, factionalized, and riddled with contradictions to such an extent that the comfortable and easy 'state versus society' framework no longer seems adequate to explain a complex reality. To the question 'Was it a revolution from above (the state) or below (society)', revisionists answer 'both'. It might not be too bold to suggest that revisionists agree that to study and understand the *process* as a developing phenomenon is more important than to try to find 'first causes', to fix moral blame, or to decide whether everything came from above or below.

William Beik wrote of another place and time that:

> Thus historians have moved from viewing the state as a triumphant organizer of society to viewing it as a fragile organism struggling against a vast, turbulent society, and finally to the realization that forces in society were influencing, if not defining the very function of the state.[57]

One might disagree with the characterization of the Soviet state as 'fragile' given its ability to inflict violence and coercion. And one also need not immediately agree that the Soviet state was simply a creation of society. But it is surely important to investigate political sociology, society and its relation to the state in order to understand Stalinism.

This was a weak state, not a strong one. The recourse to violence to centralize power, establish control, and mobilize resources is proof of that. Strong, secure regimes do not need mass violence to rule. Mao Zedong once said that his control was limited to trying to push the tides one way or the other while trying to hold the system together. The same thing might be said of Stalin.

Consider in this regard the 'defensive' functions of Stalin's personality cult. One of the most striking elements of the Stalinist system was the intense glorification of the leader as hero. 'The Great and Wise Teacher', the 'Friend of Mankind', and 'The Greatest Human Being Who Ever Lived' were among the epithets seriously applied to Stalin by his lieutenants and by society at large.[58] Although we know next to nothing about his personality, Stalin may indeed have thrived on the worship. Yet it seems equally obvious that the cult had important cultural and political uses for the leadership: it provided a common point of contact in a fragmented, conflict-ridden society. Such leader cults are not uncommon in less developed societies with weak states that desperately need legitimacy. Writing about emerging nations in modern Africa, Immanuel Wallerstein has noted that:

> The role of the hero is first of all to be a readily available, easily understood symbol of the new nation. . . . He legitimizes the state by ordaining obedience to its norms out of loyalty to his person . . . The problem of integration is essentially one of getting people to shift loyalty from a structure based on tradition ('do it because it has always been done this way') to a new artificial entity, the nation-state, whose only justification for authority lies in its constitution ('do it because it is the rationally agreed-upon law'). . . . The charismatic justification for authority can be seen as a way of transition, an interim measure which gets people to observe the requirements of the nation out of loyalty to the leader while they learn to do it for their own sake.[59]

The Soviet system in these decades could hardly be called a strong 'civil society'. There was little legal or social cohesion and no widely accepted 'social contract'. Most of the components of civil society or of the modern state were missing: a reliable bureaucracy, a unitary and consistent notion of citizenship or polity, ideological (or religious) integration, or even a sense of psychological inclusion. The cult of personality was a small bandage covering a deep and widening wound. The rise of the cult was not a reflection of centralized control; the opposite was the case.

Shifting our focus from the state to those who ruled it, it is quite clear that Stalin's lieutenants were powerful men. In all large organizations, the person at the top makes decisions based on the information and choices presented to him. Chiefs of staff control access, ministers present options and a variety of servitors control information. Of course, Stalin was no 'prisoner of the Kremlin'. He tried to maintain 'uncontaminated' and unbiased sources of information (with varying degrees of success) and certainly had the 'last word' on all questions, if he chose to speak it. Ezhov did not decide whom to arrest among the top strata – although he may have presented Stalin with finished criminal dossiers – and no members of the politburo could launch a major policy without Stalin's approval.

However, there is now abundant evidence that Stalin's lieutenants represented and spoke for distinct policy alternatives. Their policy positions are well documented in studies covering the years 1920–50.[60] These studies frequently portray a Stalin who preferred not to decide important questions unless forced. His role seems to have been that of moderator or referee, choosing from among numerous policy possibilities, although R. W. Davies is right to emphasize the differences in this condition at different periods. Many things went on without him or despite his wishes and plans.

Even in the crucial realm of 1930s foreign policy, recent evidence suggests that Stalin 'took only a sporadic interest', allowed it to drift, and entrusted it to subordinates: '. . . on the whole, Stalin abstained from direct intervention and contented himself with merely reviewing and approving. . . . Even the process of review was occasionally delegated to others.' The same author speaks of the 'ramshackled nature of foreign policy decision-making under Stalin.'[61] As Sergo Mikoyan's valuable insight also suggests, Stalin allowed his lieutenants to work generally unmolested as long as he was kept informed. Mikoyan's father argued even on big issues. If we are ever to understand the policy process in Stalin's time, it seems important to understand the views and actions of his lieutenants. Those around Stalin may have trembled but they did not always obey.

The refocus away from Stalin's person is no attempt to shift blame.[62] It rather represents an attempt to come to grips with the totality of the phenomenon, to highlight important but heretofore unstudied aspects, and to suggest that society and politics are not merely figments of one man's psychology. To approach the questions 'What caused Stalinism?' or 'What made Stalinism possible?' from the stand-point of political sociology is to investigate the socio-historical experience of Russia before 1929 and to search for factors that contributed to the full-blown Stalinism which followed.[63] Without prejudging whether or not social norms and forces influenced the state more than vice-versa, a review of some of them could in itself suggest some important interpretive issues.

There have been many attempts to examine some of the ingredients which, when combined in the early 1930s, produced Stalinism. Some of these ingredients, including Stalin's suspicious and sickly personality (to paraphrase Khrushchev), the legacy of Great Russian chauvinism and autocratic tradition, and the Leninist ideological heritage, played major roles. But since they have constituted the backbones of the literature on Stalinism, there is little point in repeating them here.

As Theodore Von Laue has stressed, in making a different argument than that posed here, Russian society and its recent history were brutal and brutalizing.[64] Backwardness and corresponding social violence were endemic parts of Russian life and were compounded by war, revolution, civil war, and a fierce determination to modernize. All of this characterized the 1890–1930 period and, more than Leninist ideology or Stalin's cleverness, was responsible for the system we call Stalinism. And although the 'decisive trifle' of Stalin's pathological psyche was a contributing factor, neither it nor socialism were the main causes; backwardness and customary violence were.

Many of the elements we associate with Stalinism – mass arrests and brutality, the routine killing of opponents, persecution of the relatives of one's enemies, xenophobia, and the arbitrary discarding of legality – were not, as some suggest, defined and created by Stalin's personality. They were in fact the products of the long and short term history of Russian society. As Stephen Cohen has written, 'The main carriers of cultural tradition are, of course, social groups and classes. . . . Indeed, the Stalin Cult, in some ways the major institution of Stalin's autocratic system, was a dramatic example of both cultural tradition and popular support.'[65]

It would be absurd to imagine that one person, however powerful, could create these attitudes and practices from scratch, although he could and did manipulate them. The real basis for Stalinism, the real villains, were the social and political situation produced by rapid economic modernization and its corresponding revolutionary upheaval. Without putting too fine a point on it, or relying on dubious ethnic arguments based on 'national character', one can see in Russian society and history a number of long-term conditions which would directly contribute to the violence and terror of the Stalinist period.[66] These characteristics are familiar to anyone who has read Russian novels or studied Russian ethnography. Stalin was a product of a violent plebeian culture, not vice-versa.

If one begins at village level, with popular culture, one encounters the cosmos of the Russian peasant. Now, of course, not every Russian (and practically no one in ruling circles) was a peasant in 1929. But the flight or destruction of most of educated Russia after 1917, and the fact that industrial workers and the majority of party members were only a generation or less removed from the peasantry, meant that the culture of the 'awkward class' remained a powerful force. Particularly at lower levels of the party and state apparatus where most collectivizing, purging, and repressing took place, traditional people retained traditional attitudes. Not surprisingly, even politburo members, including Stalin, thought and acted more like Russian peasants than like Western political leaders.[67]

Superstitious, xenophobic and deeply suspicious of 'outsiders', the peasant was largely untouched by Western rationalism, legalism, education, toleration, or even the precepts of 'scientific socialism'. His world was one in which the kin group or village ('us') was clearly demarcated from the kulak, the moneylender, the private farmer, the merchant, the zemstvo specialist, the intelligentsia, or the government official ('them').[68] For centuries, whether they be narodniks 'going to the people', intellectuals, or government reformers, 'they' had brought deceit, exploitation, slavery, and sometimes death to 'us'. Foreigners, anciently regarded as non-believers and later suspected as agents of the landlord or capitalist spies, also clearly belonged in the 'them' category. To the peasant, the outsiders were tricky city slickers. To the intelligentsia, many of whom felt love and concern for the masses, the peasants were nonetheless the *temnye liudi*: the dark masses.[69]

Formal legality, the gift of the intelligentsia, could not replace customary law and usage. The informal legal tradition stressed group over individual rights, kin over state loyalty and an expedient, rough-and-ready 'setting things right' over procedural niceties. The communal tradition and will of its majority always took precedence over the opinions, rights, and even life of the individual.[70] This was *a priori* neither a 'high' nor 'low' cultural level, but it was different from the experience and outlook of the intelligentsia.

The peasant's life was constantly visited by violence and death. Children and adults died young and apparently without reason; nobles, officials and cossacks exploited and brutalized the peasant and his kin. Exposed to brutality, society reacted brutally. Without pushing the image too far, alongside the popular egalitarian and democratic tradition, we find the traditional village fist fight, widespread wife-beating, personal assault, and murder by shotgun, axe or pitchfork.

The use of terror against 'enemies' of the collective did not start with Stalin. Recent research has shown how *samosud*, or peasant informal justice, was often extremely violent. Tarring, whipping, fatal mob beatings and stabbings, stakes driven through offenders' bodies and even 'premeditated collective murder' were not uncommon in Russian peasant villages before 1917. Witches were identified and killed by the community before and after the Revolution. Peasant self-justice also carried a strong 'us' versus 'them' character. Aside from the fact that peasants considered the official courts ('their' justice) too lenient, we can also note that retribution against offending members of the collective were usually ritualized and non-lethal, while that handed out to outsiders was hostile and more violent.[71] Such ancient defensive attitudes would provide the milieu and the impetus to the Stalin-period terror, which was seen to be directed outward against 'aliens', 'spies', 'traitors', and the like.

Over the centuries, when economic and social pressures became too great or when exploitation reached the breaking point, the *temnye liudi* were capable of exploding in mass actions of uncontrolled violence. The revolts associated with Bolotnikov and Stenka Razin in the seventeenth century and with Pugachev in the eighteenth century lashed out against all who consciously or accidentally stood in the way. 'Blind and pitiless', rather than passive, the peasants were furious and merciless in taking their revenge against 'them', and the intelligentsia was permanently terrified by the experience.[72] As Rybakov's Stalin mused, 'The intelligentsia had handled the people with kid gloves and the people had then thrown them out like so much garbage.'[73]

Moving from long-term background features to more recent historical experiences, one finds that these traditional attitudes were reinforced and unleashed after 1917. The revolutions of that year pitted 'the democracy' first against the Tsar and then against the liberal intellectual of the Provisional Government. The often violent seizure of the land by peasants, the street fighting during and after the July Days and the fighting in October pitted class against class and sharpened the dividing lines between peasants and officials and between workers and the bourgeoisie.

But it was the Russian Civil War (1918–21), more than the revolutions, that unchained the social hatreds and unleashed the violence and retribution which had existed just below the surface of society and consciousness. Much of the *atmosphere* of Stalinism derives from the Civil War: government by campaign, the fortress-storming metaphors of Bolshevik crusades, their military language and slogans, the expeditionary nature of work in the countryside, and even Bolshevik fashion – the wearing of military tunics (Stalin's permanent wardrobe) and shaving of heads – comes from this period. It was during the Civil War that the ultra-leftist Bolshevik economic policy of War Communism took shape, and this was the period which saw the Bolsheviks ban factionalism, unleash the Cheka, and outlaw opposition. All of these phenomena would be replicated during the Stalin Revolution of 1929. The formula 'opposition = treason' predated Stalin's rule. The anti-Bolshevik foreign intervention of the period also set Russian xenophobia in stone and established the permanent feeling of 'capitalist encirclement' and fear of espionage and assassination.

The class conflicts latent in pre-revolutionary Russian society exploded during the Civil War. The Whites tortured, shot and impaled captured Reds. The Red Army and the Cheka were equally savage in their treatment of White Army soldiers and those identified with the old regime such as nobles, priests, traders and kulaks. The depth of the class hatred and brutality are hard to comprehend. Recall Isaac Babel's account of the White father who captured his Red son:

> And they took us all prisoners because of that treason and my brother Fedor came to Dad's notice. And Dad began cutting him about, saying: 'Brute, Red cur, son of a bitch,' and all sorts of other things, and went on cutting him about until it grew dark and Fedor passed away.[74]

or the Red peasant who captured the landlord who had beaten him:

> But I wasn't going to shoot him. I didn't owe him a shot anyway, so I only dragged him upstairs into the parlour. . . . Then I stamped on my master Nikitinsky, trampled on him for an hour or maybe more. . . . Shooting is letting him off, and too damned easy for yourself. With shooting you never get at the soul, to where it is in a fellow and how it shows itself. But I don't spare myself, and I've more than once trampled an enemy for over an hour. You see, I want him to get to know what life really is, what life is like down our way.[75]

Although the class bitterness of the Civil War preceded the Stalin period by several years, the legacies of illegality, killing, intolerance with opposition, violent class hatred, and treason could not be easily put away in just ten years.[76] Virtually all the adults, both leaders and common folk, who lived through the 1930s remembered or participated in the Civil War. Huge numbers of those inducted into the party in the 1920s were Civil War veterans and service in the conflict was a main credential for recruitment into the secret police.[77] What cultural and experiential baggage did these veterans of class mayhem bring to their tasks? The social explosions of the 1930s cannot be understood except in light of the heritage of the Civil War. These deep hatreds, which had nothing at all to do with Stalin's personality, have explanatory power when we wonder how the terror of the 1930s became so pervasive and widespread. Class conflict, more than homogeneous servility, gave birth to Stalinism.

After the Civil War, class antagonism continued in more muted form. *Spetseedstvo*, or working-class baiting of 'bourgeois specialists', was endemic in Russian factories in the 1920s. Workers resented the restored position and relatively high wages of the class enemy. The government's official persecution of the bourgeois specialist after the Shakhty Trial only validated and unleashed a process which already existed in society. Similarly, the periodic economic crises, increases in bread prices and unemployment in the 1920s were blamed on the peasantry (whose market manipulations supposedly pressed the cities and prevented industrial expansion) and led to urban proletarian hostility toward the class from which they had so recently emerged.[78] In the countryside, tensions between communists and peasants on the one hand and the survivals of the rural nobility, kulaks, and 'class-alien elements' on the other continued.

The persistence of class-based and quite un-liberal attitudes was again manifested in the discussion of the new Stalin Constitution of 1936. This constitution, as is well known, became a kind of grim joke in the Soviet Union. Ostensibly, it was quite a democratic text full of guarantees of equal civil rights, universal suffrage, judicial normalization, and general political relaxation. But the terror, arbitrariness, and personal dictatorship of the subsequent Stalin years, made its provisions quite hollow.

On the other hand, the *process* of its adoption can tell us interesting things about the Stalinist political process and about popular attitudes in the mid-1930s. In the autumn of 1936, the Moscow leadership mobilized an 'all-Union discussion' of the new constitution. Workers, peasants, and others were invited to make criticisms, comments and suggestions on the draft. Certainly, many people said what they thought the leaders wanted to hear and only a brave few used the opportunity to make what the government called 'anti-Soviet' remarks. Indeed, we might well dismiss the all-Union discussion as a propaganda exercise had not millions of others apparently felt free to criticize several provisions of the officially proffered document and to make whatever suggestions came to mind.[79]

What is interesting in this case is the skeptical plebeian reaction and general non-acceptance of many of the concepts of Western liberalism embodied in the text. By November 1936, 1,651,592 people in Leningrad, Smolensk and their environs had made comments or suggestions.[80] A sampling of 2,600 of these shows that two of the four most common suggestions were the requests that local village soviets be given the right to arrest people without the sanction or participation of the state procurator (which the constitution had demanded), and that former nobles, Tsarist gendarmes, kulaks, priests, and other 'class alien' elements *not* be given the right to vote.[81] A collective farmer from Leningrad region believed (contrary to law and to Stalin's orders) that ideally, 'any citizen of our country can arrest such persons who wreck construction'.[82] A peasant from Kaluga warned that 'Kulaks and priests must not be given electoral rights', and at one collective farm meeting, everyone who spoke wanted to limit or deny electoral rights to priests, former gendarmes, *pomeshchiki*, and policemen.[83] Stalin himself had to publicly intervene to defend the idea of suffrage for the class-aliens.

Other remarks from the masses suggest the prevalence of the popular attitudes that made Stalinism possible. The worker Kombarov from Leningrad said that 'Using free speech, meetings, and so forth to oppose the socialist state constitutes a betrayal of the country and should carry heavy punishment.' Another peasant, showing the traditional Russian genealogical approach to things, thought that 'relatives having connections with traitors should face the full severity of the law.'[84]

Politically, the pre-Stalin Soviet period also saw the rise of attitudes and structures which were at the heart of Stalinism. Taking first the idea of capitalist encirclement, we find in the popular psychology of the Civil War and the 1920s another germ of the terror: the war scare. The diplomatic and cultural isolation of the Soviet government created a dynamic of its own in Bolshevik politics which influenced policies on many fronts.

The recent discovery and publication of high-level Politburo documents shows this at work.[85] Politburo debates on such topics as trade policy and the treatment of the Trotskyist opposition took place during war scares. We now know that arguments were made and decisions taken on these issues based on Bolshevik assessments of the international position. Hard-liners, including Stalin, argued that strict control and repression of the Trotskyists would strengthen the Soviet diplomatic position.[86] Potential enemies and allies alike would supposedly see a unified Soviet government that was willing and able to control political challenges and that was therefore firmly in control of its own country. Enemies would be more reluctant to attack a united government and others would perhaps see a more reliable potential ally.

It is well to recall that some of the periods of most intense repression in the Stalin period coincided exactly with war scares: 1927–31, 1937–9, 1947–52. Stalin and his cronies emphasized, magnified, and used these panics for their own political purposes but war hysteria did not spring fully formed from Stalin's head and was not totally counterfeit. The fright of the 1930s was followed shortly by the Nazi invasion and the hardening of the late 1940s took place in a period of US-Soviet nuclear confrontation. 'Capitalist encirclement' was a real and omnipresent danger in the Stalin period. When memoirists today remember the Stalin years and try to explain the atmosphere, they inevitably mention it.

Now, the war scares – whether manufactured or not – certainly do not in themselves explain or justify the repression that accompanied them. But they do go a long way toward explaining how persecution could seem reasonable, necessary, or expedient from a national security point of view, to those in the apparatus or in society at large. The war scares also explain how hard-line arguments made by Stalin, Ezhov, and others could seem convincing.[87]

In the realm of politics, the late 1920s and early 1930s also saw the emergence of another element of the political sociology of Stalinism: the entrenchment of local political machines. The vast size of the country presented the Bolsheviks with a severe governmental problem. The destruction or evaporation of local governmental institutions in 1917 and during the Civil War meant that the new Soviet regime had to construct a nationwide system of local political agencies from scratch. A crying lack of education and administrative expertise among the rural population meant that a network of Bolshevik party committees became the *de facto* government for most of the population, replacing and supplanting the network of soviets. These local and regional party committees *were* the government for most of the population. Especially in the 1929–32 period when Moscow relied on them to carry out collectivization and industrialization, these officials became 'little Stalins' in their bailiwicks. They were glorified locally and each had his own cult of personality.[88] They had the power of feudal 'great lords': their 'nobility' derived from their distinguished revolutionary pasts.

A great deal of work has been done in the West on the relative power and influence of Moscow versus local political organizations. We now have studies of the local judiciary and of the local process of collectivization. While Moscow gave the orders, it seems that local party bodies, far removed from the capital, carried out policies independently and frequently at odds with those desired by Moscow. Campaigns – including purges – could be stalled, sped up, aborted, or implemented in ways which suited local conditions and interests.[89] Local judicial bodies conducted trials and pronounced sentences wildly at variance with the procedures prescribed in the centre but in accord with the political interests of local machines.[90] Local agents of agricultural collectivization were sometimes genuinely 'dizzy with success'. They often jumped the gun in initiating the process, outran central targets, violated and ignored directives which did not suit them.[91]

Although these studies are on different subjects and periods, they share certain interpretive conclusions: that local government and party agencies exercised real political power in many spheres and that the lives and fates of local, common folk, were at least as much in the hands of local forces as of Stalin's clique.

The feudal nature of power relations in the 1920s and 1930s presented the Moscow leadership and the general population with severe problems and contradictions. Moscow needed the regional secretaries, but at the same time feared and resented the power they deployed locally. Local *proizvol* (arbitrary misconduct) and disobedience of central directives were endemic, particularly in collectivization and in the purges of the 1930s. It discredited the regime as a whole, but what could be done about it? A frank discussion of local abuse might well expose the regime's own undemocratic foundations to an undesirable public discussion.[92] Wholesale replacement or annihilation of miscreant local officials further destabilized an already precarious political situation in the countryside and in any case did not correct the built-in structural-geographical-political problem.

If politics is the exercise of influence by one group over others, then it was practiced at all levels of the political and social structure: from above and from below. Certainly some political forces, like Stalin's clique, were far more powerful than others and the state played a major role. At the same time, the vitally important specific and personal decisions of life and death for most of the population were made locally. How many 'kulaks' were to be deported from which villages? Who had the power to arrest whom? Whose name appeared on the purge list? Which local faction controlled the NKVD? If one is interested in either a social history of the common folk or in 'total history', one should look less at those at the pinnacle, who tried to push the tides one way or another, and more at the forces that were really important to the fates of most people.

To know with certainty the agency of repression is not to understand its social content, the reasons for its spread and scope, its impact or meaning. If, for example, implementation of political, judicial, and agricultural policies in the country was so dependent on local conditions and alignments, how can one be certain that the actual results, on the ground, were an accurate reflection of Stalin's wishes? Even if one assumes Stalin's personality was the only or main factor in the *initiation* of policies, one must still explain the obvious disparities between central orders and local outcomes: for example the failure of local agencies to adhere to Moscow's collectivization (and later, purge) targets.

Why was it that during the membership *chistki* (purges) of 1933–6, local leaders expelled so many more members than Moscow wished? Why was it that practically no local officials were purged until the power of their 'family circles' was broken in 1937? What were the personal and political interests of those local officials who decided who was to be purged and when? How much of the terror, including the selection of victims, was 'just local stuff'?[93]

The complex political sociology of the system involved *kolkhozniki*, factory workers, rank and file party activists, local party *apparatchiki*, regional first secretaries, and several factions in Moscow. Each group had its own interests and agendas and, with varying limits, the means to realize them. One cannot begin to explain all of the terror – including the means by which the terror spread, its magnitude, and its impact – without trying to understand the local social conflicts in which it functioned and which governed its actions. Local actors may not have decided national policies but they certainly determined their results. R. W. Davies is right to draw our attention to 'autonomous or uncontrolled behaviour at various levels'.

Consider the party membership purges (*chistki*) of 1933–6. At the lowest level, that of party cells, the membership targeted the peasantry's traditional class enemies as well as those with dubious Civil War pasts. This included former tsarist policemen, wealthy peasants, former noble landowners and their associates, White Army participants, locally known crooks, members of the intelligentsia and generally unpopular types who had entered the party. As the Smolensk Archive transcripts of these grass-roots *chistka* meetings show, this process victimized innocent bystanders, relatives and even past associates of the above categories: the 'genetic' peasant approach again. Local party secretaries tried to protect their political machines by defending those of their number who were targets of rank and file wrath and by running up the purge score. These secretaries expelled 'passive' (non-participating or non-duespaying) members, those who could be tripped up on ideological questions and particular members who had made trouble for the machine.[94] This was not at all what the Stalinist centre had in mind, as its subsequent furious reaction showed.[95] Indeed, the Moscow leadership spent a good deal of time trying to clean up the mess that local conduct of the membership screenings had caused. Beginning in June 1936 and picking up steam after January 1938, the centre encouraged those expelled to appeal to higher authorities. Party committees, local control commissions, the Party Control Commission and the Central Committee itself were all involved in considering appeals for reinstatement. Hundreds of thousands were readmitted. Nationally, by 1 June 1938, 51.6 per cent of all purge penalties and expulsions that were appealed were reduced or vacated by higher authorities.[96]

When the Ezhov vigilance campaign began in mid-1936, local party secretaries were happy to direct the enemy accusation against has-been ex-oppositionists.[97] When Stalin and the Moscow leadership demanded further vigilance against local machines, the local leaders were still able to protect themselves by turning police attention to helpless and unprotected common folk who were accused of suspicious connections and singing counter-revolutionary songs. When rank and file party members managed against all odds to spontaneously overthrow local leaders, the provincial leadership took in the ranking victims and protected them from police trouble. When *rank and file* party members were expelled on the other hand, the machine-controlled NKVD frequently arrested them.[98]

In Smolensk, for example, as long as the party obkom controlled the local NKVD (whose chief sat on the Smolensk Party Buro and was part of its *nomenklatura*, or personnel list), no important members of the oblast and raion party *leadership* were arrested. Only when the Smolensk machine was attacked by Moscow in June 1937 and a new NKVD chief sent in were party leaders arrested. Who controlled whom locally was once again the key to understanding the impact of the event on real people.

At the top, after June 1937, Stalin and Ezhov carried out bloody operations against elites in the army, the party, and the economic bureaucracy. Any real or perceived opponents of Stalin's rule were wiped out in police operations. In order to weaken particularly entrenched and stubborn opponents in the regional party bureaucracy, Stalin encouraged grass-roots populist attacks from below on the middle-level apparatus. It was at this point that society exploded. Things got out of control and 'local excesses' were the norm. Once the 'enemies of the people' campaign was sanctioned from above, all of the traditional, embedded factors discussed above asserted themselves.

Peasants and rank and file party members accused and purged each other, accusing each other of being *byvshie liudi* (former people) from the old regime, such as kulaks, former gendarmes and White Army soldiers. Relatives of enemies of the people were also swept away as common folk used familiar genealogical and kin categories as their reference points in defining enemies. Blind and pitiless peasants and others also lashed out at the local intelligentsia in traditional assertions of cultural and social resentment.[99] Like Russian Madame Defarges, they sat in crowds to jeer at the accused 'high' bigshots in local purge trials. Peasants naturally jumped to the conclusion that 'our' dead livestock had been poisoned by 'them' – the educated specialists. Their thinking coincided precisely with Stalin's, who years later had to be convinced by Khrushchev that fungus and disease, not sabotage, was the problem.[100] In some collective farms, 'one half expelled the other half'.[101]

As Davies has noted, the Soviet *nomenklatura*, or official stratum, created a kind of stratified class society, and the age-old social resentments against 'them' naturally suggested hostility against the apparatus. Before the mid-1930s, the 'enemy', in both official Soviet and customary peasant usages, referred to the traditional *social* enemy: the kulak, the nobleman, the White Army officer, and so forth. By 1937, though, Stalin had identified 'enemies with party cards', suggesting that the bureaucrat was the class enemy. This intervention, among others, created the catalyst for wholesale violence of all against all with a strong populist component. But his action in this instance was only the spark: to understand the reasons for the depth and spread of the violence we must look beyond Stalin's personality.

Rank and file party members lashed out at their secretarial leaders, accusing them of bureaucratism, corruption and dictatorial methods. Factory workers attacked their managers with the same kind of populist anger. Even the newly prompted Red Specialists came under fire in the pitiless assertion of radicalism. In response, the threatened official strata fought back by blaming their subordinates. Party secretaries expelled huge numbers of rank and file members in order to protect themselves and display their vigilance. Collective farm chairmen desperately ejected troublesome peasants from the *kolkhozy* for the same reasons. It was a war of all against all and the battle lines reflected social conflicts, some of them decades or even centuries old.

The more we learn about collectivization, the more a similar picture emerges.[102] Stalin had initiated a movement with vague instructions and ambiguous targets. As the process unfolded on the ground, though, it rapidly degenerated into chaotic and violent struggles based on local conditions. Party secretaries, anxious to feed their industrial workers, extend their own rural powers and increase their budget allocations truly became 'dizzy with success'. For their own reasons, and encouraged by Moscow's irresponsible cheerleading, they routinely exceeded dekulakization and collectivization targets, sponsored intense religious persecution and illegally arrested vast numbers of recalcitrant peasants.[103]

Again at the micro level, local peasants and party activists dekulakized unpopular 'outsiders': those who had violated communal traditions by getting ahead, members of the rural intelligentsia, and other traditional enemies. Things were out of control; everyone was arresting everyone. Of course, Stalin and his clique share ultimate responsibility for these 'excesses'. Their strident rhetoric and sloganeering had sparked the fire in the first place and in their attempts to build momentum for dekulakization and collectivization they had (until March 1930) encouraged 'energetic' measures.

As they would do five years later during the *chistki*, the Stalinist centre intervened during collectivization in an attempt to control the process. Stalin's March 1930 'Dizzy With Success' article was the best known such attempt. Sending in the supposedly disciplined and tempered proletarian 25,000ers was another and the Stalin-Molotov May 1933 decree limiting arrests and detentions was a third.[104]

In the collectivization, *chistki*, and *Ezhovshchina* phenomena we find the same dynamics at work: the anatomy of a radical Stalinist transformation. First, the leadership announces the campaign, pressure for which had been developing in the party. The announcement is vague and confused and the documents show signs of poor planning and internal conflict. Nevertheless, in order to overcome traditional inertia of local interests, enthusiastic measures are demanded in strident language as the party is shoved to the left.

Second, as the decision percolates down, local officials at all levels variously delay, speed up, reinterpret, or twist the idea to suit both local conditions and their own interests. Implementation of the campaign, quite regardless of Stalin's presumed intentions, alternatively reflects historical class hatreds, Civil War legacies, zealotry, personal rivalry, and the needs of official 'family circle' cliques.

Third, things rapidly get out of control. Insofar as anyone is directing events, it is the local party secretary. But much is beyond his power, not to mention Stalin's. The Stalinist centre intervenes through jawboning speeches, exemplary indictments of particular organizations and individuals, and official decrees. More often than not, the intervention is on the side of restraining local chaos and enhancing Moscow's control over the territorial apparatchiki: Stalin now shoves them to the right. Moscow tries to protect favoured groups, break local 'family circles', and conveniently pose as the friend of the persecuted 'little person'.

Finally, the central leadership decides to attenuate the campaign or end it altogether. Once again, this requires multiple statements and interventions. Halting a campaign was much more difficult than starting it precisely because of the strong influence of local attitudes, multiple actors, and omnipresent confusion. The entire process is characterized by zig-zag pushes of the political/social leviathan to the left and right in an attempt to direct it.

One could, however, easily argue that none of this matters; that social conditions, attitudes, and conflicts are irrelevant because Stalin 'pulled the lever' in order to carry out a plan to terrorize all of society, to make everyone feel fear in order to cement his personal dictatorship.

There are three problems with this theory. Firstly, as we have noted, knowing who pulled 'the lever' does not tell us anything about how and why the phenomenon spread or about who was purged when and by whom. Surely these are important questions.

Secondly, it is clear that *after* the holocaust began, Stalin and his cronies, while continuing to massacre their colleagues at high levels, made several attempts to control the process below. Several times Moscow intervened to restore the party membership of rank and file persons expelled by local officials.[105] Stalin had to intervene personally to stop the anti-specialist zeal of local party members in industrial centres.[106] A highly publicized January 1938 Central Committee resolution, which Stalin must have approved, condemned the wild orgies of vigilance at lower levels. Whether or not these interventions on the side of 'little people' were pure demagoguery is a matter of conjecture, but it is well to remember that his pronouncements carried the aura of divine revelation. If he wanted universal fear, such statements would have been counter-productive. It is just as reasonable to believe that, like Mao, Stalin had little desire to direct the fire towards the masses of loyal subjects but was rather unable to control events as he wished.

The third objection to the theory that Stalin planned everything to create a climate of universal fear relates to the process of arrest itself. Except for a few well-publicized show trials in Moscow and in the localities, most arrests were carried out quietly and without publicity. The press in the period, while filled with editorials about maintaining vigilance, carried practically no lists or even mentions of those arrested. It is almost as if the authorities wanted to keep them a secret: hardly an effective plan to generate universal terror.[107]

Was there 'universal fear' during the purges of the 1930s? The answer is both yes and no. It seems clear that members of the intelligentsia and official stratum were terrified. As writer Isaac Babel said, 'Today a man only talks freely with his wife – at night, with the blankets pulled over his head.'[108] The stories about people committing suicide when they heard the nocturnal knock on the door may not be apocryphal.

At the same time, though, an approach to the question based again on class suggests important differences. People outside the intelligentsia and bureaucracy (and many within it) do not seem to have been very frightened. Konstantin Borin was a tractor driver, Stakhanovite, and Supreme Soviet deputy in the 1930s. Several of his chiefs and associates fell victim to the terror. He fearlessly intervened to help those he knew to be innocent. Despite the victimization of those around him (including some of his fellow Supreme Soviet deputies), Borin was neither terrorized or terrified. He recalled that he 'was not afraid of being arrested because I knew that I was not an enemy of the people. I did not know that practically everyone arrested thought the same way about himself.'[109] Dupe or careerist; the point is that he was not afraid.

Many memoirs from the period, which can be used to report the impressions of their authors, do not suggest a universal climate of fear.[110] Jack Miller, a student in Gosplan's All-Union Planning Academy in 1937, lived and worked with officials and students in that heavily purged agency: 'The purge, which throughout this period was mounting to its climax, worried them not at all in any way apparent to me, either for their own safety or for pity.' But for members of the intelligentsia teaching at the Academy, 'the impact of the purge upon them was entirely different.'[111] It is also useful to remember the stunned and incredulous reception Nikita Khrushchev got at the 20th Party Congress when he told his audience about the scale of arrest in the 1930s. Their recorded expressions of 'indignation', 'consternation', and genuine shock suggest that not even such highly placed persons – most of whom were alive at the time – realized the scale of the operation; widespread and chilling fear would have left different memories.

For now, peering through the glass darkly as we must, we might profitably borrow a framework from another period.[112] At the end of the 1920s, we find almost all the necessary, long term 'preconditions' for Stalinism, for repression and, eventually, for a major explosion. The gunpowder had been combined. Customary and *temnye* social suspicion and violence, lack of a substantial legal tradition, bitter class hatred, a vicious, unrestrained, and recent civil war legacy, hostile international encirclement, continued economic uncertainty, a messianic drive for development and modernization, and a contradictory, unstable political framework were the ingredients.[113] We will never know whether they in themselves were sufficient to produce terror and chaos because a series of short-term factors intervened to touch off the explosion.

Added to these preconditions, a series of 'precipitants' from the purely political realm touched off the repression, purging, and violence of the 1930s. They included a full-blown spy and war scare, short-term disputes over economic planning, treatment of the former opposition, and the relationship between the central and territorial party apparatus. These conflicts, which reached a head between 1934 and 1937, raised the political temperature of the country and the party and involved factional infighting on several fronts. For a considerable time, Stalin remained aloof from them, keeping his options open, refusing to take sides, alternately favouring both, and preferring to act as moderator. Eventually, though, he did tip the balances by choosing sides from late 1936 and early 1937.[114] Stalin's personality and personal role, then, were the 'triggers' which ignited the tinderbox.

There has never been any doubt that Stalin's intervention set off the terror; on one level he was certainly to blame. But his actions, although necessary, are not sufficient to explain the entire *process* and its outcome any more than Mao's personality is sufficient to explain the unfolding of the Cultural Revolution in China. It is no accident, to use a Stalin-era formulation, that Maoists were the last Stalinists. While it is fashionable to stress Stalin's shabby treatment of Mao, Stalin's picture adorned Chinese Communist Party meetings and parades long after Khrushchev and the Soviets began the process of de-stalinization. Perhaps Maoists felt a certain empathy toward the Soviet Stalinist experience. There are certainly strong parallels. Both countries were backward, wanted to modernize quickly and had huge populations divided and sub-divided along complicated class lines. Both societies had peasant traditions of class violence, superstition, anti-intellectualism, and xenophobia. Both endured bloody revolutions and civil wars which were followed by prolonged periods of international isolation. And, in both places, supreme leaders tried to resolve political factionalism by instigating populist action against the bureaucracy.

When all is said and done, is Stalinism really a surprising result of this historical situation? No one would argue that Stalinism was inevitable. But a backward country with a legacy of social hatred, passing through a violent revolution and trying to modernize, was likely to produce an unstable revolutionary society with deep tensions and conflicts. The ideology of socialism was neither the problem nor the cause: it should not be the issue today. The histories of several modernizing countries in the twentieth century demonstrate that such problems frequently lead to political violence and social chaos, even when there is neither socialism nor Stalin.

What is perhaps surprising is that scholars have for so long insisted on studying the Soviet example ahistorically and strictly in terms of psychology and ideology.

The early Russian Marxist G. V. Plekhanov observed:

> . . . every man of talent who actually appears, every man of talent who becomes a social force, is the product of social relations. Since this is the case, it is clear why talented people can . . . change only individual features of events, but not their general trend; they are themselves the product of this trend; were it not for that trend they would never have crossed the threshold that divides the potential from the real.[115]

One need not go so far as Plekhanov in underplaying the power of individuals and still doubt that one man's personality could create social classes, determine national culture, and overcome deep social reality. Stalin as a personality was not the dominant factor of his era any more than Russian society or history were fated to produce a Stalin. The question whether Stalin or Soviet political economy controlled the other is as badly put as the chicken and egg argument; we can only have personal opinions about which created which. Sweeping statements about everyone being terrorized, Stalin having total power or society being a passive tool are simplistic and useless. Our tasks should be to tease out the entangled strands of the state-society knot, to weigh the pressures society put on Stalin and vice versa, and to analyse the precise relations as we find them.

Discussion

In his fascinating and valuable contribution, Sergo Mikoyan makes the case for Stalin-era mass psychosis and 'psychological enslavement', candidly and honestly listing himself among the former slaves. He tells us that people at the time were psychologically controlled even though they believed they were acting on their own. Of course, I am not in a position to question Mikoyan's self-evaluation, but for this very reason I must express doubts about mass psychosis as an historical explanation of anything. By definition, and aside from individual clinical hypnosis, I wonder if it is possible. Do we have the right to say that our ancestors functioned within a 'false consciousness', if, as Mikoyan admits, they *believed* they were making their own choices? I do not think so. Some future historian will undoubtedly say the same thing about us today: that we now only believe we are acting autonomously, but that the 'truth' is otherwise. Is the reality perceived by our consciousness today any more genuine than that created and inhabited by Soviet citizens in the 1930s? It is far too easy, and not a little patronizing, simply to assert that those with beliefs and social backgrounds different from ours, whether in the past or present, are psychological slaves because they do not share our values. People in the 1930s were undoubtedly lied to. But they continued to act rationally according to their perception of their interests. There is no such thing as historical mass psychosis or hypnosis.

Secondly the contributions of both Alec Nove and Sergo Mikoyan discuss the issue of historical possibilities and viable alternatives to Stalinism. Nove is somewhat skeptical about them, Mikoyan less so. Both in the West and in the former Soviet Union today, such considerations are quite prevalent: Was NEP viable? Could it have continued? How would things have turned out? The most sophisticated of them use mathematical methods to project future possibilities from the 1920s.[116] Such work is often valuable and always interesting.

But there are other less scientific speculations which have a different purpose. As Nove observed, many writers have also posited lost alternatives to Stalinism in order to show that it was not inevitable. The idea is that if Stalinism were not foreordained by the Russian Revolution and that other roads were possible, then Stalin's personal role was mostly to blame, not 'the system' which could have gone right. It is said that the other point of view, wrongly called the inevitability theory, suggests that if Stalinism were inevitable or inherent in the system, then Stalin's *personal* responsibility or importance are somehow reduced. In other words the system produced him and is at fault.

Many historians trained in the western mode have problems with such types of analysis for two reasons. First of all, the connection between an alternative scenarios approach and the need to disassociate (bad) Stalinism from (better?) Leninism suggests a clear polemical agenda behind historical study. If there were alternatives, then Leninism need not have led to Stalinism. Second, inevitability is not a common concept in the arsenal of most professional historians. Either historical events and phenomena happened or they didn't. If they didn't, they are not historical events but possibilities, scenarios, or fantasies. Although they make good reading, they are not history.

These attempts to analyse the relationship between Stalin and the Soviet system on the basis of other possible realities are quite useless.

Whether we like it or not, things turned out the way they did. Alternatives did not take place because they were 'not viable for some reason or other, whether economic, political, or social. The proof is in the pudding.'[117] For some, this smacks of inevitability or determinism. Nove is worried that we cannot reach the truth by simply concentrating on antecedents of what actually happened. He suggests that when we have 'listed' them (and historical analysis should surely be more than listing!), we will have a set of conditions that could have produced some other outcome. The preconditions to Hitlerism *could* have been the preconditions to some other outcome.

Agreed. But they weren't. We are not relieved of responsibility to examine causes by the possibility that they could have caused something else. Smoking, air pollution, and certain diets cause cancer. Of course, sometimes they don't. But when we see malignancy, we should focus on the centrality of known causes, not speculate on whether these pre-existing conditions might have had more benign results. Insisting that we focus study on the causes of an existing cancer in a patient (rather than on the possibility that cancer might not have developed) makes no statement about its inevitability. It is perfectly appropriate, even necessary, to deal with the equally malignant Stalinism in the same way: by studying causes and components (including, of course, Stalin's dangerous personality) without worrying about might-have-beens or the peculiarly Germanic concept of historical necessity. Inevitability, whatever that may mean, need not enter into the process. The consideration of 'other possible worlds' must always remain speculative. That is why we have the disciplines of philosophy and theology.

Of course, serious historical analysis requires that we trace both the components of the phenomenon as well as its antecedents. History is about causality. But our focus should always be on explaining what actually happened. Most historians would probably agree with E. H. Carr in the work referenced by Nove:

> . . . one can always play a parlour game with the might-have-beens of history. . . . But plenty of people, who have suffered directly or vicariously from the results of the Bolshevik victory, desire to register their protest against it; and this takes the form, when they read history, of letting their imagination run riot on all the more agreeable things that might have happened, and of being indignant with the historian who goes on quietly with his job of

explaining what did happen and why their agreeable wish-dreams remain unfulfilled.[118]

Third, Alec Nove seems to me to underestimate the importance of local events; he doubts that one can deduce 'causes' from below.[119] Specifically, he implies that provincial doings were not important enough to influence or decide on terror. As far as it goes, the idea is reasonable. But Nove's concern is exclusively with causes: Who started it? Did it come from 'above' or 'below'?[120]

Causality and agency are slippery things. If in 1921 Lenin was forced by social realities beyond his control to implement the New Economic Policy, can it be said that he 'caused' NEP, or even phenomenologically 'initiated' it? Which came first, the chicken or the egg? (Philosophy again!) Certainly Stalin, 'from above', launched collectivization and the *Ezhovshchina*. But he and his circle did not make their fateful decisions *a priori*, in a vacuum and without confronting rigidly imposed social and political parameters and constraints, some of their own making, others not. As Moshe Lewin wrote of the decision to collectivize:

> The market mechanism of NEP, which had worked wonders at the start simply by following its natural course, had in the end led the regime into an impasse. . . . When faced with a dangerous 'procurement crisis' he [Stalin] reacted, as was to be expected, by using the lever whose use he best understood; he resorted to force . . . When he manipulated this particular lever in January 1928, Stalin did not know where the process set in motion by his 'emergency measures' would ultimately lead him.[121]

As Lewin noted, the personality of the leader was only one of the factors (and an important one) leading to collectivization. Of course, we can again chase chickens and eggs by arguing that the Bolsheviks created the policies that created the circumstances that apparently forced them to act.

Certainly Stalin pulled the lever, but the *origins* of collectivization are also to be found in the social, economic and political environment that he did not create. If our purpose is merely to find the person who 'started it' in order to blame him, we can be satisfied with Stalin. If our purpose is rather to understand more profoundly the origins of phenomena and historical events in their totality, we must widen our focus. Surely we agree that history is at least an interplay between subjective and objective factors.

Finally, I wish I could be as 'crystal clear' about what happened in the

1930s as Sergo Mikoyan is, but we still have few sources and a lot of work to do. Fortunately, some important documents (or descriptions of them) are creeping to light in such publications as *Izvestiia TsK*. Most of these documentary revelations are aimed at illustrating Stalin's direct role in the repression, a point more startling to Russian readers than to Western ones. Some of these revelations raise as many questions as they answer and sometimes paint an unclear picture.

New evidence casts doubts on rumours and myths that have become prevalent. Thus the new documents provide no evidence for the existence of a bloc of Stalinist moderates who tried to restrain Stalin's alleged careful plan for terror.[122] Similarly, the belief that 282 delegates (or sometimes 123 or 125 or 2–4 or 5–6 or 3, depending on the rumour) voted against Stalin at the 17th Party Congress in 1934 has been questioned by recent research. A special investigation by Central Committee staff in 1989 concluded that 166 ballots were indeed missing, but because the numbers of ballots printed and delegates voting are unknown, 'it is impossible definitely to confirm' how many, if any, voted against Stalin. A 1960 investigation concluded that 166 delegates simply 'did not take part in the voting.'[123]

Continued release of documents from the 1930s may also weaken the tradition of writing history by anecdote. With great respect for both Anastas and Sergo Mikoyan, we can note that new information seems also to raise the question of the role of Anastas Mikoyan. True, as Volkogonov has suggested, his role was clearly more benign than those of Molotov, Kaganovich, and Ezhov. At the same time, though, Anastas Mikoyan was involved in the repressions rather more than the single episode mentioned by his son. We now know that at the February 1937 plenum, Anastas Mikoyan gave a 'long speech' attacking Bukharin and Rykov, which was 'in fact a co-report' to the vicious remarks of Ezhov accusing the rightists of being spies and assassins. Mikoyan then chaired the subcommission that condemned Bukharin, and which very nearly voted to shoot him outright.[124] Later in that year, in December, Mikoyan was master of ceremonies at a celebratory meeting at the Bolshoi Theatre to mark the founding of the Cheka and glorify the ongoing depredations of N. I. Ezhov. At that occasion, Mikoyan's speech was quite laudatory and stressed Ezhov's fine personal qualities and widespread popularity. Certainly his subsequent career and much other evidence show that Mikoyan, like Khrushchev, was a human among monsters, and it is possible that his 1937 activities were necessary to save his life.[125] Such were the times.

Notes

1 Svetlana Allilueva, *Twenty Letters to a Friend* (New York, 1967); Nikita Khrushchev, *Khrushchev Remembers* (Boston, 1970); Seweryn Bialer, *Stalin and his Generals* (New York, 1969) contains useful excerpts from Soviet military men who had contact with Stalin; see also Milovan Djilas, *Conversations With Stalin* (London, 1962); a Soviet example is A. Iakovlev, *Tsel' zhizni* (Moscow, 1967).

2 Anatoli Rybakov, *Children of the Arbat*, trans. by Harold Shukman (Boston, 1988); Anton Antonov-Ovseyenko, *The Time of Stalin: Portrait of Tyranny* (New York, 1980). On the reliability of Antonov-Ovseyenko, see L. van Rossum, 'A. Antonov-Ovseenko's Book on Stalin: Is It Reliable?', *Soviet Studies*, No. 3, 1984, 445–7.

3 For example see Alexander Orlov, *The Secret History of Stalin's Crimes* (London, 1954), Boris Bazhanov, *Avec Staline dans le Kremlin* (Paris, 1930) and *Bajanov révèle Stalin* (Paris, 1979). For a critique of Bajanov's credibility see Robert H. McNeal, *Stalin: Man and Ruler* (New York, 1988), p. 346.

4 Iurii Borev, *Staliniada* (Moscow, 1990).

5 *Istochnikovedenie* is today practically a separate branch of historical scholarship in Russia. Literature on it in Russia far outweighs that in the English-speaking world. To sample it, try I. D. Koval'chenko (ed.), *Istochnikovedenie istorii SSSR* (Moscow, 1981) or M. A. Varshavchik, *Istoriko-partinnoe istochnikovedenie: teoriia, metodologiia, metodika* (Kiev, 1984).

6 Patricia Kennedy Grimsted, 'Archival Resources for Social History of the 1920s and 1930s: Soviet Archival Developments and Reference Aids for the Social Historian', *Russian History*, Vol. 12, Nos. 2–4, 168.

7 Stephen F. Cohen, 'Stalin's Terror as Social History', *The Russian Review*, 45: 1986, 381, and Alec Nove, 'Stalinism: Revisionism Reconsidered', *The Russian Review*, 46: 4 October 1987, 417.

8 For careful analyses of memoirs as sources see: Robert W. Thurston, 'Fear and Belief in the USSR's "Great Terror": Response to Arrest, 1935–1939', *Slavic Review*, 45:1986, 213–44; Hiroaki Kuromiya, 'Soviet Memoirs as a Historical Source', *Russian History*, 12:2–4, 1985, 293–326; V. S. Golubtsov, 'Vospominaniia, dnevniki, chastnaia perepiska', in Koval'chenko, *Istochnikovedenie*, 465–80.

9 For critiques of the Letter's authenticity, see J. Arch Getty, *Origins of the Great Purges: the Soviet Communist Party Reconsidered, 1933–1938* (New York, 1985), pp. 214–16; Roy A. Medvedev, *Nikolay Bukharin* (New York, 1980), pp. 115–18; McNeal, *Stalin*, p. 355. See also the recent critical testimony of Bukharin's widow: Anna Larina, *Nezabyvaemoe* (Moscow, 1989), pp. 272–89.

10 For criticism of Orlov, see Getty, *Origins*, pp. 211–12, and McNeal, *Stalin*, pp. 360–2.

11 This has been the practice so far. We ignore the 'Letter' when it suggests that Ezhov or Kaganovich had the most to gain from Kirov's death.
12 Exceptions to this generalization include the memoirs of Khrushchev and the sanitized recollections of Anastas Mikoyan. Yet, perhaps because the authors were participants in unsavoury events, they do not tell us what we would like to know about the crucial process of decision-making in the inner circle.
13 See, for example, Matt F. Oja, 'Fictional History and Historical Fiction: Solzhenitsyn and Kis as Exemplars', *History and Theory*, 27:2, 1988, 111–23.
14 One expert noted that although the book is rich in social history and texture, it 'cannot be said to add a great deal to our understanding of Soviet politics'. John Barber, 'Children of the Arbat', *Detente*, no. 11, 1988, 8–11; for other views of the value and problems of the novel see R. W. Davies, 'Soviet History in the Gorbachev Revolution: The First Phase', in R. Miliband, L. Panitch, and J. Saville (eds), *Socialist Register 1988*, pp. 37–78; and A. Latsis, 'S tochki zreniia sovremenika', *Izvestiia*, 17 August 1987, 4; Vadim Kozhinov, 'Pravda i istina', *Nash sovremennik*, no. 4, 1988, 160–75.
15 Compare Shatrov in *Znamia*, no. 1, 1988, 26–8, with A. Orlov, *Tainaia istoriia stalinskikh prestuplenii* (New York, 1983), pp. 135–6. This odd 'feedback loop' between western anti-Soviet cold-war propaganda works and recent *glasnost* literature is not uncommon. Some Russian writers, in private conversations, are even quoting Winston Churchill on Stalin.
16 See A. Butenko (following Rybakov in *Children of the Arbat*), 'Political Leadership and the Struggle for Power Under Socialism', *Moscow News*, no. 9, 1988, 12, for the claim. For Stalin's speech see *Pravda*, 2 November 1927.
17 B. W. Wolfe (ed), *Khrushchev and Stalin's Ghost* (London, 1957), p. 154.
18 See Stephen F. Cohen, *Rethinking the Soviet Experience: Politics and History Since 1917* (New York, 1985), ch. 1. The tendency is less pronounced in other countries with Soviet studies disciplines: Britain, France, Germany, and Japan.
19 See Peter Kenez, 'Stalinism as Humdrum Politics', *The Russian Review*, 45:1986, 395–400.
20 Leon Trotsky, *The Revolution Betrayed* (New York, 1937). See also Robert H. McNeal, 'Trotskyist Interpretations of Stalinism' in Robert C. Tucker (ed.), *Stalinism: Essays in Historical Interpretation* (New York, 1977). Although Trotskyism is alive and well among some politically committed people in the West, it has few adherents among mainstream scholars. Alec Nove, both in previous writings and in the present volume, has dealt extensively with Trotsky and Trotskyist interpretations.
21 See, for example, Stephen F. Cohen, 'Bolshevism and Stalinism' in Tucker (ed.), *Stalinism*, pp. 3–29.
22 Roy A. Medvedev, *Let History Judge* (New York, 1971) is the most important example of the Khrushchev interpretation.
23 On the continuity thesis generally see Stephen F. Cohen, *Rethinking the Soviet Experience* (New York, 1986).
24 Particularly important documents are Lenin's 'Testament' and his final writings on the prospects of the Soviet system. The ultimate sources of legitimacy are therefore Lenin's early 1920s views and prognostications for the future.

25 The Russian Marxist G. Plekhanov wrote that 'The effect of personal peculiarities . . . is undeniable; but no less undeniable is the fact that it could occur *only in the given social conditions.*' 'We know now that individuals often exercise considerable influence upon the fate of society, but this influence is determined by the internal structure of that society and by its relation to other societies.' G. V. Plekhanov, *The Role of the Individual in History* (London, 1940), pp. 40, 43–4.

26 For excellent discussions of perestroika and history see R. W. Davies, 'Soviet History in the Gorbachev Revolution: The First Phase', *The Socialist Register 1988* (London, 1988), pp. 37–78; and Thomas Sherlock, 'Politics and History Under Gorbachev', *Problems of Communism*, May–August, 1988, 16–37.

27 M. Gorbachev, *Izbrannye rechi i stat'i*, Vol. 3 (Moscow, 1987), p. 163.

28 'Printsipy perestroiki: revoliutsionnost', myshleniia, i deistvii', *Pravda* editorial, 5 April 1988.

29 *Ogonek*: no. 26, 1988, 25, for the call for Stalin's expulsion; no. 32, 7, for Aleksandr Veinstein's suggestion that the remains of 'the main criminal of all times and peoples' be removed from the mausoleum; and no. 3, 1988, 4, on Stalin's birthplace.

30 Vadim Kozhinov, 'Pravda i istina', *Nash sovremennik*, no. 4, 1988, 160–75.

31 For criticism of Kozhinov, see Vladimir Lakshin, 'V kil'vatere', *Ogonek*, no. 26, 1988, 10–11, and Roy Medvedev, 'Roots of a Phenomenon', *Moscow News*, No. 24, 1988, 13–14.

32 '[T]here can be no doubt that Stalin was a monster and that if there ever existed a real "enemy of the people" it was him. His crimes will be remembered for ever and we need the entire concrete truth about the epoch of his omnipotence as much as we need air.' Igor Shafarevich, 'Logic of History?', *Moscow News*, No. 24, 1988, 12.

33 A. Tsipko, 'Istoki Stalinizma', *Nauka i zhizn'*, Nos. 11–12, November 1988, 45–55; No. 1, January 1989, 46–56.

34 See Andrei Nuikin, 'Idealy ili interesy', *Novyi mir'*, no. 1, 1988, 205 for a characterization of Stalin's coming to power as a counter-revolutionary state coup (*perevorot*). Iuri Afanas'ev has also characterized Stalin's programme as 'counter-revolutionary' and suggested that the system he created (and that existing today) are not socialist. See *Pravda*, 26 July 1988. None of those in this school are avowed Trotskyists or Bukharinists.

35 'Printsipy perestroika: revoliutsionnost', myshleniia, i deistvii', *Pravda* editorial, 5 April 1988.

36 *Pravda*, 26 July 1988, in rebutting Afanas'ev, took the 'serious mistakes' line but suggested that Stalin had helped to save socialism.

37 For discussions embodying the 'administrative system' approach, see A. Bek's novel *Novoe naznachenie*, serialized in *Znamiia*, nos. 10–11, 1988 and G. Popov's review essay on it ('C tochki zreniia ekonomista') in *Nauka i zhizn'*, No. 4, 1987, 54–65. See also Nuikin, 'Idealy ili interesy'.

38 A rather strident defence of Stalin was published as a letter from Leningrad teacher Nina Andreeva in *Sovetskaia Rossiia*, 13 March 1988. It is widely believed that Andreeva's original letter was rewritten by several neo-Stalinist hands before

publication and therefore represents a collective manifesto. *Pravda* published a long denunciation on 5 April 1988.

39 For discussions of the role of historians, journalists, and the relationship between them, see D. S. Likhachev, 'Ot pokaianiia-k deistviiu', *Literaturnaia gazeta*, no. 37, 1987, 2; 'Istoriia i literatura. Materialy nauchnoi konferentsii', *Voprosy istorii*, no. 6, 1988. (*Voprosy istorii KPSS*, a more cautious historical journal, published only a truncated version of this important conference in no. 6, 1988, 152–3); 'Stopping History or Marching On?', *Moscow News*, no. 10, 1988, 12–13; and a roundtable of historians in *Pravda*, 14 June 1988, 2.

40 Even old Marshal Zhukov was not immune from repeating rumours, such as the one that the high command of the Red Army was executed in 1941, not in 1937. See Anna Mirkina, 'Marshal pishet knigu', *Ogonek*, no. 16, 1988, 13.

41 V. P. Danilov, 'Diskussiia v zapadnoi presse o golode 1932–1933gg. i demograficheskoi katastrofe' 30–40kh godov v SSSR', *Voprosy istorii*, no. 3, 1988, 116–30.

42 There are some recent exceptions: Dmitrii Volkogonov, *Triumf i tragediia* (Moscow, 1989); Iu. S. Kukushkin (ed.), *Rezhim lichnoi vlasti Stalina* (Moscow, 1989); V. I. Demidov (ed.), *Leningradskoe delo* (Leningrad, 1990).

43 Roy Medvedev, 'Roots of a Phenomenon', *Moscow News*, No. 24, 1988, 13 (emphasis added). Such statements are surprising from the Soviet historian who in his writings has done the most to uncover the deeper causes of Stalinism.

44 A perceptive analysis of this issue is provided by Henry Reichman in 'Reconsidering Stalinism', *Theory and Society*, 17 (1988), 57–90. See also Gabor T. Rittersporn, 'Rethinking Stalinism', *Russian History*, 11:4 (1984), 343–61.

45 H. R. Trevor-Roper, *The European Witch-Craze of the Sixteenth and Seventeenth Centuries and Other Essays* (New York, 1968), pp. 114–15, and quoted in Lynne Viola, ' "The Second Coming": Class Enemies in the Soviet Countryside in the 1930s', paper presented to the 1988 meeting of the National Seminar on Russian and Soviet Social History, Ann Arbor, Michigan. My thanks to Roberta Manning for reminding me about witch crazes and their like in history.

46 Cohen, *Rethinking*, p. 68. Theorists of totalitarianism avoided the question because, for them, the regime dominated society through force quite regardless of popular sentiment.

47 For alternative views that discuss forms of worker support for Stalin, see Sheila Fitzpatrick, *Education and Social Mobility in the Soviet Union, 1921–1934* (New York, 1979) and Hiroaki Kuromiya, *Stalin's Industrial Revolution: Politics and Workers, 1928–1932* (New York, 1988).

48 The newspaper *Moscow News* has been a forum for a wide-ranging debate on the causes of Stalinism. Evgeniia Albats, 'Not to be Pardoned', *Moscow News*, No. 19, 1988, 13, is a remarkable but not entirely unsympathetic interview with a former NKVD interrogator. An angry response to her position came from Anatoly Aleksin, 'No Statute of Limitations', *ibid.*, No. 28, 1988, 2.

49 Natan Eidelman, 'Under Stalin's Spell', *ibid.*, No. 30, 1988, 2.

50 See V. Z. Drobyshev's comments to a roundtable of historians published in *Kommunist*, No. 12, August 1987, 72; V. Loginov in *Literaturnaia gazeta*, 28 October 1987; and Fedor Burlatskii writing in *Pravda*, 18 July 1987. The reference to the Tatar Yoke is from Burlatskii.

51 Roy A. Medvedev, *Let History Judge* (New York, 1973), p. 428.

52 See Dmitrii Volkogonov, 'Fenomen Stalina', *Literaturnaia Gazeta*, 9 December 1987.

53 It is revealing that the opponents of this Soviet view (members of the *Pamiat'* society and others who champion the traditions of the Russian peasant) repeat many of the arguments of Chaadaev's opponents in the nineteenth century, the Slavophiles.

54 Following Stalin's own characterization.

55 Moshe Lewin, 'The Social Background of Stalinism' in his *The Making of the Soviet System* (New York, 1985), pp. 260–6. See also Sheila Fitzpatrick's discussion of the 'above' and 'below' question in her 'New Perspectives on Stalinism', *Russian Review*, 45 (1986), 357–413.

56 See Getty, 'State, Society, and Superstition'; Roberta T. Manning, 'State and Society in Stalinist Russia', *The Russian Review*, 46:4, October 1987, 407–11. Although none of the revisionists are avowed Marxists, the type of political economy they propose, in which elements in the superstructure reflect or represent elements in society, is Marxist in approach and method.

57 William Beik, *Absolutism and Society in Seventeenth-Century France: State Power and Provincial Aristocracy in Languedoc* (Cambridge, 1985), p. 17.

58 The classic treatment of the cult is Robert C. Tucker, 'The Rise of Stalin's Personality Cult', *American Historical Review*, 84:1979, 347–66. See also his *Stalin as Revolutionary, 1879–1929* (New York, 1973). See also Graeme Gill, 'Personality Cult, Political Culture, and Party Structure', *Studies in Comparative Communism*, 17:2, 1984, 111–21. To sample the prose, try one of the commemorative volumes issued on the occasions of Stalin's birthday.

59 Immanuel Wallerstein, *Africa: The Politics of Independence* (New York, 1961), p. 99.

60 See Jonathan Harris, 'The Origins of the Conflict Between Malenkov and Zhdanov, 1939–1941', *Slavic Review*, 35:2, June 1976, and 'Stalin's Division of Labor: "Party-State" Relations in the 1930s', unpublished paper. (My thanks to Professor Harris for permission to cite this work.) See also Sheila Fitzpatrick, 'Ordzhonikidze's Takeover of Vesenkha: A Case Study in Soviet Bureaucratic Politics', *Soviet Studies*, 37:1985, 153–72; Werner G. Hahn, *Postwar Soviet Politics: The Fall of Zhdanov and the Defeat of Moderation, 1946–1953* (Ithaca, NY, 1982); William O. McCagg, Jr., *Stalin Embattled, 1943–1948* (Detroit, 1978); Timothy Dunmore, *The Stalinist Command Economy: The Soviet State Apparatus and Economic Policy, 1945–1953* (New York, 1980). There are several other examples.

61 Jonathan Haslam, *The Soviet Union and the Struggle for Collective Security in Europe, 1933–39* (New York, 1984), pp. 52–3.

62 One of the features of revisionist scholarship is its reluctance to deal in any detail with the question of blame or guilt. Most revisionist scholars either consider the question settled or outside the scope of their research. They have been criticized for this lack of moral statement by scholars who believe that moral stands have a central place in historical writing. See, for example, the contributions of Stephen Cohen and Peter Kenez to the published discussion on revisionism in *The Russian Review*, 45:4, 1987.

63 On political culture and tradition see Robert C. Tucker, *Political Culture and Leadership in Soviet Russia from Lenin to Gorbachev* (New York, 1987).

64 Theodore Von Laue, 'Stalin in Focus', *Slavic Review*, 42:1983, 373–89 and 'Stalin Among the Moral and Political Imperatives, or How to Judge Stalin', *Soviet Union*, 8:1, 1981, 1–17, argues that the Russian backwardness, responding to the challenge of modernization posed by the West (which is to blame), led to brutality and Stalinism.

65 Cohen, *Rethinking*, p. 69.

66 See Roger Pethybridge, *The Social Prelude to Stalinism* (New York, 1974), for a valuable discussion of some of these points.

67 We know, for example, of the indecorous conduct of Stalin and his cronies at their midnight feasts. Similarly, eyewitness accounts and film footage of Stalin in company with the more urbane and cosmopolitan Roosevelt and Churchill during the Second World War suggest his social discomfort and nervousness in the presence of these aristocrats.

68 Stalin's conventional usage of expressions like 'our people', referring to party members or those who supported the Soviet power, *versus* the 'enemy' was an echo of peasant attitudes.

69 See Jerry Hough, 'The "Dark Forces", the Totalitarian Model, and Soviet History', *The Russian Review*, 46:1987, 397–403, for the development of this idea in the Stalin period.

70 The Bolsheviks' dominant legal thinking in the 1920s (class-based justice rather than individual rights and equalities) was thus perfectly consonant with Russian tradition. The ease with which the state 'legally' expropriated and destroyed the NEP-men at the end of the 1920s illustrates the flexibility of legality, the poor development of property law, and the inclination to subsume legal procedures in the name of some overriding collective purpose.

71 Stephen P. Frank, 'Popular Justice, Community, and Culture among the Russian Peasantry, 1870–1900', *The Russian Review*, Vol. 46, 1987, 239–65.

72 'They' were usually defined as boyars, nobles, or evil advisers. The tsar was often, and wrongly regarded as good: 'If he only knew. . . .' See Daniel Field, *Rebels in the Name of the Tsar* (Boston, 1976). Similar expressions were heard with regard to Stalin in the 1930s and Mao Zedong in the 1970s.

73 Rybakov, *Children of the Arbat*, p. 278.

74 Isaac Babel, 'The Letter', *Collected Stories*, ed. and trans. by Walter Morton (New York, 1955), p. 48.

75 'The Life and Adventures of Mathew Pavlichenko', *ibid.*, p. 106.

76 Visitors to the American south a century after the US Civil War know that the heritage of that conflict's hatred and bitterness remain. Imagine how powerfully such sentiments lingered in Russia less than a decade after a much more brutal conflict.

77 Merle Fainsod, *Smolensk Under Soviet Rule* (Cambridge, Mass., 1958), pp. 160–2.

78 See Lynne Viola, 'Notes on the Background of Soviet Collectivization: Metal Worker Brigades in the Countryside, Autumn, 1929', *Soviet Studies*, No. 2, 1984, 205–22, and *The Best Sons of the Fatherland*. See also William J. Chase, *Workers,*

Society, and the Soviet State: Labor and Life in Moscow (Urbana, Illinois, 1987).

79 See J. Arch Getty, 'State and Society Under Stalin: Constitutions and Elections in the 1930s', *Slavic Review*, Spring 1991.

80 Tsentral'nyi gosudarstvennyi arkhiv oktiabr'skoi revoliutsii i sotsialisticheskogo stroitel'stva SSSR (hereafter TsGAOR), fond 1235, opis 41, delo 127, p. 145.

81 TsGAOR, fond 3316, opis 41, dela 127–9.

82 TsGAOR, fond 3316, opis 41, delo 127, p. 13.

83 TsGAOR, fond 3316, opis 8, delo 222, list 26; fond 3316, opis 41, dela 207, list 230.

84 TsGAOR, fond 3316, opis 41, delo 127, pp. 9, 13, 84.

85 Mikhail Reiman, *The Birth of Stalinism*, trans. by George Saunders (Bloomington, 1987). See also Sheila Fitzpatrick, 'The Foreign Threat During the First Five Year Plan', *Soviet Union*, no. 5, 1978, 26–35.

86 Menzhenskii, head of the Cheka, seems to have pressed earlier and harder than Stalin for tough measures on the opposition.

87 Of course, one can make a counter argument here. If the international position was so dangerous in the 1930s, it would appear to make little sense to plunge the government into chaos, persecute the military or other elites, and thereby weaken the country in a time of peril. At such points, one is constantly reminded how little our logic resembles that of dictators in the 1930s. Stalin and his leadership clearly believed that such persecution would *strengthen* the country. In one limited sense, he was proved right in so far as Adolf Hitler believed that the purge of Tukhachevskii and his fellow army officers had strengthened Stalin's centralized control. Joseph Goebbels, *The Goebbels Diaries, 1942–1943*, ed. and trans. by Louis P. Lochner (New York, 1948), p. 355.

88 In Smolensk, factories, enterprises and one entire district were named for First Secretary I. P. Rumiantsev. Merle Fainsod called Rumiantsev 'the Great Lord of Smolensk'. See *Smolensk Under Soviet Rule*, Ch. 2.

89 See Merle Fainsod, *Smolensk Under Soviet Rule*, Cambridge, Mass., 1958; J. Arch Getty, *Origins of the Great Purges: The Soviet Communist Party Reconsidered, 1933–1938* (New York, 1985), Chs. 1–4; Patrick Flaherty, 'Stalinism in Transition, 1932–1937', *Radical History Review*, 37:1987, 41–68; Roberta T. Manning, 'Government in the Soviet Countryside in the Stalinist Thirties: The Case of Belyi Riaon in 1937', *The Carl Beck Papers in Russian and East European Studies*, no. 301, 1985; Gabor T. Rittersporn, 'The State Against Itself: Social Tensions. Behind the Rhetorical Apotheosis', *Telos*, 46:1979, and 'Rethinking Stalinism', *Russian History*, 11:4; Nobuo Shimotomai, 'Springtime for the Politotdel: Local Party Organization in Crisis', *Acta Slavica Iaponica*, IV:1986, 1–34, and T. H. Rigby, 'Early Provincial Cliques and the Rise of Stalin', *Soviet Studies*, III:1, January 1981, 3–28. For a fascinating look at 'localization' of party organizations in the 1920s, see Daniel Brower, 'The Smolensk Scandal and the end of NEP', *Slavic Review*, 45:4, Winter 1986, 689–706.

90 See Peter H. Solomon, 'Local Political Power and Soviet Criminal Justice 1922–1941', *Soviet Studies*, 37:3, July 1985, and Gabor T. Rittersporn, 'Soviet Officialdom and Political Evolution: Judiciary Apparatus and Penal Policy in the 1930s', *Theory and Society*, 13:1984.

91 The interplay between local and central policymakers during collectivization is explored by R. W. Davies, *The Socialist Offensive* (Cambridge, Mass., 1980) and by Lynne Viola, *The Best Sons of the Fatherland* (New York, 1987).

92 Gabor T. Rittersporn, 'The State Against Itself: Social Tensions Behind the Rhetorical Apotheosis', *Telos*, 46:1979, and 'Rethinking Stalinism', *Russian History*, 11:4, 1ff.

93 This was the way one military commander described the order for his arrest, which he avoided by simply leaving town. Petro G. Grigorenko, *Memoirs* (New York, 1982), p. 85.

94 'Passives' were not mentioned or targeted in the instructions for the 1933 *Chistka*, but were nonetheless the largest single group expelled in the operation itself.

95 From the 'outside', though, it was and is easy to mistake this mass purging at the hands of local secretaries for a Stalin plan to terrorize everyone. For whatever it's worth, Sasha Pankratov, hero of *Children of the Arbat*, was expelled at the instigation of the *leadership* of his party cell.

96 N. A. Zolotarev, *Vazhnyi etap organizatsionnogo ukrepleniia Kommunisticheskoi partii 1928–1937gg.* (Moscow, Mysl', 1979), pp. 178–81.

97 At the February 1937 Central Committee plenum, the regional party secretaries on the Central Committee did, after all, vote to expel and condemn Bukharin, Rykov, and the other rightists. None of them defended the oppositionists. See *Izvestiia TsK*, no. 5, 1989.

98 This fascinating process is documented closely in Belyi Raion of the Western Oblast'. See Smolensk Archive files WKP 111 and WKP 321 and the account in Getty, *Origins of the Great Purges*, pp. 151–3. See also Roberta T. Manning, 'Government in the Soviet Countryside in the Stalinist Thirties: The Case of Belyi Raion in 1937', *The Carl Beck Papers in Russian and East European Studies*, no. 301, 1985.

99 New research on the impact of local peasant attitudes on the purges is appearing. See Lynne Viola, ' "The Second Coming": Class Enemies in the Soviet Countryside in the 1930s', paper presented to the 1988 meeting of the National Seminar on Russian and Soviet Social History, Ann Arbor, Mich. Also see Roberta T. Manning, 'The Case of the Miffed Milkmaid or How the Great Purges Came to the Sychevka Pedigreed Livestock Breeding Station', unpublished paper presented to the Third Workshop on the Social History of the Stalin Period, Austin, Texas, 7–8 March 1986.

100 See Manning, 'The Case of the Miffed Milkmaid' and Khrushchev, *Khrushchev Remembers*, pp. 110–14.

101 *XVIII s"ezd vsesoiuznoi kommunisticheskoi partii (b) 10–21 marta, 1939g.: stenograficheskii otchet* (Moscow, 1939), pp. 519–23.

102 The following account owes much to Lynne Viola, *The Best Sons of the Fatherland*.

103 It is interesting to note that today, many of these fierce collectivizers (Postyshev, Chubar', Sheboldaev, Rumiantsev, and many others) have nonetheless emerged as rehabilitated heroes simply because they later became victims of the *Ezhovshchina*. A similar thing has happened to Alexander Kosarev, who had ruled the Komsomol with an iron hand and who had carried out his own purges before his fall. See *Ogonek*, no. 7, February 1988, 26–9.

104 See Lynne Viola, 'The Campaign to Eliminate the Kulak as a Class, Winter 1929–1930: A Re-evaluation of the Legislation', *Slavic Review*, 45:3, Fall 1986, 503–24.
105 Getty, *Origins*, chs. 4 and 7.
106 *Pravda*, 11, 15 May 1937, 31 October 1937 for examples.
107 See McNeal, *Stalin*, pp. 200–2.
108 Ilya Ehrenburg, *Men, Years, and Life*, vol. 4 (London, 1963), p. 195.
109 See 'Privlechenie k sudebnoi otvetstvennosti direktora MTS Matiukhova i dr. za sryv raboty kombainera-ordenonostsa Borina', *Sotsialisticheskoe zemledelie*, 17 July 1937, 1; and Konstantin Borin, 'A Time to Reap', *Moscow News*, No. 12, 1988, 16. My thanks to Roberta Manning for the first citation.
110 See Robert W. Thurston, 'Fear and Belief in the USSR's "Great Terror" '; Hiroaki Kuromiya, 'Soviet Memoirs as a Historical Source'.
111 Jack Miller, 'Soviet Planners in 1936–37', in Jane Degras (ed.), *Soviet Planning: Essays in Honour of Naum Jasny* (Oxford, 1964), p. 119.
112 In what follows, I have borrowed Lawrence Stone's framework (*The Causes of the English Revolution, 1529–1642*, New York, 1977) which he used to explain the causes of the English Civil War of the seventeenth century.
113 There were, of course, other preconditions to Stalinism which space forbids us to discuss: generational conflict between old Bolsheviks and 'new men', a network of personal grudges and resentments, party/army rivalries, and others.
114 The nature of these debates and the way in which they, with Stalin, sparked the terror were the subjects of my *Origins of the Great Purges*. Even on the subject of repression, Stalin sometimes seemed unsure. Although he took a hard line toward Trotskyists and Zinovievists, he was for a long time undecided on Bukharin and Piatakov. In summer 1936, he actually appointed Piatakov to be a witness at the first show trial. But less than two weeks before the trial, Piatakov was removed and himself arrested based on evidence suddenly produced by Ezhov and Iagoda (*Ivestiia TsK*, no. 9, 1989, 37). After receiving for five months Ezhov's written 'evidence' denouncing Bukharin, Stalin declined to sanction his arrest. Even at the notorious February Plenum of 1937, photostatic evidence shows that Stalin's first impulse was to simply exile Bukharin, without sending him to trial (*ibid.*, no. 5, 1989, 82). Of course, in the end, both Piatakov and Bukharin were killed, but the road to their demise was not a straight one.
115 G. V. Plekhanov, *The Role of the Individual in History* (London, 1940), p. 52.
116 See, for example, L. I. Borodkin and M. A. Svishchev's fascinating use of Markov chain modelling to study small production during NEP: 'Sotsial'naia mobil'nost' v period nepa. K voprosu o roste kapitalizma iz melkogo proizdvodstva', *Istoriia SSSR*, no. 5, Sept.-Oct., 1990, 105–20. Svishchev has used the same method to project possible futures for NEP agriculture: 'Was the Great Break-Through Historically Inevitable?: A Simulation Model of Social Mobility During the Period of NEP'. My thanks to Svishchev for permission to cite this unpublished paper.
117 Lynne Viola, 'Back on the Economic Front of Collectivization of Soviet Agriculture Without Soviet Power', *Slavic Review*, 47:4, Summer 1988, 221.
118 E. H. Carr, *What is History?* (New York, 1961), pp. 127–8.

119 Nove also expresses such doubts in 'Stalinism: Revisionism Reconsidered', *The Russian Review*, 46:1987, 412–17.

120 I discussed this problem of 'first causes' in Soviet history in 'State, Society, and Superstition', *ibid.*, 391–6.

121 Moshe Lewin, *Russian Peasants and Soviet Power: A Study of Collectivization* (New York, 1968), pp. 516–17.

122 This hypothetical bloc, variously said to consist of Sergo Ordzhonikidze, Pavel Postyshev, and perhaps others was used to explain the zigs and zags of Stalin's policy: supposedly he faced resistance from this group and frequently had to back down. But documents suggest that, for example, no one defended Bukharin and Rykov at the February plenum.

123 The whole story about votes against Stalin comes from a single testimony, that of V. M. Verkhovykh in 1960. Other 1934 congress participants have contradicted his claim. See *Izvestiia TsK.*, no. 7, 1989, 114–21. Anastas Mikoyan's 'confirmation' of the rigged voting is hardly that; he reports rumours he heard in the 1950s, although he was present at the 1934 congress.

124 *Ibid.*, no. 5, 1989, 76–9.

125 *Pravda*, 21 December 1937, p. 1. On the other hand, several other Stalin intimates did not find it necessary to so visibly involve themselves in order to survive; one thinks of Kalinin, Khrushchev, Andreev, Iaroslavskii, and even poor Voroshilov who praised the military high command at the very moment that other Stalin cronies began to attack it. See *Izvestiia TsK*, no. 4, 1989, 45.

CHAPTER 5

Stalinism As I Saw It

Sergo Mikoyan

To the memory of my father-in-law, Alexey Kuznetsov, a small town young communist enthusiast of the 1920s, a hero of the 900-day defence of Leningrad, blockaded by Hitler's wehrmacht *in the 1940s, a man whose life and untimely death, caused brutally by Stalin's secret police at Stalin's order, reflected the light and the dark, the romance and the remorse, the hopes and the despair of Soviet communists for decades after October 1917.*

This chapter is supposed to provide a critical commentary on the analysis offered by the distinguished authors of the previous chapters. My task may look easier than theirs. But in some respects it is more difficult.

First of all, for several decades my professional job as a historian drew my attention away from the Soviet Union to other countries, mostly across the Atlantic. Second, unlike my co-authors, Stalinism in its worst features was for me not an object of academic study from abroad, but my natural environment for at least the first twenty-four years of my life. I lived not just in the heartland of Stalinism, but in the family of one of Stalin's closest associates. I lived inside the Kremlin walls, walls which isolated 'The Great Genius of All Times and Peoples' from some two hundred million people living outside (but unfortunately not the other way around). I could see a short man in the uniform of a Marshal, followed or surrounded by a group of people including my own father who practically every night (or rather early morning) came back straight from His home.

Could these circumstances – and many others which it would be inappropriate to narrate here because of the space they would have demanded – leave me the smallest opportunity to remain an absolutely objective, calm and academically minded scholar about the matter which for a long time was the substance of my very existence?

Of course, readers of this book need not fear endless recollections on the theme 'Stalin and me'. But this short introduction should make any reader prepared for anything which might seem prejudiced or not absolutely objective. Perhaps nobody can ever be absolutely objective. Still, this case is clearly something special even though Stalinism could not have been treated without any emotion by anybody who is human. (Thank God, computers have not been asked to play Stalinism, as they are playing chess.)

But what is Stalinism? That question, put by Sheila Fitzpatrick in her chapter, is very important to answer, however difficult it might be.

The new term *Stalinishchina*, mentioned by Sheila Fitzpatrick, appeared just because 'Stalinism' began to be understood in the Soviet Union much more broadly than the system which existed under Stalin himself. That system featured the almighty OGPU-NKVD-MVD-MGB, the deception and naivety of millions, ideological rigidity, turning to fierce fanaticism, widely spread and overwhelming, subduing without pity the honesty and common sense even of people who were known to be decent, human and intelligent – all of these lie in the term *Stalinishchina*. We felt it necessary to introduce a new word because it had a definite negative sound in Russian, with a strong accent of contempt and disgust. But many began to express the opinion that Stalinism was born not with the dictatorship of Stalin – in 1929 or towards the end of 1920s – but much earlier, perhaps in October 1917 under the name of victorious Bolshevism. Stalinism did not die with Stalin in March 1953, and we cannot celebrate its complete burial even today.

Whichever trend prevails in future, one assumption is absolutely excluded. In my opinion S. Fitzpatrick is wrong in saying that it is 'anyone's guess' if a more positive view of the Stalin era is possible in future, even in the case of, as she puts it, 'the outside pressures on historians – from the Soviet political leadership, [or] from the public'.

The fact is that even the Pamyat society, always known to defy democratic and humanistic trends, even the Russian chauvinists, grouped around the journals *Nash Sovremennik*, and *Molodaya*

Gvardia, are trying to overcome their former allegiance to Stalin and his era. The article by Fomenko in issue No. 8, 1990, of *Nash Sovremennik* is very typical and sounds like a manifesto of their recent ideological development (the Ukrainian name of the author has no significance because in Russia there are a lot of authentically Russian people with such names). They have discounted not only Stalin, but Marxism-Leninism and socialism altogether. The idea of the Russian empire (of course without the word 'empire' – this is the only disguise they think reasonable to retain) leads them back to Tsarist Russia, to the Russia of the Provisional Government and sometimes, cautiously, to the Russia of the Constituent Assembly, disbanded by the Bolsheviks in January 1918 with the notorious words of the Kronstadt sailor Zhelezniakov: 'The guard is tired. I ask you to clear out the premises.'

So far as convinced Stalinists are concerned – and I know some of them among the educated part of the former Party apparatus and 'the Party intelligentsia' – even they will never again be able to openly take a pro-Stalin posture, even if they temporarily obtain access to the (political) commanding heights of the country. Let us recall that for a decade after Khrushchev's fall even such a Stalinist dogmatic and almighty ideologist as Suslov could only prevent any *mention* of Stalin. Nowadays it is (and will be) absolutely suicidal for any political figure to call for a more positive view of Stalin. In future much can happen in the USSR. But even the most extreme scenario of the full (in any case doomed to be short-lived) triumph of dogmatic and conservative apparatchiks will not put Stalin back on his pedestal, from which he was thrown down to the dirt, where he rightly belongs.

What, indeed, is Stalinism? A more exact formulation of the question is: what belongs to Stalinism, what was a part of it, what remained afterwards as his legacy and what still remains?

Surely, the core of it was *Stalinshchina* i.e. the Great Terror, the Great Fear. Let us try to understand the logic of those who after the beginning of glasnost re-vitalized the discussions of the post-1956 period, which had been slowed down and then suspended by Suslov and his ideological clique after 1964. We mean, of course, the public discussions. The discussions in private never stopped, the analytical work continued. More and more people were stimulated by life itself to think about it, despite the official position of silence or careful one-sided rehabilitation, when it came to Stalin's appearance in films or books concerned with the war or even some pre-war achievements of industrial and technological development.

In this book my colleagues give a broad picture of bibliographical trends, including those in the contemporary Soviet Union. I would like to suggest our readers put themselves in the boots of a common Soviet man or woman or even a teenager interested in listening to adults, reading politics and thinking for himself (my younger son was a reminder that youngsters can do this even earlier than teen-age). Why? Because basically all of them have lived through some periods or aspects of Stalinism. It was they who actually decided the fate of Stalinism as such, though not yet to the very end. Everything depended on their ability to overcome the brainwashing of the previous decades, the breathtaking revelations of the Khrushchev era and the conspicuous silence of the Brezhnev years.

None of this was easy, even for those authors who are now cited in this book and reflect different trends in the ideological struggle, as well as in the historical analysis of these times. The striking difference of historical analysis of Stalinism inside and outside the Soviet Union may be explained by the substance and the meaning of the discussions. For the Soviet people the discussions necessarily mean the fierce struggle for the most vital issues of their everyday life now and in the future. For us the past has not yet become the pages of a history book.

Beginning with the awakening of 1956, people could choose between two extreme points of view (critically analysed by my colleagues in this book):

(a) Stalin alone was responsible for everything bad, just as earlier his name was connected with everything great. The Marxist–Leninist ideology, the Communist Party, the socialist system – all these were not to be blamed, but rather to be pitied for all the harm Stalin had brought to them.

(b) Stalinism had been pre-determined by historical, political and social circumstances, and was a direct outcome of the October Revolution of 1917. Stalin's personality played some – but not a significant – role.

Incidentally the second point of view worked both for defenders of Stalin and for opponents of Marxism–Leninism (at least Leninism).

As Alec Nove correctly writes, Lenin until recently was a difficult theme on which to be totally frank and critical. This was true as far as published works were concerned. It was also true of our psychological readiness to investigate our private analysis of our past. But it takes less time to free your mind than to achieve the determination to make your thoughts known to the public and of course to overcome the barriers of editorial and official censorship.

I remember the discussions between my friends and colleagues in and after 1956. Cautious critique of Lenin was psychologically restricted to recalling, for example, 'The Resolution About Factions' of 1921, forbidding the creation of factions (which Lenin introduced, being afraid of a split in the Party just after it had triumphantly won a bloody civil war in a predominantly peasant country with a hostile 'capitalist encirclement'). Usually we approached such delicate topics by the standards of those times, based on the understanding that *subjectively* Lenin's actions should be understood in the context of the given, difficult situation, but *objectively* they led to an easy way for Stalin to finish with more or less organized opposition against him.

The intelligentsia could not be statisfied with the first extreme point of view (mentioned above), offered at that time by Khrushchev and reiterated by him in his memoirs in spite of the fact that in these memoirs he did much to 'correct' history and his own image, not bothering very much about the trustworthiness of his recollections. As the authors of this volume put it, the explanation was ridiculous indeed.

It is important here to mention something which has not been mentioned in the previous chapters of this book. This is the role of the process of thinking and analysing for the sake of a better understanding by our intelligentsia as a whole, not only by writers, sociologists and historians (who have been read, re-read and cited abroad widely), but specifically the scientific intelligentsia, which was often ahead of those for whom the study of the history of our society was their profession. When Yuri Afanasiev was still denouncing 'bourgeois historians' and Fedor Burlatski was helping to formulate the political documents of the CPSU or of the State, substituting 'black' for 'white' (both often being much more frank, if not cynical, in private talks), physicists and mathematicians were dicussing some essential issues without any prejudice. This does not mean that I am accusing anybody of hypocrisy. I certainly have no right to do this. And the problem is much more complicated than simple hypocrisy or place-hunting. The minds of people engaged in political science were deformed, they needed more time to liberate their minds, to get rid of 'the inner censor' and to get used to writing what they really thought. It was different with the mental processes of people engaged in exact sciences. Andrei Sakharov is of course the best example. But I used to meet many of them, putting so called 'difficult questions' bluntly, logically and uncompromisingly. Their advantage was not necessarily a moral superiority, which no doubt was the case of Sakharov himself. It was freedom from dogmas and stereotypes, professional non-commitment to any ideology and a fresh, unbiased search for a clear answer. Others – in social sciences and in political practice – were accustomed to adjusting common sense and evident facts to *the cause of socialism*.

Unfortunately my own father, Anastas Mikoyan, despite having plenty of common sense, inner honesty and decency, was fanatical enough to subdue these inborn qualities to the goals of *the Party* (formulated and defined by its 'collective leadership' or by personalized leaders). About his role as a Party functionary, and later one of the leading figures in the Party and in the State, I will have more to say. But as a person he was just one of those who moved within a narrow space, or rather a cage, formed by such sacred things as *the interests of the Party, the allegiance to Party discipline, the interests of socialism, the interests of Soviet power*. I have met thousands of quite honest and decent people bound by these or similar ultra-durable fetters.

The proportions of fanaticism and place-hunting, self-denial and hypocrisy, conformism and obsession for power at any price, fear and stubbornness to the point of stupidity, were different in different people. We need somebody of the stature of Dostoevsky in the understanding and interpretation of human behaviour to form conclusions when it comes to somebody other than a simple butcher in the OGPU-NKVD. But whatever the motivations were, they constituted the foundations of Stalinism, under Stalin *and* after him. I consciously draw a parallel between the behaviour of Stalin's *okruzhenie* (circle) and that of the intellectual *okruzhenie* surrounding Khrushchev or Brezhnev. The latter served the dictators, who were not murderers. The former had to deal with a first-rate murderer. Extenuating circumstances for the latter are evident – they did not serve a murderer. But 'extenuating' circumstances can also be found for those who constantly felt the coldness of a gun barrel at the back of their heads. After Stalin, disgrace meant just a less prestigious job, retirement or even 'diplomatic exile' (which in the USA is paid for after the electoral campaigns of presidents). Under what conditions is it more forgivable – if it can be forgivable at all – to sell one's soul?

But let us come back to the common people in trying to evaluate Stalinism. Khrushchev's naive intention of putting all the blame on one man, even on so unique a combination of demonic qualities, leaving the theory and the 'new' practice of the Communist Party looking correct and innocent, was understandably not convincing. Moreover it managed to compromise to some extent the process of de-Stalinization. The question inevitably rose: Why only Stalin? Maybe Khrushchev is trying to duck his share of responsibility?

If not Stalin alone, who else? This natural question led the official party documents of the perestroika years to use the expression 'Stalin and his entourage' ('associates' may be a better word for the Russian *okruzhenie*). Even such independent minds as Anatoliy Butenko and Roy Medvedev in 1986–8 provided names and characteristics of those who helped Stalin, assuming that their help played a significant if not decisive role. Actually they gave the names of those from the Politburo who somehow managed to live through the Stalin years as well as those of some satraps from the OGPU-NKVD. There was some logic in such an approach, but not too much of it as we could understand afterwards from numerous documents about the political behaviour of many people doomed to be executed or to perish in the *Gulag*. Anyway, the circle was too narrow to make the concept of its being the fault of those who did not die an adequate explanation (Roy Medvedev's book on Stalin was not published in the Soviet Union at that time, so people judged his views by his later articles and essays). For a country with almost two hundred million people the message that one evil genius with a dozen or so accomplices had been a strong enough force for unprecedented atrocities and total subordination could not be a sufficient or convincing explanation.

The easiest way, technically, was to make the list longer. One could just combine lists of participants of the 13th[1] to the 17th Party Congresses. Morally, however, this was more difficult because those people mostly perished in the torture-chambers of the NKVD and in the frozen soil of the *Gulag*. Anyway it could only give another two to three thousand names. What about the Party, people began to ask. I was asked the same question many times while lecturing in 1987–9 in Moscow and Leningrad, Kiev and Odessa, Dnepropetrovsk and Donetsk, Gorky and Kirzhach, Obninsk and Narva, Ivanovo and Novosibirsk, Tallinn and Dushanbe.

The fact is that the Communist Party in the 1920s was the only institution where democracy existed, even flourished, where discussions were hot and open, defiant and straightforward, sometimes given to strong expressions bordering on insults. However, there was one man who was invariably treated with respect by everybody; his name was Lenin. But even he had to explain, to reason, to convince, and very often to argue. How could such a party permit their leadership to 'betray' the Revolution, as Trotsky put it?

Next or simultaneous questions were: was Stalinism a *betrayal* of the revolution at all? Or was it a logical, possibly overly cruel, *development* and *continuation* of it? In other words: are Stalinism and Bolshevism identical conceptions?

Again, let us not forget that the Party was for some time a sort of enclave of freedom in a totalitarian state. Unjust persecution of different groups of the population was not only tolerated but recognized as 'necessary'. Faked trials of invented, non-existent 'parties', which led to deaths and confinements of leading economists, engineers and others, did not cause any significant feeling of indignation among Bolsheviks. Certainly they might have believed the OGPU. But why were they not touched by repressions against former white officers, Mensheviks, SRs and other innocent people?

The evident answer is: the logic of the Civil War – more than anything else. Actually the War did not stop in the minds of its main belligerents: the reds, whites, pinks or even greens.[2] The harsh feelings of being exposed to death, the habit of solving problems with a Mauser in the hand, the continuous sense of a decisive struggle against some kind of enemy, practically without any limit as the means of struggle is concerned. A. Tsipko is right when he told a journalist of *Ogonyok*[3] that such an approach and behaviour was immoral, as was the readiness of Bolsheviks to unleash a civil war. But he forgets to add that practically all civil wars have similar features: France, the USA, Mexico, Colombia and many countries of Asia and Africa without any presence of Marxists provide us with a lot of examples of these inhuman features as necessary characteristics of civil war in general. What is also typical is that they do not end completely after an armistice or a peace treaty. In reality they usually do nothing of the kind except after defeat or capitulation. A. Tsipko is not correct in suggesting that only Bolsheviks were ready to unleash such a war in Russia in 1917–18 (in the same issue of that weekly there is an article by Yuri Davidov, who reminds us that 'the whites' were in no way better than 'the reds').

But the nightmare of collectivization was actually carried through by local Party activists, nine years after the end of the Civil War. The leadership of the ruling party and some rank and file members were no doubt responsible for the fact that the spirit of civil war was still there. Unfortunately only a minority of Bolsheviks were able to realize that collectivization was the turning point, when the Party had to discover that its own inner democracy began to disappear very rapidly and implacably. Now there was almost no hope of spreading it in the country in the foreseeable future. This was 'the moment of truth'. After that the Party itself was doomed to lose its inner democracy in favour of the rigid and pitiless dictatorship of one man. At that time nobody believed the vicious circle would be locked, that the pole-axe would fall on the Party itself, 'the Great Purge' would come to those who dreamed of everybody's happiness.

In this respect I agree with Tsipko, cited by Alec Nove, that the Bolsheviks failed to see the cost of suppressing all dissidence, 'they did not see the possible consequences of the total power of the party apparatus, a total power which they all sought'. I lived in a family of such Bolsheviks and met many others like it, both before and after the *Gulag*. And I disagree with Klyamkin, who looks back with hindsight at what happened in the past when he writes: 'The party majority was predestined to suppress inner-party democracy.' Even his correct thesis, that 'it became clear [already in Lenin's time] that democracy within a mass party without a democratic society cannot be sustained', implies two ways of solving that contradiction. Which one won is clear now. But in those times Bolshevik-idealists hoped democracy would spill over from the Party to society as a whole in the process of the stabilization of Soviet power and of the implementation of basic socio-economic reforms. (I am convinced the Bolshevik idealists composed the majority in the 'old guard' and that is why they had to be eliminated by Stalin or to be turned into obedient associates with menace of perpetual pillory as 'the enemy of the people' and inevitable death together with their families.) Of course they would not have permitted 'the loss of the achievements of the Revolution', but their interpretation of the socialist path could have differed significantly. However, the atmosphere of a fierce inter-party struggle, masterfully instigated and manipulated by Stalin, pushed aside and postponed the understanding of the immediate necessity of democracy until sixty years later.

Alec Nove mentioned one of the Pamyat writers, who in his turn was citing words by Feodor Raskolnikov uttered in 1918 and in his devastating and superbly written open letter to Stalin in 1938. But, as many now agree, this is not a real contradiction, it is a demonstration of utopian ideals. History has different experiences, even of utopias coming true.

Raskolnikov's 1938 letter is a manifesto which could have been signed by hundreds of thousands of Bolsheviks. It gives us more understanding of the inner world of the 'old guard' Bolsheviks, than judgements of contemporary authors, whose emotions, no matter how understandable, grow into obsessions, thus damaging their scientific value.

So, what about the process of learning in our country? When Tsipko wrote his well-known article in *Nauka i zhisn'* he gave his answer to millions of people whose intellectual quest was moving to the core of the issue. So did Klyamkin, Nuykin, Seliunin, Butenko, Ambartsumov, Latsis, Andreev and many others. It was not them who put the questions; they began to answer them when the whole country was demanding the truth to be sought and told. But the very nature of that path to the truth, which is complex in the extreme, is not such that several articles or even books can suffice to find it.

Several scholars inside and outside the Soviet Union point out that if the footprints of Stalinism lead to the October Revolution of 1917, to Bolshevism, then the latter can be traced back in Russian history. This leads to more and more questions, some of which can be found in the chapters by Alec Nove and by Arch Getty. The further back we go into history, the more complicated and less convincing are the answers.

For instance it is difficult for me to agree with historians Alexander Yanov and Victor Seliunin, or with the novelist Vasili Grossman, that Ivan the Terrible, Peter the Great and Stalin were all enslavers of the people, evil geniuses of Russian history, who proved that any process of modernization in that country was necessarily combined with suppression of freedom. I cannot understand how Ivan the Terrible can be connected with any normally understood historical modernization. The triumph of his bloody absolutism is not necessarily a modernization. In any case it was Ivan III, grandfather of the Terrible, who actually became the creator of a united Russian state. On the contrary, Maliuta Skuratov and his *oprichniki*, acting on the instructions of the Terrible, can be regarded as the fathers of the first genocide against most educated families. The sad fate of Feofan Grek was a clear enough indication of the attitude of the Terrible to education and knowledge in general. Also, why should Peter the Great be considered an enslaver?

Such an analogy, seen by some Russian authors and which has impressed Alec Nove, seems to me too artificial. The system of Russian serfdom had been in the making for decades and was finished by Peter's father Alexey Mikhailovich, who incidentally was called 'The Quietest' (*tishaishi*). Under Peter, serfs attached to manufactures and metallurgic plants had only been moved there from villages with a view to a more useful and 'modern' way of employment; whereas Stalin turned free farmers into serfs. Besides, the opening of the 'windows to Europe' (unlike Stalin's 'iron curtain'!) could only have given opportunity for fresh winds to blow to the country, for freedom for significant numbers of serfs. Peter was an ardent supporter of those common people who were able to abandon traditional beards and study sciences. And who can deny that development of sciences brings about more freedom of thought? He promoted everybody, including young and old aristocrats ready to be involved in the process of modernization. On the contrary, Stalin eliminated those who were dangerous for his personal dictatorial power, which is why he preferred 'men from below'. The fates of Peter and Stalin's sons are absolutely incomparable (though that of Ivan's son, killed by his father, can be remembered). The first tried to play a political role and was against the main cause of his father's life. The second had nothing to do with politics, he was so unhappy about his father, 'the Great Leader', openly despising him, and he tried to commit suicide before the war. After he returned from the hospital Stalin commented in the presence of my father: 'Even this thing you could not do properly!' Stalin's refusal to exchange him for von Paulus was a foul attempt to conceal his inhumanity behind a pompous phrase: 'I do not exchange a fieldmarshal for a captain.'

Of course the analogy between Ivan and Stalin is striking. But where in that scheme (modernization–unfreedom) is Alexander I, without whom the modernization of the Russian society could not have been so fast? Our great poet and amateur historian Alexander Pushkin mentioned it, and 150 years later his admirer and scholar Nathan Eidelman proved it by his thorough historical analysis. The Decembrist movement, the freedom-loving literature, poetry and historiography were born in the years of that Emperor.[4] Where is Alexander II, the great reformer, killed by the leftist extremists? And where is another great reformer, Stolypin (also killed, but by rightist extremists), with his wise and important economic and social modernization? The repressions after the Revolution of 1905–7 were actually insignificant and in any case dictated by Nicholas II. But even those repressions were counterbalanced for the history of the modernization of our state by the appearance of the first Russian parliament after the Novgorod 'veche' of the eleventh to thirteenth centuries. The Duma was perhaps not very effective in real politics, but democratic enough to have four Bolsheviks as its members.

It is easy to explain history if one approaches it selectively and does not deal very comprehensively with remote or recent years. Those years often become in our country victims of a biased approach, when history has to approve the conclusions 'necessary' for the present. So, Pokrovsky could have been satisfied: not only Stalin and other Soviet leaders looked at history as he had advised, but many authors of our days fail to avoid the temptation of writing a partisan 'history'. However, in this case historians repeat the mistakes of writers and playwrights, who, as Arch Getty justly comments, give rise to diverse and free-wheeling literature that often bears little allegiance to the basic rules of historical investigation.

Past centuries are of only limited use for an analysis of Stalinism. So, what features of the system should be regarded as parts of Stalinism and which of Bolshevism? The distinction – if it exists – is crucial for understanding the roots and nature of Stalinism. After we understand the distinction, which from my point of view certainly exists, it will be perhaps easier to explain *Stalinshchina* too. The word 'Bolshevism' has to be treated, without any prejudice, as the term for the political movement which appeared in 1903 within the social-democratic movement of Europe. The main reason for a split in the Russian Social-Democratic Party with those who from now on became known as 'Mensheviks' was a different approach to issues of organization and Party discipline. Of course differences grew from year to year. But until October 1917 Bolshevism was not corrupted by power and its fanaticism led to self-sacrifice rather than to sacrificing others for its cause.

The Monopoly of Power of the Communist Party

Certainly it was created by Bolsheviks immediately after October 1917. Lenin and all the leading Bolsheviks, as well as the vast majority of the second echelon and maybe of the whole Party, saw no necessity to seriously share power even with their allies. But does this mean the one-party system was then considered the only possible version of the development of society? I don't think so, though I understand how lonely I may remain with such an opinion.

The first attempt by Lenin to ignore not only the Mensheviks, who had very little support in the population, but SRs also, who had more support than Bolsheviks themselves and who were considered comrades in the whole struggle, caused a strong protest from several leading Party Central Committee members. Some resigned from the Party Central Committee which in those times was very small and played the role of the future Politburo. Others resigned from the first purely Bolshevik government. Lenin had to retreat, and three 'left SRs' were introduced in the government. This was the first cornerstone of a potential 'multi-party' system. It became evident that there existed two main tendencies among leading Bolsheviks as to the attitude to other socialist parties. Unfortunately Lenin and many of his followers at the time did not yet understand the importance of the multi-party system. The SRs were too radical to play only a nominal role of co-rulers, the role Lenin agreed to. They began to fight in the non-democratic manner of the Bolsheviks, as they once fought the monarchical regime. In October 1920, the SR party was officially legalized, though not for long.

Again, we cannot ignore the absence of democratic traditions in Russia. Everybody knows that democracy existed here for just a few months after the February Revolution 1917. Russian political culture had little practical experience of solving conflicting points of view in a civilized manner through a parliamentary system. It was the Mensheviks who regarded these traditions as essential for real democratic development. But their leaders were either dispersed to different places or advised to emigrate immediately after the end of the Civil War.

It was the uncompromising polarization of the Civil War that brought intolerance of others' opinions and the absence of any wish to resolve differences by discussion. This applied both to the Bolsheviks and the SRs. Mensheviks, as a truly social-democratic tendency, were much more ready for political co-existence. But it is important to remember that the first government and the first political face of the regime were not one-party. More peaceful relations between Bolsheviks, SRs and the NEP could have brought more meaning to the multi-party system. With all the difficulties, domestic and international, the multi-party system threatened the Bolshevik grip on power. No party having won a civil war is inclined to voluntarily give up power. So the Bolsheviks' insistence on a one-party system, even before Stalin's dictatorship, was the legacy of the Civil War. The NEP demanded insurance against the loss of political power – even though in economics too *komandnye vysoty* (commanding heights) were secured by the Bolsheviks.

So the transition to a one-party system was a result of the Bolsheviks' state of panic during the first years of the Soviet power. On the part of Lenin this was also a proof of an intoxication with power, so easily won (which was 'lying in the streets', as M. Heller writes)[5] that he was not yet able to think about the consequences of such dictatorship.

It can be easily argued that the monopoly of power *had* to lead to a one-party system. But my objection is that without a bloody civil war, without *force* being so decisive on the political scene of the Russian empire in 1917–20 and without the reality of hostile and aggressive international encirclement, Bolshevism could have been more tolerant to at least two parties: the SRs and the Mensheviks. And to a number of local, regional parties too. The understanding which undoubtedly came to Lenin in his last years – that Soviet power was faced by the horrible, mortally dangerous 'barrack' system – could have led not only to naive proposals about more participation of workers *ot stanka* (from the bench) in the Central Committee or more workers' control. Lenin's approach to his own brainchild – the NEP – *had* to lead him to some sort of 'political NEP', if only he had lived as long as Stalin.

Lenin's new ideas were not shared by the majority of the higher echelon of the party. A secret letter was sent to provincial committees in 1923 disavowing the last proposals of the mortally sick leader, claiming his illness was affecting his judgement. The strength of Lenin's prestige was enough to overrule the Politburo (as he often did), and to change the trend despite the stubbornness of those to whom he had become a 'hindrance'.

I am convinced that in this respect my father was a typical

representative of the second echelon of the Party leaders. By his way of thinking we may make judgements about predominant tendencies in the party. Perplexed by the multiple controversial opinions, fears, gloomy forecasts and recipes, they listened to Lenin – what he will say, they would do. He knew better, looked farther, understood deeper. There were hundreds of such people voting at the Party Central Committee and the Congresses and doing the concrete job of influencing the whole party.

It is my view as a historian that personality is often decisive, especially in Russia and especially during the stormy periods of its history.

The Command-Administrative System in Economic Life

The NEP is good evidence that Bolshevism could have accommodated itself with a multi-sectoral economy. Of course it would have influenced Bolshevism itself, maybe even altering its ugliest features which we were to see afterwards. And why not? Any ideology is interpreted, followed and implemented by people, usually by a few leaders. I disagree completely with the assertion of some Soviet historians, repeated in some of the chapters of this book, that the Bolshevik 'old guard' was poorly educated. Not at all! In their ranks it was considered shameful not to read history, philosophy, political economy, and all those areas which today make up 'political science', even if they had no opportunity to do it at universities. The first Bolshevik government was perhaps the most intellectual in the contemporary world. The higher party echelon consisted mostly of people with a college background, including the best universities of Russia and Western Europe. They read books in two or three languages besides Russian. And of course as they were human, they could change. The latter thesis is especially important. To think otherwise is to confine oneself to something I would call '*political racism*'. Otherwise not only the architects of Perestroika would remain absolute phantoms, from the point of view of their historical role, but also the historians of our country, who are now exploiting that kind of 'racism', would look rather dubious themselves, taking into account many of their own pasts.[6]

An additional argument for the possibilities of changes in Bolshevik practice is that one could find in the volumes by Marx, Engels and Lenin everything to 'prove' diametrically different ideas. As a matter of fact we used to do so for decades. Why could it not have happened, not according to the interests of our successive leaders but to the development of society, with the maturity of predominantly young revolutionaries, with their constant contacts with common people?

It can be argued that a sound attitude to economics was close to being achieved; in 1926–7 it may have been just around the corner. And I do not agree with Klyamkin, cited by Alec Nove, that to the question 'Could the NEP have been preserved?' the only answer is 'no'. There were debates on this issue but their outcome was only decided by Stalin. We should ask ourselves why Stalin altered the course of the ship of state so drastically, apart his 'predilection for spicy dishes' (as Lenin said about him). His main motive was political pre-dominance over other leaders of the Party and the quest for total dictatorship in the country. Let us not forget that his 'year of great change' threw the country's economy back so violently that Soviet agriculture has never been able to recover. The economy as a whole suffered, in spite of the successes of industrialization. The speed of industrialization – the main justification for the end of the NEP – was accelerated artificially and suffered because of shortages of agricultural goods. There are sound reasons to think that industrialization would have been helped by more moderate policies. So how can we believe there was no other alternative? No other way to develop your right hand but to disable your left hand?

Alec Nove reminds us that the principal motive of the collectivization was to mobilize a larger agricultural surplus. But the result was quite the opposite. Any *surplus* disappeared for decades.

Let us recall the group of economists led by Chayanov. Why could they not have been heard by the Party apparatus? Only because somebody decided that their views were hostile to socialism. But they could just as well have been regarded as very helpful for the socialist state, searching for a sound economic policy in the village.

A. Mikoyan, the People's Commissar of Trade after August 1926, was so impressed by the possibilities opened by the NEP that he argued openly with Stalin, at the Party Congress and other meetings, in favour of *trade* as the way to get grain from the village. Only when he realized that economic issues were interpreted by Stalin, not on their own merit, but as a means in his *political* struggle did he follow all the zig-zags of Stalin's 'general line'. Those very zig-zags are also evidence of the absence of any *one* dominant theme for the Bolsheviks in the 1920s. I even believe that Stalin himself could have been a defender of the Bukharin line in connection with the NEP and peasantry much longer if only Trotsky could have established a united front with Zinoviev and Kamenev as a strong leftist opposition to his power for a longer period.

Bukharin was no less a Bolshevik than Stalin but his approach led to a more complex power structure. It allowed for more humanism, in spite of all those harsh words which dogmatic historians may find in Bukharin's speeches and writings. Writings are often rather deceptive. And speeches even more so. When we extract documents from the library dust, we unfortunately are very often inclined to ignore the pulse of the past years, the purpose and the concrete conditions of the moment a speech was pronounced or an article written; we are not even interested to whom the message was sent, or how the author meant to be heard and understood. Words are given to people not only to express their views, but to conceal them, or even to combine one with the other. This happens not only in our everyday human behaviour, but in political behaviour as well. Politics is always made by human beings. And human beings, unlike robots, have confused thoughts, changing or modifying ideas, undergoing unpredictable transformations, deviations from their usual 'ego', etc. Maybe that's why Cardinal Richelieu said once: 'Give me six phrases, written by anybody, and I shall hang him.'

The Totalitarian System of Ideology and Government

The two variables mentioned above determine the third one. But before Stalin acquired the leading role in the Party apparatus, totalitarianism was still in question. Stormy discussions such as those concerning the role of the trade unions showed that the development of syndicalism was also a real possibility, which would not have let the totalitarian structure be formatted and solidify. This was something like the Solidarity movement in Poland 60 years later. Other discussions also do not permit us to look at Bolshevism as something monolithic. Thoughts were in conflict, people looked for answers to new questions, put forward by life itself and not envisaged by Marx. The Party lived within society. It was not isolated from the vital issues of the new society, every step of which was a step into the land of the unknown. Different tendencies could have prevailed, different people could have influenced the direction of developments. I cannot fully agree that the majority of the Party supported the extremist line, which Stalin finally decided to declare 'the General Line'. The general line itself fluctuated according to the needs of the struggle for power.

Ideas about the theoretical possibility of the development of post-revolutionary society in Russia lead me to think about the ideals of Marxists in Russia before the revolution. I could draw an analogy with early Christianity. There are some common utopian features between Christianity and communist theory. Defence of the poor, of the humiliated and humble, preference for rags rather than riches, is a ıconcept dear to millions. The money-changers were driven out of the temple by Jesus himself. 'Peace to huts, war to palaces!' was proclaimed by the French Revolution in 1789. Martin Luther hated the Catholic church for its open services to the nobles and the rich. I cannot agree with A. Tsipko, who blames the Bolsheviks for their appeal to 'have-nots'. This is not a question of blame, but a perpetual human aspiration for social justice, for equality (let us not forget that *égalité* immediately followed *liberté* in 1789), for dignity of the pariahs of any society. To declare all outcasts and 'have-nots' a mob or a rabble with vile instincts to divide everything, and to accuse Bolsheviks of sharing such instincts is simply not just. It is only easy for those who have never been in, or who have successfully left, such strata of society. How it is best to help the poor is another story. A. Tsipko is correct that to take away and to divide has always been a first and primitive temptation of the poor, which should never be encouraged.

There is certainly a great difference between the methods of the early Christians and those of the early Bolsheviks. The latter were decisively in favour of the use of force though Lenin assumed that force would not be necessary if the 'ruling classes' would give up their ruling position. However, as early as during the seventh century St Augustine offered a new theory, which permitted the use of force for a 'just cause'. He even introduced the theory of a 'just war', which centuries later was attributed to Lenin.

How often has force been used in history in the name of sacred goals of Christianity. Crusades of the Middle Ages, the Inquisition and the mass extermination of Indians in America by 'conquistadores' are a few among many examples. But there was always a conflict between the human tendency, faithful to early commandments, and a forceful, aggressive tendency. In Italy there was St Francis and the unbridled, unruly papacy; in Spain Torquemada and Bartolome de Las Casas; in contemporary Latin America the archbishop of El Salvador Arnulfo Romero and archbishops of Paraguay obedient to Stroessner. Everywhere and always there has been struggle. Unfortunately the humanistic tendency has usually been the loser.

The same fate overtook the idealistic, utopian intentions of the 'early Communists'. It is therefore no surprise that the speed of such transformations, like the speed of all the historical and technological changes, has accelerated in modern times.

However, let us come back to the 1920s. Finally, fanaticism triumphed. The fear for the unity of the Party, as many authors rightly point out, prevailed over the idea of democracy. But where and for whom and why were these magic words 'unity of the Party' so important? We can rely on memoirs, transcripts of numerous party meetings of various levels, articles in the press, and so on. My conclusion is that the unity of the Party as a whole was not in danger. There was a 'danger' of a fierce fight for power between five persons, each of whom dreamed, to some degree, of taking on the role of Lenin (as far as possible). Those people mixed their own ambitions with the fate of the country, their quarrel with each other and the danger of a split in the Party, their intrigues with cardinal deviations from 'Marxist-Leninist thought'. They involved local leaders and 'activists' in their struggle, pretending that their theoretical games and personal issues were tremendously important and menacing to the future of the country. True, the nation's fate was being determined at the time but absolutely not in the way it was declared.

Actually the differences between Politburo members in political and economic spheres were natural for such a historical experiment and should have been resolved quite peacefully, in discussions among colleagues, who were supposed to share common ideals.

The following are some of the circumstances which, in my opinion, transformed the internal discussions into a battlefield and then a tragedy for all of the country:

(a) The tradition of intolerance, which can be traced to Lenin's theoretical fights with his opponents, his rejection of 'false' ideas and the tendency to keep the Party theoretically and ideologically monolithic. We know that in Lenin's case these fights very rarely led to extra-polemical, 'organizational' outcomes. But for his successors it was easy to use differences in order to excommunicate somebody, compromise him as a 'bad Marxist' or 'bad Leninist'.

(b) The organizational structure of the Bolshevik party with its principle of 'democratic centralism'. It was easy for any demagogue to win the majority and to demand a full capitulation of his opponent. Moreover, the latter had to 'confess' his mistakes because the majority is always right. So people were taught to lie, because naturally the voting could not change their opinion, although they had to pretend that it did. The organizational structure of the Party was superb for underground work, for revolution, but it was quite inappropriate for a party engaged in building a new society. And here we must put the responsibility on Lenin, who did not understand it, until it was too late, and even when he began to understand did not see any other way out except removing Stalin from the post of General Secretary.[7]

(c) The psychology of the Civil War helped to demonize those who were 'mistaken'. The capitalist, hostile encirclement was used to expose as heretics those who were objectively weakening the country in the most dangerous international situation.

(d) Fanaticism, which helped before 1917 and was partly understandable during the Civil War (though it made possible pitiless and excessive repressions), finally turned out to be the crucial destructive force for democracy, the Party, and the country. Now there was actually no salvation for either one or the other.

During the first half of the 1920s there were still opportunities for the Party to abandon its confrontation with society (according to its concepts, with the exception of the working class, society was full of fluctuating and unreliable 'elements'). The local party leaders were mostly sincere in their attempts to develop the country, to make life better, and to 'strengthen the alliance with peasants'.

As an example I'd like to give some characteristics of the work of Anastas Mikoyan in South-Eastern Russia, or the North Caucasus. Both names were used subsequently for a huge territory from the Rostov oblast to the frontier with Georgia and from Novorossiisk to Dagestan, populated by 10 million people. This is not because my father was necessarily better or worse than other local party leaders, though both could have been true; still, I think he was typical. Anyway, here are the issues that I know.

In 'his' area of responsibility lived Cossacks, whom Sverdlov in 1919 considered to be enemies of the state and demanded that they obey or face being massacred. Mikoyan came there in 1922 and immediately began to return to the Cossacks their former status, traditions, self-administration and the right to use their traditional sabres in riding. He convinced the local authorities that the war was over and the Cossacks were citizens, like all other people, with the right to decide day-to-day problems of their *stanitsi*. He insisted in Moscow that several thousand Cossacks be permitted to come back from Turkey, where they had fled after the defeat of the 'white' armies of Denikin and Wrangel in 1919–20.

There were numerous ethnic groups in the mountains of the area and not all were friendly to the new order. Mikoyan helped Voroshilov, commander of the military district, to defend against those who continued to fight the Russians. But his strategy from 1922–5 was to incorporate the mountain peoples into the agrarian economy of the area, defend them against migrants from Russia, draw them into the activity of the local authorities and take into account the traditional special respect to elderly men. He even insisted they should elect senior representatives of those peoples to the local soviets. Tribesmen who accepted Soviet authority were allowed to keep their traditional cold steel. Why could such a strategy not have prevailed throughout the country?

International influence could also have helped lead towards democratization. Soviet Russia became a Mecca for leftist groups, especially from Europe. They brought with them European political culture and they played a very active and dynamic part in social and political life. Up to sixty thousand engineers and workers came to the Soviet Union to help to develop its industry. They could and should have become the exponents of a civilized approach to different aspects of life.

All this *could* have happened. We could in fact have had Perestroika 60 years earlier.

No doubt some readers will call this wishful thinking or even an attempt to defend Bolshevism. In denying the latter I would say there is no doubt about the responsibility of Bolshevism for creating the possibilities and even incentives for a very different development towards a totalitarian system and a dictatorial regime. Here I fully agree with Alec Nove's theory that Stalinism as a system *made possible* the scale of the repressions which were senseless even from Stalin's point of view.

But I do not regard those events as having been inevitable. E. H. Carr is right, of course, that historians like to call something 'inevitable' after it has happened. Precisely this kind of approach dominates our Soviet historic studies. The Marxist tradition of looking for a predetermination (*zakonomernost*, 'law-given development') is very strong. Maybe it is natural: all those who are writing now were taught 'historic materialism'. My own experience tells me how difficult it is to substitute common sense in place of dogma.

Stalinshchina, i.e. The Terror

This topic has been analysed, discussed and described by so many people in so many books, articles, memoirs, letters, diaries, that it is difficult to add anything significant. Though I do have something personal in this connection to add, it is more important to ask why there was so much destruction of friendly political strata? Why so many people, not connected with politics at all? Why so many 'commanders of production', so badly needed for the country's development? Why so many commanders of the armed forces, so indispensable for the coming war?

Part of the answer lies in the legacy of the Civil War, the fear of hostile capitalist encirclement and the absence both of democracy in the country, law and of a humanitarian tradition among the masses. These were the conditions, but still there was no necessity or, indeed, inevitability. Stalin could not have realized his horrible plot without these conditions but the conditions would not have been materialized without him.

To stage other scenarios of any historical development instead of the one which was staged by life itself is easy for those who have enough imagination to write their own scripts. But it is difficult for those who wish to take into account all the main actors and the premises of the historical record, while being perceptive enough to exclude the impossible. I base my own scenarios on everything I have accumulated from what I have heard, read and thought over. They are as follows.

Scenario 1. Lenin does not die at the age of 54 but lives ten to fifteen years more and remains healthy enough to have effective control of the situation. I expressed my point of view as to what he would do or try to do. My vision of possible future development was coming back to the social-democratic trend. It was still fresh in the memory. The alliance with the Second International was broken only eight or ten years before; the importance of such significant support in the world could not be overlooked. It was Lenin who broke with that trend inside and outside of the country. And it was Lenin who could easily change course towards a new alliance with social-democracy. (After the work was ready as a draft I found a supporter of this hypothesis: Alexander Tsipko wrote in *Daugava*, in the article I have cited earlier, on page 86, about 'a turn of our revolution towards the realism of social-democracy, drawn by dying Lenin, [which] could have worked well').

An important 'detail' should be added to this general assumption: the leadership, the highest echelon of the Party, would not be the same as in 1924. There is no doubt that Stalin would have been pushed aside. Bukharin would rise in importance. And new people would inevitably appear in that upper echelon. Nobody knows who, but such people as Kirov, Frunze (who, I believe, would not have died so unexpectedly and early after an ulcer operation allegedly because of the narcosis), some of the younger party functionaries from all over the country, or new 'socialist businessmen'.

Lenin liked people who could make things move and not only make speeches but organize concrete work to be done. That is why I think people like Zinoviev and Kamenev had little chance. A new generation of leaders could have changed for the better the dogmatism, the rigidity and fanaticism of the 'old guard'.

But such small historical details as the bad health of one man could not be 'corrected' by any *zakonomernost'*. However, it could instead doom the whole society for the next scenario.

Scenario 2. This is the one which became the reality, with Stalin at the head of the Soviet Union.[8]

The party purges and strengthening of Stalin's dictatorship plus the mass deportation of 'kulaks' were a perfect preparation for the future 'harvest of sorrow'. At last Stalin could plan the destruction of all his enemies whom he feared, hated, despised, envied, or just did not like, or thought they knew too much, or were not obedient enough. The machinery to do this – the OGPU – was firmly under control. The only thing missing was the atmosphere of mass psychosis in which everything that was once impossible becomes easy. The example of Hitler had a very convincing effect. Even such a politically developed, civilized nation as the Germans could become steeped in hatred and hysteria.

Because Stalin knew the Party well, he was not deceived by the chorus in his honour. He knew the inner strength of the Party even after Trotsky was gone and Zinoviev, Kamenev and Bukharin were out of the leadership. He knew better than anybody who he was just ten years ago. He knew he could not speak, write and reason as well as many other well-known people from the party elite. He knew that the party members thought too much of themselves and their right to elect whom they please. The votes were secret! Besides he could not exclude a 'palace conspiracy', if the results of the decision of the Politburo were supported by others. He knew how many people hated him or did not consider him the best man for the job.

He was very attentive to the new names in the Politburo. He was sure about Molotov and Kaganovitch. He was not afraid of Ordzhonikidze, Zhdanov, Andreev and Mikoyan. But he was not sure about Rudzutak, who was not at all ambitious but had been unofficially proposed by Lenin to become General Secretary. He was not sure about the Ukrainians: Skrypnyk, Kossior, Postyshev and Grin'ko.

He was definitely afraid of the rising star, Kirov, and tried taming[9] him. In *Pravda* (edited by his faithful servant Mekhlis) a *feuilleton* was published about a party boss who comes from Baku to Leningrad with a big dog, which made it desirable for the owner of the dog to have a large flat. ('The name was not used, but everybody understood . . .' – recollected A. Mikoyan.) Then somebody finds in a newspaper from the North Caucasus dated 1913 an article by Kostrikov (the real name of Kirov), which can be interpreted as celebrating the 300th anniversary of the Romanov dynasty. Who was looking for something compromising about Kirov, secretly scrutinizing everything written, said or done by him? And by whose order? Anyway, at the Politburo the issue was being discussed. After some questions by different people Stalin himself proposed not to make a fuss about this episode. 'Just his style!' commented Mikoyan.

Kirov was rather passive during the Politburo. He usually did not express his opinion. Such modest, even strange behaviour could not reassure or deceive Stalin. Was Kirov not very emotional and articulate when speaking at mass gatherings, as everybody said?

In the Spring of 1934 at the 17th Party Congress, Kirov had three votes against his membership of the Party Central Committee and Stalin – 282. Zatonsky, responsible for all the dozen or so counting commissions, and Kaganovich, overseeing them on behalf of the Congress Presidium, consulted Stalin secretly and the official figure declared for the General Secretary was also three. Two dozen local party leaders approached Kirov, offering to elect him General Secretary. True, Kirov himself told Stalin about such a proposal and said that he had rejected it. But . . .

On 1 December Kirov was shot by a certain Nikolaev. Weeks before, Nikolaev had been arrested for several days for having a gun and a plan of the Smolny Palace drawn by himself. But the newly appointed (by Yagoda) deputy chief of the Leningrad OGPU let him free.

The organizers of the murder were named even before any investigation. They were 'the Leningrad and the Moscow centres of the Trotsky-Zinoviev block'. Mass indignation is very easy to transform into mass hysteria. The 'Great Purges' had begun.[10]

Scenario 3. Trotsky is the leader of the party and of the country. He is not tremendously enthusiastic about democracy but is satisfied with his authority, knowing that he is the most well-known and eloquent leader. The extermination of party members does not take place, with the rare exception of the corrupted elements. He confines himself to the expulsion from the Party of those who threaten his personal power. He is less scrupulous where non-party members are concerned.

The NEP is curtailed but not so fast and forcefully as under Stalin because of the opposition in the Party, led by Bukharin, with his growing popularity. The peasantry have little hope of special attention. Force is still used rather than economic incentives if there are some problems with grain. But the scale of the anti-peasant offensive cannot be compared with that of scenario 2, again because of opposition within the Party. Trotsky himself is not able to reach such an unlimited scale of repression. The opposition in the Party compels him to be more or less restrained.

After several years of power Trotsky is no longer elected General Secretary (here I disagree with A. Tsipko, who does not believe Trotsky would have allowed himself to be removed by a normal party procedure).[11] A much more moderate 'general line' is adopted. The next leader is probably N. Bukharin.[12] But it may be, as in scenario 1, somebody of the next generation of party leaders.

Scenario 4. In 1926, when Stalin for the second and the last time offers his resignation, the leadership, instead of being afraid of Trotsky and of 'the split', recalls Lenin's unofficial advice and elects Rudzutak as General Secretary. This leads to a de facto restoration of factions. A soft politician, without any obsession about a special 'general line', Rudzutak is inclined to have as much discussion as possible before adopting any significant measure. The local party leaders become accustomed to less stress on command and more on looking for sound compromises. The most intelligent and those close to the interests of common people remain. Dogmatists lose prestige and elections. The atmosphere of tolerance to different opinions spreads over the party ranks and the press tells the whole of the country about the discussions. Glasnost makes its contribution. New active leaders of local and central importance appear. They are educated, articulate and free of dogma and fanaticism. The struggle between them and the bureaucracy is not easy, but much easier than it would be sixty years later.

Why could not Kirov become the Gorbachev of his time? Why could he not start perestroika when the search for new roads was still unresolved and it was a hundred times easier to change 'the general line' than in the 1980s and 1990s?

Let us recall those years. All matters discussed within the Party are, in their turn, discussed openly, by the press, by intellectuals, by active representations of peasants, of the NEP economy and others. The NEP remains the reality, and it turns out to be a source of stable development. A mixed economy takes shape with a growing private sector in light industry and services. Political factions play the role of opposition parties, attracting influential non-party groups and individuals. A tendency to social-democracy appears, in the beginning rather cautiously, then more openly.

Scenario 5. Bukharin is the leader of the Party. The NEP is officially declared 'the general line'. Developments within the Party, in the economy and in society are the same as under Scenario 1. I'd like to add that such developments could have influenced the international context for our country as well.

The Comintern would not alienate social-democrats in Germany. Instead of attacking them most fiercely, E. Thälman and his German Communist party could have understood where the main danger was coming from.

These scenarios, except, of course the second one, are obviously vulnerable. But it is also unsound to declare that there were no alternatives to what actually happened. I cannot believe there was only one possible 'alternative'.

So, I exclude the possibility of *Stalinshchina* without Stalin. *Trotskyshchina* can be imagined, but it could not have stood a serious comparison with 'the harvest of sorrow' our country experienced.

Still, why was that harvest so excessive even from the point of view of Stalin's interests of obtaining absolute dictatorial power and exterminating those whom he meant to destroy? (I can offer a contribution to the statistics of the terror: my father told me that just before the 22nd Congress in 1962 the KGB told the Party Central Committee that between 1 January 1935 and 22 June 1941, seven million people had been shot. A further 12,700,000 were arrested or otherwise dealt with.)

In this book one can find many possible reasons. I believe practically all of them are described correctly. The relative weight of each of them is quite impossible to determine. The main thing is that nobody – Marxists, Leninists, Stalinists, 'Communist-democrats', Russian patriots or fierce enemies of Marxism – can feel at ease when they prefer to give exclusive emphasis to one factor. There is no doubt that without Marxism there would be no Bolshevism. Without Bolshevism and its leader Lenin there would be no October Revolution. Without the October Revolution there would be no Soviet power and no ruling Communist party in Russia. Without that base for his efforts Stalin could never have been able to have a single person shot.

But all this proved to be possible *in Russia*. And its background, its history has direct relation to *Stalinshchina*.

Plekhanov was absolutely right when he insisted that the flour for the cake of a Russian revolution had not yet been ground. And Lenin was wrong when, while actually admitting that, he wrote about the possibility of Russia, led by his party, creating a state of 'preparedness' for socialism. This means the October Revolution was premature. It led to a civil war which the Bolsheviks had to win. When they did so, they were confronted with a contradiction, correctly noted by Tsipko and cited by Alec Nove. The growing dilemmas of the new society could only have been solved by victorious revolutions in Germany, Hungary and elsewhere in *civilized* countries.

Marxism was to blame. But why in some other countries did Marxism produce social-democratic parties, able to achieve many of Marx's ideals without spilling the blood of a single person? Examples of the opposite case in modern history include Pol Pot in Cambodia, Mao Tse-tung in China, Kim Il Sung in Korea. But there are also the cases of Hitler in Germany, Duvalier in Haiti, Stroessner in Paraguay, Pinochet in Chile, Idi Amin in Uganda, Saddam Hussein in Iraq; we know about 'Jakarta 1964'. All of them hated or ignored Marxism. Maybe the human race has something important missing in its genes, something which prevents animals, even beasts of prey, from killing their own species.

Lenin is even more to blame. He began 'the red terror' even before F. Kaplan shot at him and 'the red terror' was officially proclaimed. The official journal of the CPSU recently published documents which show that Lenin gave orders to organize court-martials with capital punishment for 15,000 priests.[13] Of course the Orthodox Church was at the time an obedient servant of the monarchy and of the most conservative and ruthless 'whites'. Their activity could seriously endanger the new regime. But this consideration cannot justify capital punishment for one and all, without the most scrupulous investigation of the alleged guilt of each of them. And Lenin was a lawyer by training!

Still, Leninism cannot be reduced to 'the red terror'. To argue that Stalin of the 1930s was 'Lenin today' is to underestimate Stalin as a personality. The terror which existed during the Civil War, when a new regime was in mortal danger, was one thing (though I still cannot justify it). But the Great Terror, without any danger for the regime, was absolutely another. It is not correct to deduce from such a terror that the Soviet state in the 1930s was still weak (as one of the contributors to this book does). In fact Leninism or Bolshevism (the two terms I believe mean almost, but not absolutely the same thing) as a political tendency in RSDRP gave birth to different channels of thought concerning future developments. Lenin's last actions and writings were supposed to encourage a more 'liberal' version. Lenin wrote in August 1921 to G. Miasnikov: 'Yes, whoever does not understand the substitution of the slogan "the civil war" by the slogan "the civil peace" is ridiculous if not worse'.[14]

In December 1921–February 1922 Lenin proposed and realized the transformation of the Cheka into the OGPU with important restrictions. It could no longer keep people imprisoned for interrogation for more than a month, was obliged to pass them to the courts and could not implement capital punishment without the decision of the court. Of course all this looks like a naive attempt at elementary respect for the basic demands of law, or even less. But in those times it meant the beginning of a very important process which was supposed to be developed. It was the beginning of the path to a legal order, which in the end took more than six decades to reach.

So I believe that society and its ruling elite was ready for different versions of political development. Why did the Russian Communist Party permit the most horrible of them to win?

Stalin began his paranoic hunt for human lives, happiness and dignity without any consideration of any 'danger' for the country. Quite the opposite: his actions brought more harm to the country in ten years than any foreign or domestic danger could bring in a century.

Why did Russia permit him to create the conditions under which a human being was no more precious than an insect? Why did so many people participate in the blood-bath, in trampling on the dignity, in turning human beings into something much worse than cattle? (Cattle are taken care of until their slaughter but in the *Gulag* human beings are doomed to starve to death.) Why was Russia for many decades able easily to manage without a hint of law, of human rights, of respect for the 'sacred' word *Narod*? Why did almost everybody think (and I am afraid many still think) that they had a right to decide the future, the life, the freedom, the fate of the property of other people?[15] All these questions are actually the answers for Kozhinov and other 'Russian patriots'. In my opinion Nikolai Chernishevsky was much more of a patriot when he exclaimed with bitterness: 'A miserable nation! Nation of slaves . . . From top to bottom – all of them are slaves.' Lenin cited these words as an example of positive patriotism, full of determination to change the conditions which had created such a society. Anton Chekhov said he had been 'squeezing a slave out of himself'.

Maybe the most important question for the present time is: Why did so much of Stalinism outlive him for decades? (R. W. Davies explains this very well in relation to the 'command system'). One of the answers would be that the legacy I mean is that of Bolshevism as a whole, not of Stalinism. But this is not a very satisfactory answer. For one thing, why after six years of perestroika, under the conditions of practical absence of the high authority, when everything is possible, do such legacies of Stalin as *kolkhozy* and *sovkhozy* still exist? Why is the population of the villages predominantly against the few private farmers, who are desperate in their efforts to work and earn money? Why does the rural population mostly support the chairmen of *kolkhozes*, who are sometimes much worse than landlords in Tsarist Russia? The roots of the spirit of collectivism must lie in certain features of the Russian peasantry. It is difficult to believe that the resistance of the conservatives alone can stop local mass movement nowadays.

There are still, of course, other instances of Stalinism's legacy in our reality. The apparatus is still connected with the Communist Party local committees. The assumption that Stalinism and Bolshevism are the same thing does not explain anything. There are very few people eager to defend Bolshevism in matters where it equals Stalinism. The masses of the people are now more able to be independent actors in political life than they were after the Civil War. 'Bolshevism is a certain condition of the human soul', one of our sociologists said recently.

The Russian people are often very conservative until convinced of the need for change. Once convinced, however, their response may know no limits. This may explain many things in the past and in the present, irrespective of whether it is pleasant to 'Russian patriots'.

Like Alec Nove, I cannot agree that 'Stalin's triumph was due to mass support for his extremist policies'. But I would like to add something that very few historians notice. Stalin began to gain credibility by repeating how humble he was in theory (which was true) and that he was just a loyal follower of Lenin (which I think was untrue). Anyway, his stake in the game was the name of Lenin. This secured the initial support of the Party and that part of the population impressed by Lenin, a truly outstanding personality of Russian and world history.

But Lenin was no longer an 'extremist' (by the standards of those times) after the Civil War ended. Surely, extremism was only strong within some Bolshevik groups. The NEP had begun the process of pacifying those who were hostile to anything 'private'.

A. Tsipko's assertion, that Stalin 'never departed from the elementary propositions of Marxism in his articles and speeches', does not impress me very much because, first of all, it is not exact. One can find among Stalin's 'inventions' or 'developments' of Marxist theory many things which would have made Marx, as Russians say, 'turn upside down in his coffin'. Second, Stalin was never terribly attentive to the correlation between what he said or wrote and what he actually did. One usually did not coincide with the other. I cannot agree with Tsipko, that 'were he [Stalin] unable to find Marxist ideas on which to base the expropriation of the village, he would hardly have obtained the support of the party'.

The situation in the Party has been described above. The possibility of finding contradictory phrases in classical Marxist texts is as easy as doing so with the sacred books of Christianity. Stalin defied Lenin's attitude to the NEP, whereas Lenin was much closer and dearer to the Party than was Marx in every respect.

R. W. Davies reminds us how Engels saw socialism. 'Society', wrote Engels, would 'reorganize production on the basis of a free and equal association of producers'. And Lenin supported it not only in 1914 but also in saying that 'socialism is a society of civilized cooperators'. Who can claim that Stalin paid any attention to these basic formulations? The same applies to Lenin's thesis that competition between socialism and capitalism will finally be decided by productivity of labour. We know very well that Stalin saw more perspectives in forced labour and that he stressed the quantity of employed people. This is an additional proof that actually Stalin cannot be called a socialist in the strict sense of the term. If it is difficult to understand the term 'feudal capitalism' (only Japan before 1945 comes to mind as something of the kind), it is even more difficult to agree that 'feudal socialism' can be reconciled with Marxist-Leninist theory.

Another notion by Tsipko which attracts my attention is one concerning 'the old guard' and its historic guilt for 'during Lenin's lifetime voluntarily handing over to Stalin the vast power created by the revolution'. We use the expression 'the old guard', but sometimes people mean different things. In this case it is evidently the Politburo of 1922. In other cases it is the Party in its pre-revolutionary composition. The difference would be great! We may also mean the Party Central Committee in the post-revolutionary years, with or without several hundreds (or thousands?) of local and central 'activists'. So we need some explanation each time we use this term.

Alec Nove's opinion about the potential role of Trotsky did not completely convince me. But it showed that I may still base my assumptions about that leader on old prejudices and on those kinds of citations from Trotsky's speeches and writings which I have advised myself not to take necessarily very seriously.

R. W. Davies believes that a very difficult question to answer (as in any political system) would be 'Did Stalin lead from the front or was he pushed from the back?' He gives a very interesting analysis of the role of other people in economic planning. Still, it is far from being the most difficult question concerning the Stalin system. Other people could express their opinions, but only within the general understanding of the matter held by Stalin. They could discuss 'how' or even 'how many', or 'what in the beginning and what afterwards'. But they had to be permitted or directed by Stalin in all important matters. Any attempt to do something significant without his permission, even within the authority of a certain People's Commissar (or later minister), would have been regarded by Stalin as dangerous independence of thought and action. Maybe in the early 1930s such a tradition was not yet formed. The worst years were of course 1937–9, while the easiest were 1941–5. But generally until Stalin's death nobody dared do something really important without fear of some kind of punishment. For example, in the winter of 1944–5 the Byelorussian authorities asked A. Mikoyan to give a loan from state reserves to boost the republic's seed grain supplies for the coming spring. The republic had just been liberated from German occupation and there was a shortage of seeds. They promised to give back 30 per cent more grain. Mikoyan was responsible for such matters. So he thought it necessary to give the grain because, first, the republic would in this case have a much better harvest and, secondly, the state reserves would have been benefited. He did not tell Stalin, maybe hoping he would never know. But Stalin was informed and became furious. He cancelled the decision and personally wrote the decision of the government to take the grain matters out of Mikoyan's authority, since he was 'squandering state property'. True, some time later Mikoyan was again made responsible for grain resources because Molotov, who had replaced him, 'of course could not deal with such matters' (Stalin's opinion of Molotov as an executive was rather low).

Another example occurred in the early 1950s. Khrushchev made a speech about *agrogorod*, agro-cities (rather a utopian idea but still an idea). Stalin ordered the publication of an article in *Pravda* which severely criticized the speech.

Mikoyan remembered that until Ordzhonikidze's death both of them could decide many important issues together. Stalin just demanded to be informed. But as the years went by he showed increasing intolerance of independent actions. However, when he was duly informed 'he generally did not hinder our work', remembers Mikoyan.

In connection with R. W. Davies' observation on how Bolsheviks like Ordzhonikidze could modify their revolutionary enthusiasm by acquiring some of the professional realism of the older specialists, I would like to say that there were two attitudes to specialists (*spetsi*). These were neglect, jealousy and envy on the one hand; and respect, attention and defending them from 'revolutionary phrasemongering' (to use Lenin's words) on the other. There is no doubt that the vast majority of 'commanders of production', like Ordzhonikidze, Mikoyan, Zaveniagin, Mikhail Kaganovich (Lazar's brother and People's Commissar of the aviation industry, who committed suicide on the day he was to be arrested for 'espionage'), Vannikov, Tevosian, Ginzburg, Malyshev, Serebriakov, Mil'chakov, Klimov, Tupolev and many others, adopted the latter attitude. The former one was demonstrated by *vydvizhentsi*, new people who were often raised to high positions without serious consideration as to their abilities and knowledge. Their attitude can be understood as based upon their inferiority complex. Instead of trying to learn (the necessity for which some of them understood), many preferred to criticize the *spetsi* for lacking decisiveness, being slow and lacking an understanding of the 'demands of the party'. It was that attitude which made many excellent specialists victims of repressions.

A. Mikoyan tells in his unpublished memoirs how much he got from old specialists when he came to Moscow in 1926 to replace L. Kamenev as the People's Commissar of Internal and Foreign Trade. He was thirty that summer and stubbornly resisted Stalin's wish to promote him (also to candidate membership of the Politburo). For about six weeks he exchanged angry letters and cables with Stalin and Rykov, who argued that his name was proposed by many Party Central Committee members. The reason for his resistance was obvious. Mikoyan did not think that he would be able to cope with an all-Union and even international scale of work. His experience had been limited to one area albeit a large one. When finally he had to obey the nomination (only after it was published in newspapers!) he understood that without constant learning, advice and teaching on the part of specialists he would not be able to work at the required level. This attitude continued in all his future work.

One episode, connected with Stalin, may be illuminating. Around the end of 1945, Mikoyan, the deputy Prime-Minister and the minister of foreign trade, was expecting in Moscow a visit from Harold Wilson, then a young new Trade minister of the Attlee government. The topic for discussion was the Soviet war debt to Great Britain. The interest burden was high and my father was considering what could be done about it. My father always invited specialists before important decisions or negotiations were due. They were free to discuss everything. This time he presented them with the question: how could we bargain for better conditions? What could be done at the talks with the British minister? In his group of consultants on such matters there was an old professor whose name was Mai. Mai said: 'I don't know the political aspects of the debt problem, but the interest on France's debt to Britain is much less than ours. The difference amounts to several hundred millions of pounds.' Mikoyan picked up such ideas. He demanded exact calculations, adding: 'The political aspect will be my job.' Then he came to Stalin's office and told him everything. Stalin was sceptical and did not advise that the question be posed because he did not believe for a moment that Great Britain would modify the agreement signed at the beginning of the war. Mikoyan insisted that he would try because there was nothing to lose. 'Well', said Stalin, 'do try, but you will see that I am right'.

The talks took place, and the story was told to me not only by my father, but by Harold Wilson himself, who came to Moscow in the 1960s and 1970s as Prime Minister and publicly declared that Mikoyan had been his teacher in trade negotiations (the Soviet press of the Brezhnev years was not allowed to publish such words; even the TV interview was 'edited' and those words cut out). The main argument of Mikoyan was that the Soviet contribution to the defeat was incomparably greater than that of France, so why such discrimination? Wilson argued for several days, then flew to London to report to Attlee and the Cabinet. He came back to Moscow and finally said yes. Stalin was amazed and, of course, satisfied. This episode, like the unwillingness of Mikoyan to be promoted in 1926 and 1938, resisting appointment to the deputy-premiership, partly helps to explain why he survived the purges. Only partly, because obedience was absolutely obligatory. But these qualities helped Mikoyan not to become a real satrap of Stalin, as Alec Nove mentions, for example not to prove his faithfulness by direct participation in the repressions. Stalin made him involved only once, sending him to Armenia with a letter to the Central Committee of the Republic's party, accompanied by Malenkov, and with Beria who joined them a day later from Tbilisi. These very circumstances suggest that Stalin did not consider Mikoyan an ardent supporter of repressions (though Mikoyan had to put his signature on a list of 'the proved enemies of the people', given to him by the local NKVD; the fact that he dared to cross out several other names did not save those people). Maybe this was the reason why he was made to deliver a speech on the twentieth anniversary of the Cheka-OGPU-NKVD.

Obedience in economic and other professional matters did not exclude some discussions, if one felt brave enough to argue. Some preferred not even to argue. For instance Malenkov never argued, though he was very close to Stalin. He had a constant fear of the man.

Mikoyan argued even on serious matters. For example, when the Marshall Plan was announced, Gunnar Myrdal, then Executive secretary of the UN Economic Commission for Europe, came to Moscow to discuss with Mikoyan the possibility of the USSR's participation in it. Mikoyan said he supported the idea completely but added: 'You understand that such a question cannot be decided by me alone. So, let us meet in a couple of days.' Myrdal, talking with me in Stockholm in 1978, said Stalin's name was not mentioned, but he understood with whom Mikoyan would have to talk. My father had earlier told me the same story and that he had spent hours trying to convince Stalin. My father said:

> His only reaction was: 'We shall be dependent on the West'. In vain I argued that we were independent enough politically, and that with the help from the USA we would be able to restore the economy of the European part of the country, which was in ruins, much faster and on a new technological level. Which would have only made us more independent! But Stalin, a clever man, able to understand economic issues when one explained them to him, could be also stubborn as a donkey, to the extent of being a fool.

In this connection he told also how Stalin had made him sell the network of gasoline stations in Austria, which the USSR obtained as reparations after the Second World War. Mikoyan was in charge of all foreign economic ties, including the important Soviet Property Abroad Administration (the uranium mines in Germany and Czechoslovakia were particularly significant). So he argued that the gasoline stations in Austria, got by our country through sheer luck, would bring growing annual profits in hard currency. To lose such an opportunity meant to lose it for ever. But Stalin evidently resented any ties with foreign countries if they could be avoided.

In July 1941 Mikoyan ordered several trainloads of grain and other food products escaping German occupation, to be directed to Leningrad. Zhdanov, informed about it, protested to Stalin directly, not bothering to discuss it with my father. The argument was that the city had no warehouses and that it had enough reserves of food. This was only two or three months before the 900-day blockade of the city! Of course, Mikoyan told me, he did not foresee the siege, he just thought that such a big city could use many buildings, like movie theatres, indoor stadiums, museums and palaces as warehouses. If Leningrad did not need the food reserves it would have been easy to redistribute them to other places. When Stalin called and told him about Zhdanov's objections, Mikoyan explained what he had in mind. But Stalin wouldn't agree, saying: 'Zhdanov knows his city and its needs better than you do. Direct those trainloads to other places.'

Some mention should be given to 'Yakovlev's Stalin'. The memoirs of the well-known aircraft designer are 'pro-Stalinist'. Such was the opinion of both Mikoyans, including Yakovlev's colleague, the MiG fighter-designer Artiom Mikoyan. Of course Stalin was able to understand sound arguments and to take correct decisions. But he was just as able not to listen to sound opinion and to take wrong decisions. Concerning the atmosphere of fear and intrigues connected with Yakovlev, Artiom Mikoyan told of a notable episode when Yakovlev's very fate was at stake. At a meeting in Stalin's office, the host was informed by the Air Force command that the new Yak-3 fighters often fell apart in the air because the surface fabric split and broke.[16] It was not the first report of this kind. Yakovlev was not able to explain why all his attempts to obviate the difficulty had been unsuccessful. After the report Stalin said in the most menacing tone, after which people usually had only minutes or hours of freedom: 'For whom do you work, comrade Yakovlev, for our country or for Hitler?' The audience was totally silent, Yakovlev became white as snow and could not utter a word. The situation, and Yakovlev's fate, were saved by Artiom Mikoyan who stood up and loudly said: 'Comrade Stalin, we give you our word, that we shall find out what is wrong. Give us two weeks.' First of all, to say 'we' meant that in the case of failure the guilt would automatically fall on him also. Stalin kept silent, his anger was still there. Then he said: 'You have only two weeks. Remember this.' After which a group of designers flew to the main plant and scrutinized carefully all the stages of the production. They worked like rank-and-file inspectors for eighteen hours every day. Finally they discovered that the khaki paint of the upper part of the body was covered by a lacquer which could not withstand the extreme frost of the 1941–2 winter, especially at high altitudes and in flight.

After Stalin's death only the degree of menace and the consequences changed. 'The voluntarism' of the boss continued, the intrigues did not disappear, the habit to 'destroy barons and baronies', as Sheila Fitzpatrick puts it, was taken over by Khrushchev. The important difference was, however, that nobody was arrested or shot. But decisions were often taken unilaterally, flatterers triumphed and those who maintained their views in spite of the anger of Khrushchev either lost some of the factories and designer bureaus in favour of their competitors or were moved to another job (*naznachenie!*). Some were even forced into retirement. Such a 'space adventurer' as Vladimir Chelomey managed to undermine the prestige and the scope of activity of Sergei Korolyov, the father of the Soviet space breakthrough. Having the son of Khrushchev, Sergei, then a young and credulous engineer, at his 'firm', and making him a Hero of Socialist Labour, Chelomey managed to charm Khrushchev. Let us not forget that even a man of principle like Admiral Nikolai Kuznetsov was demoted from full admiralship twice: by Stalin at the end of the 1940s and by Khrushchev in the 1950s. This also belongs to the legacy of Stalinism.

To add to R. W. Davies's conclusions about the household plots as a recognized and long-lasting feature of the socialist economy, it is useful to keep in mind that in 1953 Khrushchev was the first to remember the grave fate of the peasants. He carried out important measures which made possible an increase in agricultural production and the liberation of the peasants from their serfdom (many Western specialists make a mistake when they attribute this to Malenkov, who merely mentioned new policies in a speech at the Supreme Soviet). But seven to eight years after, the same Khrushchev made an attempt to deprive the peasants of their household plots, which even Stalin did not do. Such was the strength of the Stalinist approach both to taking cardinal decisions and to the long-suffering Russian peasantry.

I find it difficult to agree with one of Professor Davies's conclusions when he says: 'By the mid-1930s the political system and social structure had already acquired their own laws of behaviour, and *even the most powerful dictator found it difficult to manoeuvre them*.' First of all, the system and the structure were just as the dictator wanted them to be, in order not to undermine but to strengthen his dictatorship. Secondly, if we suppose that he considered them not good enough *from his point of view* he could easily have manoeuvred them in any desirable direction.

But I fully agree with Professor Davies that Dr Viola and Arch Getty misunderstand or underestimate the role of Stalin in the acceleration of forced collectivization. The article 'Dizzy with Success' is nothing more than the usual hypocrisy on the part of Stalin. We know hundreds of examples of that kind. However, 'dekulakization' required so many soldiers, so many trainloads and so much co-ordination of transportation throughout the country, and was so connected not only with the places where it was implemented but also with the places to which the 'kulaks' and their families were moved, that it would be absolutely fantastic to believe that Stalin was not aware of the scale of the operation. A. V. Snegov, whom I mentioned above, worked in the Ukraine. He witnessed a conversation between Ordzhonikidze and a local party leader. The Ukrainian had known Sergo, so he confessed that he tried not to implement all the tough measures ordered by Moscow and not to speed up the process, sending less than totally accurate reports. To which Ordzhonikidze replied: 'You are right. Do not pay much attention to commands of people who are far away and know the situation on the spot less than you do.'

R. W. Davies sees a disagreement between Alec Nove and Arch Getty. The former admits that 'things happened (especially in the economy) which did not conform to [Stalin's] orders or desires'. But, after all, he points out: 'there is no such thing as *totally* limitless power'. While the latter regards personal despotism as of relatively minor importance, Davies himself, however, pays much attention to Stalin's populism, to its effect on his own behaviour and the operation of the system, believing that the passive resistance of the peasants and the technological conservatism of the system proved more powerful than Stalin.

I agree that populism was used by Stalin fairly intensively. But I do not see where and how the peasants limited Stalin's power. And it is even less clear why the system, created by Stalin as he wanted it to exist and serve him, as well as to help the whole strata of the party-state apparatus, 'proved more powerful'. Stalinism included Stalin and the system. And why 'technological conservatism'? Technology has its own laws and a human being cannot overcome them. But some people would be eager to put even earthquakes under the authority of their great leader.

One small episode may help to illuminate Stalin's feeling about his own power. Once, in August, walking with Mikoyan in the park of 'Blizhnyaya dacha' in Kuntsevo, Stalin said: 'I want a lemon tree to grow here', and pointed to the open ground. Mikoyan responded: 'It cannot grow here. The first frost will kill it.' Stalin replied stubbornly: 'No, it *will* grow.' Mikoyan thought: 'Strange. He looks like a clever, very clever man. How can he talk such nonsense?' I think the episode reveals Stalin's inner conviction: nature obeys him, or must obey him. The lemon tree was planted. By late autumn it began to die and Stalin ordered a greenhouse to be built around it. Maybe a new healthy tree was planted without his knowledge.

Arch Getty provides an excellent explanation of the conditions for Stalin's despotism, but I cannot share his 'historical determinism' about those conditions, as should be clear from this chapter. And I certainly cannot agree with his evaluation of events in the 1930s. In the final part of his chapter Arch Getty writes about 'a series of "precipitants" ' and 'conflicts, which reached a head between 1934 and 1937, raised the political temperature of the country and the party . . .' Getty goes on: 'for a considerable time, Stalin remained aloof from them, keeping his options open, refusing to take sides'. For me it is crystal clear that the temperature was raised by Stalin himself, that he was behind the scenes of all the conflicts, organized and orchestrated by him as a preparation for the coming blow.

But I hardly believed my eyes when I read that in connection with the terror 'on one level he [Stalin] was certainly to blame. But his actions, although necessary, were not sufficient to explain the entire process and its outcome any more than Mao's role is sufficient to explain the unfolding of the Cultural Revolution in China'. I know my country and I know Stalin. About China and Mao I can judge only by implication. Both dictators could easily manipulate the masses thanks to the systems of 'communist' dictatorship, which gave them unique opportunities to enslave people not only politically but also ideologically and psychologically. Since I used to be such a slave myself I can testify that people could be made to do everything. At the same time they sincerely believed that they were acting on their own, fulfilling their duty, behaving according to their inner readiness to implement everything the party (i.e. Stalin) wanted them to implement. They did not sell their souls, but presented them free, with pride and joy. That kind of mass psychosis can be considered a 'clinical case'. If it is so, a whole country was a huge clinic. This sounds like a paradox or a gloomy joke, but nobody can convince me now that I was normal, because my thinking and behaviour were pre-determined by historical circumstances. We are able to look back, to evaluate our thoughts, feelings and obsessions of passed decades without resorting to text-books or monographic researches, even if they can give us a false consolation that we as a nation were not raped by an evil genius of a dictator.

Some years ago Arch Getty perhaps could have been right, saying that 'the general public in the West knows more about the details of Stalinism than the general public in the Soviet Union' (although I am a little doubtful about 'the general public' in the West). But nowadays this is no longer correct. The general public in the USSR since 1986–7 have got the amount of information that only a few people in the West would bother to read. The cause of denouncing Stalin ceased to be the result of the efforts of 'official' authors. The process long ago went out of anybody's control. Of course, it led to some mistakes, some emotional or ideological interpretations, even fantasies instead of facts. Advocacy of somebody and of something as well as the wish to apportion blame are often the goal of many authors. As a result reviewers worry more about the intentions of the author than about the sources or methodology involved.

Re-reading these thoughts by Arch Getty, shared and expressed also by Alec Nove, Sheila Fitzpatrick and R. W. Davies, I have to be aware of the possible attitude of any of my esteemed colleagues and any of the readers of this volume. I do not claim to be impartial. Moreover, I do not hope to be impartial. Too much has been connected with Stalin, Stalinism and *Stalinshchina* in my life to make any attempt at an absolutely cold and clinically balanced approach to the immense topic possible.

Epilogue

Stalinism continued to exist without Stalin for many years. This fact seems to overrule my own emphasis on the role of personalities and to support the positions of determinist approaches to the decades of the history of the Soviet Union under discussion. Still, in my opinion the long life of the system is not necessarily proof of its historical inevitability. Sure, the system was exactly what the new class, created to make it function and having become its inseparable part, painstakingly cherished, tried to develop and stubbornly defended. Sure, it was based upon the vested interests of the new class. However, the formation of the class could have been stopped and its young leaves could mutate to other kinds of flora.

One of the paradoxes of the history of Stalinism can be seen in the Khrushchev era; *Stalinshchina* was vehemently rejected but the system of the Party rule, the main cornerstone of Stalinism, was actually strengthened. Why? Without the direct fear of mass repression, shootings and tortures, new guarantees for the lasting rule of the system were needed. So the main fault of Khrushchev was inability and unwillingness to understand that 1956 had to become a starting point for a rapid revolution from above against the system. Instead he preserved almost all its key elements and even added some new ones.

Still, neither the leader nor the apparatus could stop the development of thought which was described above. And the next reformer became a revolutionary against the very system he headed. This historical fact cannot be seriously denied by anybody. Although anti-Gorbachev emotions often give birth to theories, that system was rapidly breaking up and Gorbachev wanted to save it with the help of cosmetic reforms. In my opinion such allegations belong to the sphere of personal attitude and not to objective scientific analysis or to realities, which all of us still remember very well. The system was strong enough in 1985–6 and small liberal gestures by Gorbachev would have given hope and peace of mind to many politically important stratas of society. And of course the leader would have achieved a reputation as an intelligent, young statesman with a wide horizon of thought. Such an image, in combination with the new political thinking in foreign policy, would have kept the system and its leaderships afloat. The contrast with the long years of gerontocracy would have been so positive for Gorbachev and his team, that they would have obtained a stable leading role for quite a long time. My only concession to determinism here is the assumption that sometime in the third millenium the system would have died anyway.

Its strength and ability to retain significant remnants of the mechanism, not intact but still playing a certain role in society even after several years of *perestroika*, was amazing. How long could it have lasted but for the coup of August 1991? Not too long, of course. But let us not forget that it outlived its creator by almost forty years.

Its fate was decided by the practice typical of this system as it is typical for any totalitarian system. I would like to call it 'a law of totalitarian structures'. I mean the absurdity of actions, based on presumptions and beliefs, brought to life by its own propaganda, by its traditional wishful thinking and inability to evaluate correctly existing realities. Overestimation of its power has always caused behaviour which looked simply idiotic or even dictated by secret enemies of the system, who had made their way into its elite.

The August 1991 coup proved that again. Trying to stop the dismemberment of the Union, it caused new powerful centrifugal trends and hasty actions; hoping to save the ruling role of the Communist Party, it brought its immediate end; dreaming of a backlash against democratic movement, it gave the strongest momentum to that movement; expecting to impose the old fear on the people, it liberated people from relics of that fear once and for all.

This Second Revolution in the twentieth century's history of that vast area called Tsarist Russia and subsequently the Soviet Union, will probably be named by historians the August revolution. It was very unusual, almost peaceful and bloodless, easy and simple, so that we can say that *perestroika* had made its main contribution, or even had completed its main historic task: on the one hand it helped to turn the system into a living corpse, and on the other hand it destroyed that decades-old FEAR, which helped even the final convulsions of the system look menacing and dangerous for the development of society. The process of evaporation of fear could be almost watched during the dramatic three days around 'the White House' of Moscow and elsewhere in the city. An unprecedented degree of unity and determination of people, defending democracy against the last convulsions of Stalinism, were evident to all the participants of the events, among whom I had the luck to be present. And I do not think the barricades which I helped to build separated me in a decisive way from the original ideas of other barricades, which had attracted all the passion and thought of my father more than seven decades ago.

Optimism would be natural under such circumstances. But there are still some doubts about the 'triumphant march of democracy' (using the phraseology of 'A Short History of the CPSU'). Why so? We can again cite a thought, expressed by one of the Russian writers of these times, who said: 'Bolshevism is a certain condition of the Russian soul'. And, he added, until we fully understand this we will not be able to understand anything in our past and perhaps our present.

The society was sick for too many years. But even earlier, before the October revolution of 1917, it was not free from certain viruses of extremism, intolerance, despotic inclinations, which made it possible for Bolshevism to assume its ugly features, to triumph and to last for several decades. So the question is: how free is today's society from those viruses? Were they actually cured to their roots by democratic developments, by the growth of political culture, by the bitter experience of the past? Did a sort of immunization come out of that sickness, as happens in a human body? If the answer is 'yes', we may look forward with optimism.

However, the future development of the country – and of the new-born states which are appearing in the area – is still unpredictable. It is much more sound to restrict that kind of analysis to Russia proper. The August revolution was most important for Russia (though it greatly facilitated separatist trends in the republics and elsewhere). The upsurge of democratic aspirations, the disappearance of fear are signs that society is more or less ready for cardinal changes.

The situation is more difficult in respect of political leadership. It has not yet reached those high levels of responsibility and wisdom necessary for a speedy recovery of all the structures of the whole society from a unique experiment staged by history itself on one sixth of the globe. But when the two streams match each other, that part of the globe has every chance to play a great and extremely positive role for the whole human civilization.

Socialist ideas, although deformed and often only a caricature of socialism, have left behind something important, which hopefully will lead the society not simply along the paths explored by other nations long ago. They will inevitably bequeath certain important values and features to the future nature of the society which is emerging from the abyss of Stalinism.

Notes

Note. This chapter reflects my thinking as of early 1991, when it was written and delivered to the publishers.

1 At this Congress (March 1924) in connection with 'Lenin's Testament' the will of the Politbureau was actually imposed on the delegates.; the text was read to regional delegations separately; no discussions were offered or advised.

A. Mikoyan remembered that an unprecedented unity of Trotsky, Zinoviev, Stalin, Bukharin and others so impressed the rank-and-file delegates that they did not object. The text was not distributed or given to anybody in any form and of course it was not published. So Arch Getty is wrong when he considers Stalin's use of portions of the document *several years later* as not concealing the document from the party and from the people at a moment when it could have changed the history of the country.

2 This word of course had a meaning quite different from the one that it acquired decades later; it meant anarchical peasant armies, mostly acting in the Ukraine.

3 No. 47, November 1990.

4 Nathan Eidelman was a good friend of mine for decades since our student years at one of the best high-schools of Moscow; we spent many nights – Russian nights! – talking before his early death in 1990. He had a rare ability to generalize about contemporary history, basing his conclusions on strictly objective and 'cold' studies of the past and present.

5 M. Heller, *A. Nekrich. Utopia u Vlasti* (London, 1986).

6 Not long ago being in Washington I gave a lecture about perestroika. There was a Chilean officer among the listeners who said that he would never believe in the ability of any communist to turn from communist dictatorship and 'ideological expansionism' to democracy, that the whole process of perestroika could only be a big deceit of the West, that the struggle between 'conservatives and democrats' could only be a show, staged by the Kremlin. The officer said that he would never change his belief that 'the best communist is a dead one'.

For a man who had participated in the coup d'état of Pinochet and in the bloody repressions afterwards, this was understandable. I was interested to talk with him, to get a better insight into the mechanics of the brainwashing in some armies of Latin America. This was a classical example of *political racism*. But it would be rather sad to see it in other countries and among other categories of people.

7 Arch Getty mentions that Stalin acquired the position thanks to Lenin; this is not correct. It was Kamenev and Zinoviev, thinking that Trotsky would be their main competitor in the power struggle after Lenin died, who proposed to create such post, to give the Secretariat functions it never had, and named Stalin for this job, because were sure that a man of such low theoretical grasp and non-existent charisma would never be a difficulty for them. Besides, Kamenev thought that after common exile to Siberia Stalin was still in his 'team'.

8 The following text is in no respect an imitation of A. Rybakov's writings; it is an abridged account of my understanding, formed in the 1950s by talks with my father and old Bolsheviks, who often came to our home and whom I visited myself: O. Shatunovskaya, L. Shaumian, A. Snegov, my uncles Artiom Mikoyan, H. Toumanian, A. Arzumanian, a former member of one of the 17th Congress counting commissions N. Andreasian (a friend of my father since their school years), and some others. Some of them had the experience of the NKVD torture-chambers and the Gulag behind them.

9 This is the exact word used by my father, and when I did not quite understand, he explained: 'to subdue'.

10 Arch Getty would like to have more substantial evidence against Stalin. As a historian I agree. But so far it is only possible with the help of a spiritualist to talk with those who are dead. Still, we should not forget that in the archives of the

Central Committee of the CPSU there is a thick volume of interviews with those whom Stalin was not provident enough to kill, and many other documents. The volume was compiled at the end of the 1950s by the Party Control Committee. Its former member Olga Shatunovskaya told me that it was very convincing. Alexander Yakovlev wanted to publish the volume for the 100th anniversary of Kirov but in 1986 it was *still* difficult; now it seems *already* difficult. Let us wait. The opportunity will come.

11 *Daugava*, No. 7, 1990.

12 I read A. Tsipko's article in *Daugava*, cited above, only when this chapter was practically finished. So I was astonished and pleased to see that my colleague and friend wrote that *if* Bukharin had been the leader of our party, our country would have stood a good chance of avoiding the catastrophic cataclysms which channelled its development towards an ugly kind of society.

13 *Izvestia of the CC of the CPSU*, No. 4, 1990.

14 V. I. Lenin, *Complete Works*, vol. 44, p. 78 (Russian edition).

15 Just one very simple example in this connection: once, a year or two ago, at a public discussion I got a note with the following text: 'You and the son of Khrushchev should not write articles or speak at any gathering; instead both of you should be imprisoned for the crimes of your parents.' I read this note aloud – as I did with all the notes, always – and asked the audience if they felt any difference between that thought and Stalin's killing of the wives and imprisonment of families of 'the enemies of the people'? True, the audience in its majority advised me not to pay any attention to such opinions. And I wouldn't, if only it did not reflect the reality of the times, which supposedly disappeared with Stalin. I could not but recall that, according to published accounts of eyewitnesses and victims, even in maternity-houses there were nurses who refused to help to give birth to a mongrel offspring of an enemy of the people!

16 The aluminum industry in the Northern Ural was being hurriedly created at that time under the guidance of my father, according to Stalin's order. Mikoyan had been surprised by the order, objecting that he knew little about metals. Stalin's argument was simple and short: 'You will cope with it.' 'Generally he believed that I would cope with anything', added my father musingly.

CHAPTER 6

Stalin and Stalinism – Some Afterthoughts

Alec Nove

Sergei Mikoyan's contribution is of evident importance, bearing in mind the author's family background and 'inside' knowledge. In any disagreement with the 'revisionists', represented here by J. Arch Getty and (to a lesser extent) by Sheila Fitzpatrick, I tend to back Mikoyan. None the less, I have problems with some of his arguments. Specifically, I would like to take issue on three matters: the number of victims of the terror, the relevance of the Russian historical tradition, and, finally, on alternatives to Stalin.

First, then, numbers. Mikoyan cites his father to the effect that he was told that 'between 1 January 1935 and 22 June 1941' 7 million were shot, and 12.7 million sent to Gulag and other such places. It is difficult to reconcile such figures with the demographic data that we have. As Mikoyan would surely agree, the many millions of peasants who died of hunger or in deportation mostly perished before 1935. Their disappearance shows up in the unexpectedly low population total in the census of January 1937: 162.0 million. Since the authors of the census were shot, it is reasonable to accept this as close to the true figure. The 1939 (January) census counted 170.5 million people, but it is widely accepted that this is an overstatement. Such figures as 167 or 168 million are suggested, for example by V. Tsaplin (*Voprosi istorii*, No. 4, 1989). But even this does not leave room for more than about a million shootings in 1937–8, and (despite Kuropaty) one would expect fewer, not more, shootings in 1939–40.

Or one can approach the figures in a different way. Let us compare the total said to have been shot and arrested (in 1935–40) (7 + 12.7 =

19.7 million) with the male adult population – the great terror of those years surely hit adult males disproportionately: they numbered only about 45 million. Could they have detained a third of the entire adult male population? These age-groups were to bear huge losses in the war, when we know that about 30 million were mobilized. Is it possible that the totals cited by Anastas Mikoyan relate to a much longer time-period and/or include all categories of *repressirovanye*? I have myself criticized those 'revisionists' who cite unbelievably low figures of victims. In my own calculations I reach a total of 10–11 million for the period 1932–9 (the large majority of them peasants), surely a grim enough figure!

Then there are archival data, cited by Yu. Polyakov et al. in *Sotsiologicheskie issledovaniya*, No. 8, 1990 (p. 49), which give those 'specially registered' by the NKVD in January 1939 as 3,738,822 (Maksudov has seen a total of 3,593,000 plus 366,000 NKVD personnel, which may be included in the higher of the two figures). It is true, however, that these figures exclude not only those already shot, but also a large number of exiles who were not behind wire. Also published recently are figures on numbers shot for 'counter-revolutionary offences'. Of course, they are probably incomplete, since some were shot with no trial or formal accusation at all. But we must somehow reconcile the increasing number of citations from hitherto top-secret archives with some of the very high estimates which have been made, including those by Conquest, Roy Medvedev and Antonov-Ovseyenko. To repeat, the data that are emerging are bad enough, by any historical standard, including that of Russian history.

So let us turn to that history. I already cited Kozhinov's argument that other countries, too, had bloody (sometimes bloodier) histories. And indeed Ivan the Terrible, unlike Henry VIII, did not have his wives executed, the French religious wars were bad, the Thirty Years War ghastlier. Russian history does indeed include reforming tsars, reforming statesmen such as Stolypin and Witte, and some notable rebels too, such as Razin and Pugachev, as well as great writers and so on. And yes, Peter opened windows on Europe, Stalin closed them. However, it is also right to see in Peter a prototype of the despotic-barbarian modernizer, and this is why Berdyaev saw the similarity, while Voloshin the poet wrote: '*Veliki Pyotr byl pervyi bol'shevik*.'

Both Peter the Great and Stalin gave priority to that part of economic development which served the military state: as Tugan-Baranovsky explained in his magisterial *Russkaya fabrika*, Peter's *manufaktury* provided weapons, ammunition, iron, sailcloth, uniforms, and paper for the bureaucracy to write on. He adscripted serf labour to work in these 'possessional' factories and mines, and to build his capital city 'on the bones of the peasants', as it used to be said. So he was both an enslaver and a unique species of modernizer, containing within himself many contradictions of Russia's history. That excellent economic historian Alexander Gerschenkron also saw parallels between Peter and the Bolsheviks. And Mikoyan himself agrees, in his own text, that the lack of a democratic political culture made a significant contribution to the rise of Stalinism. None the less, the historical precedents do not point only one way, agreed. There are some (admittedly rare) examples of a traditional ruling stratum revolutionizing itself, as happened in Japan with the Meiji restoration, though more common are failures to respond to challenge, as for instance in Poland in the eighteenth century and in China in the nineteenth – and one can add Tsarist Russia at the beginning of the twentieth – despite the efforts of Stolypin (and Gorbachev?).

Which brings one to the complex issue of alternatives. Agreed, we must not assume that whatever happened *had* to happen, that no alternative courses of action existed. But some alternatives were more likely than others to be chosen, and some were simply excluded, given the antecedent circumstances and the ideas (the ideology) of those who took decisions. To illustrate this last point, presented with a choice between cheese and ham, an orthodox rabbi would have no choice. . . . Mikoyan correctly notes the existence of different strands in Marxism, and Kautsky and Rosa Luxemburg regarded themselves as orthodox marxists when they criticized Lenin's one-party state. Also it is true that there were Bolsheviks (for example Rykov) who protested when Lenin tried to exclude other parties from the first Soviet government. Nor can one underestimate the great importance of the civil war, and Sergei Mikoyan is right to point to the brutalities that accompany civil wars everywhere. We would all agree that these experiences strengthened tendencies towards authoritarianism and intolerance, but it is surely also true that these tendencies were already present, and also that the seizure of power by a small group acting in the name of the proletariat in a peasant country does have long-term despotic implications. Mikoyan points out that the original Bolshevik leaders were highly educated. True, they were predominantly intellectuals. But Lenin himself worried at the end of his life about the narrowness of the party's educated stratum (*prosloika*). Below it, the party's cadres were crude men-of-the-people. For them Stalin was an appropriate leader, especially as he gave them the opportunity to eliminate the intellectuals, few of whom survived the Terror. The 'socialism' or 'marxism' of the masses was brilliantly satirized in Platonov's 'Chevengur' (which can be seen as anticipating the extremism of Pol Pot). Mikoyan seeks to defend the Bolsheviks against Tsipko's accusation that they let loose the dark masses. Here was in fact one major difference with the Mensheviks: Martov feared the consequences of a new Pugachevshchina; Lenin was willing to ride the storm. The more ambitious and able (and ruthless) of the 'men from below' became, surely, a vital element in the rise of Stalinism, and later in the specific features of *stalinshchina*.

As for alternatives to Stalin, on a personal level it is hard for me to envisage Bukharin as a political leader, given his lack of firmness and organizational abilities. Trotsky was surely excluded by his own reluctance to undertake political manoeuvring, the attitude to him of most party functionaries and by being a Jew. Rudzutak could have been a competent party secretary, but did he have the stature of a leader at a time when strong leadership was felt to be indispensable? Rykov and Kamenev each had qualities, but it was surely not an accident that Stalin found it so easy to eliminate them, and indeed in the political 'game' he outclassed everybody.

So, even in retrospect, Stalin's victory in the inner-party struggle of the 1920s can be seen as irreversible. But, accepting that there was a crisis of NEP in 1927–8, need he have acted as he did? It seems easier to imagine Stalin himself acting differently, than to imagine Trotsky or Bukharin in his place. One could imagine alternative 'Stalin-based' scenarios. He, too, had choices. In my view (and that of such Soviet historians as Afanansyev and Gefter) there was a long-term basic incompatibility between Bolshevism and NEP. Yes, as Mikoyan points out, in the mid-twenties party policy was more tolerant of the peasantry, but there is much evidence (gathered by Yuri Golland, and presented in his article in *Znamya*, No. 10, 1988) that most party cadres in rural areas opposed the policy of 'face to the village', and so had no difficulty in supporting the 'left turn' of 1928. As for the left opposition, they urged higher investments and more severe measures against the *kulak*, which would have made the crisis of 1927–8 more severe, though, to do them justice, their policies were far less extreme than those shortly to be adopted by Stalin. As for Bukharin, while he certainly opposed Stalin's 'left turn', by 1927 he too was advocating an 'offensive against the *kulak*', and this in a situation in which he must have known that party officials would regard as a *kulak* any commercially successful peasant.

I had argued in 1961, in my article entitled 'Was Stalin Really Necessary?', that the circumstances of the time did call for a strong leader and tough policies in the direction of 'primitive socialist accumulation', but that it did not follow that Stalin's *excesses* were thereby explained or justified. As already mentioned, I also proposed the notion of 'excessive excesses': coercive policies have a logic of their own, which all too often results in more coercion than is strictly necessary, but Stalin went far beyond this. Did he *have* to order *raskulachivanie*, or the adoption of absurdly over-ambitious targets for industrialization, or the ruthless procurement policy which led to the dreadful famine of 1933, or the execution of so many? Using Mikoyan's terminology, I am really saying that there were strong objective causes for 'stalinism' and not for *stalinshchina*.

Just as Ivan the Terrible was under no compulsion to institute the *Oprichnina*, or to drown so many citizens of Novgorod, so Stalin could have sent Bukharin off to teach marxism-leninism in the provinces, and left Kamenev to work in the 'Academia' publishing-house, and not issued instructions about harsher conditions in labour-camps, or to kill the bulk of senior army officers. He did, after all, choose to spare Pasternak and Litvinov. It was Gefter who argued that in 1935 Stalin faced an alternative: a policy of reconciliation seemed objectively possible, linked with the need to create an anti-Hitler coalition. And then he chose the path of personal despotism, to assert his own 'necessity', to impose fully-fledged *stalinshchina*. The point I am making is that it seems easier to imagine *Stalin* adopting different policies than to imagine scenarios with a different leader, or one in which Bolshevism itself evolved in a more democratic manner: surely all the leaders in those days saw themselves as surrounded by a vast *melkoburzhuaznaya stikhiya*, the peasants, seen as obstacles to the desired 'socialist' transformation of society, a transformation they were called upon to accomplish from above.

With Bob Davies's remarks I have no quarrel. Yes, Stalin was in a sense 'populist' in his attitudes, and the cultural counter-revolution of the thirties (in education, in history, in architecture, in literature) doubtless commanded considerable mass support. No doubt, too, that in economic policy questions Stalin had to take into account the constraints of objective reality – though he did his best to pursue the line that 'there is no fortress the Bolsheviks cannot take'. On his personal role in directing the Terror, and on its vast scope (though not on the statistics) I am on Mikoyan's side. Arch Getty has no difficulty in showing that many party officials (and others) took the opportunity to denounce their comrades, to settle old scores, to show 'vigilance' or to secure their own advancement, and that their initiatives contributed to the scale of the terror. Also that rank-and-file resentments played their role too. None the less, Stalin was surely the director-general of the process. Just as surely it was on the basis of his general instructions that *raskulachivanie* occurred, even though in specific local instances the zealousness of local comrades and the hostility to specific families doubtless affected the actual application of the policy to Ivanov, Petrov or Sidorov.

Just how much support for collectivization there was among the village poor it is far from easy to determine, and precisely on this sort of question the archives may be of little help, since there was pressure to report what should have been. Yes, the social basis for Stalinism is a topic well worthy of detailed research, and Sheila Fitzpatrick is justified in pursuing this theme. However, the thirties was a period in which the old party and state cadres, and indeed most of the men of importance in society, were being violently thrust aside. Those that did the thrusting certainly included men whom Mikoyan refers to as *vydvizhentsy*, the promoted ones. They were given the green light to oust and denounce those who stood in their way. There must be many instances, in Smolensk and elsewhere, in which the fate of many depended on 'initiatives' from below. At higher levels too, one might well be able to show that Budenny denounced Tukhachevsky, or that Beria or Malenkov initiated what came to be known as the Leningrad affair. This in no way diminishes the responsibility of the despot who set the whole process in motion.

Perhaps we could all agree with the formulation of the Soviet sociologist–historian Bestuzhev-Lada:

> In principle the mechanism of terror is more or less clear. It was similar to that of dekulakization: a directive from above, threatening punishment for non-fulfilment, 'competition' between executants at all levels, from the centre to the provinces . . . and finally personal grudges or material calculation (to get the job, the property or the housing-space of the victim). . . . The net effect

was a lava-like progression of the process, which apparently had at times to be restrained so that everyone would not be included [*Nedelya*, No. 15, 1988].

It may be useful to cite the view of Marshal Zhukov, expressed to Soviet historians: asked about the functions of the State Committee of Defence and the headquarters staff (*stavka*), he replied: 'I did not see the difference. . . . Stalin was the *stavka*, and the State Committee of defence was also basically Stalin. He commanded everything, he directed it all, his word was final' (*Kommunist*, No. 14, 1988, p. 97). But of course this does not mean that no Soviet division ever advanced or retreated without orders originating with the generalissimo (and he did not control the Germans!).

Arch Getty's paper raises a whole number of other issues, and with many of the points he makes I have no difficulty in agreeing. However:

(a) No one could measure, or prove by reference to archives, how many people were afraid. Surely here it is appropriate, as I did in an article to which he makes reference, to cite a poem, and particularly by one with the background and connections of Tvardovsky (rather than Akhmatova's *Requiem*, since she was a survivor of *byvshie lyudi*, 'former people'). Here oral history, the memoirs of those who lived through the period, are the only source we have.

(b) Getty is perfectly right to remind us that memoirs, and memories, can be unreliable and require cross-checking. But is there not also a danger in taking archival material at face value? Do not officials (and not only in Russia) sometimes write what their bosses want to hear, and this even if they are not terrified?

(c) Yes, in a sense strong regimes do not need terror. But that does not mean that terror cannot be used to create and impose a strong regime.

(d) Getty refers to 'the routine killing of opponents, persecution of relatives' etc., in a context which could lead readers to suppose that Stalinist practices were in line with the traditional behaviour of Russian rulers. But this was not so. Throughout the nineteenth century, and even under the harsh rule of Nicholas the First, executions were remarkably few (and Nicholas did not punish the relatives of the Decembrists). It is precisely because capital punishment had been so rare in Russia, in the previous hundred years, that the hangings that followed the suppressing of the 1905 revolution so shocked public opinion. And if Getty had in mind not the actions of the state but the primitive justice of the peasantry, is there in fact any evidence that murders were more common in Russia than elsewhere? In these respects what Mikoyan calls *stalinshchina* was surely unprecedented.

Preventive or 'prophylactic' repression, the arrest of those thought likely to offend, ahead of any offence, is not unknown in other countries in time of conflict. Even in Britain, several hundred Iraqis were detained in January 1991. What *was* unique to *Stalinshchina* was the scale of the repression, and the fact that it hit one's own people (in two senses: Soviet citizens *and*, disproportionately, party members). I would argue that the attitudes that made this possible relate not only to Stalin's own personality, but also to the fact that the Bolsheviks seized power and held power in what to them seemed a hostile environment; in which civil-war attitudes persisted long after the actual civil war had ended. Distrust of the peasants, distrust of the intelligentsia, of 'bourgeois spetsy', of party comrades who might express, through deviation from the party line, alien class interests, hostility to nationalisms in a multi-national state, the need for the semi-educated to cling to a simplified catechism-like version of the one true doctrine, all contributed.

Now, when all things can be publicly questioned, including the legitimacy of Bolshevism and of October, the system disintegrates.

Conclusion

So, finally, what are the key issues that require to be addressed?

The Stalinist regime was despotic, terroristic, hierarchical, with rigid control over the arts, the media, science. A pseudo-marxist ideology was used as a simplified catechism, only to be interpreted on high. There were minimum rights for workers, less for peasants. A highly centralised economy, with top priority for heavy industry. There was, from the middle thirties, a restoration of 'national' history and traditional family and educational values (though Pavlik Morozov, who denounced his father, was there to remind one that duty to the state and to Stalin was primary). The bulk of the old Bolsheviks were killed off, along with millions of others of all ranks and conditions. A new ruling stratum emerged, privileged but with a high risk of arrest. The despot was worshiped as a demi-god.

So, first of all, why did this happen? What were the *istoki*, the origins, the explanations? Some stress, the autocratic traditions of Russia, of which Stalin was certainly well aware. Or the ultra-radical traditions of the Russian revolutionary intelligentsia. Or the logic of a Bolshevik takeover of an isolated backward country 'unripe' for socialism. Or the logic of 'primitive socialist accumulation' in a country under external threat. More recently, especially in the work of Alexander Tsipko (e.g. in *Sobesednik*, Nos. 20, 21, 22, 1990) (and in *Novyi mir*, No.4, 1990), the 'blame' is assigned to Lenin, Marx, Engels. Popov, too, pointed out that Stalin's actions were generally in full conformity with the 1919 party programme. Here we see several controversial points: to what extent did Marx's own ideas (e.g. on 'labour armies' in agriculture, his moral relativism, his negative attitude to markets, his views on law and on civil society, etc) contribute to Bolshevism, the civil war, the so-called proletarian dictatorship, the one-party state? What aspects of Leninism led to, or facilitated, the emergence of stalinist despotism? Was Stalin the executor of Lenin's policies or the executioner of Lenin's comrades? Or perhaps both in some measure? Not only Tsipko but also persons as different as Vasili Grossman and Soloukhin (not to mention Solzhenitsyn) have been stressing Lenin's single-minded ruthlesness, his willingness to use coercive measures, terror.

Then, secondly, there are the issues connected with *alternatives*. What other policies, what other leaders, could have coped with the crisis of NEP, with the dilemmas which faced the Bolsheviks towards the end of the twenties? A Trotsky alternative, a Bukharin alternative, or even just a more moderate, less extreme and murderous stalinist alternative. A linked question concerns the evaluation of what the Stalin policy actually did achieve, when stripped of statistical exaggerations. Were NEP and Bolshevism compatible?

Thirdly, there is the complex of questions related to the social basis of stalinism. Thus in a symposium devoted to the subject, L. Batkin asks: did Stalin create the system or did the system create Stalin; what came first, the chicken or the egg? Or maybe both, they grew together? He both represented and created a 'new class of "rulers", lacking in ability and in knowledge, except how to rule (*rukovodit'*)', in Stalin's 'lumpen-state'. What stratum, what interests, did Stalin represent?

Fourthly, there can be differences of view about the degree of Stalin's personal dominance, the role of his associates in policy-making, the significance of conflicts among the leaders, and, perhaps more important, of the objective circumstances, obstacles, resistances, which must have underlaid these disagreements. Could a man like

Kaganovich have been personally responsible for the destruction of much of old Moscow, or Malenkov and Beria in the postwar years for the destruction of the Leningrad party apparatus. Or, whatever the court intrigues, were the final decisions always Stalin's?

Fifthly, there are questions connected with the scale of the great purge, and the numbers of peasant victims of famine and *raskulach-ivaniye*, plus Stalin's objectives and personal responsibility.

Other matters connected with Stalin's personal role relate to the war (responsibility for initial disasters, his activities as generalissimo and as a symbol of resistance).

And there is Stalin as a human being, his personal characteristics, his possible psychological abnormality. When people sought to pander to his every whim, when he could order the execution of anyone, including his closest associates, when millions of peasants could be deprived of food because he so ordered it, the human or inhuman qualities of the individual can be said to matter.

Perhaps mention should also be made of possible resistance to Stalin: the Ryutin platform, the attempt that seems to have been made at the 17th Party Congress in 1934 to reduce his power. This is linked also with the search for a rational explanation of the Great Terror: was there in fact an opposition in process of formation?

Finally, the nature of stalinism was closely linked with crisis and emergency. The historian Gefter has argued that Stalin deliberately adopted policies that made him and his methods 'necessary' – crash-programme industrialization, the terror, the renewal of repression in the postwar years – and that relaxation and stalinism were incompatible. This interpretation finds support in Molotov: in the course of interviews in which he justified stalinist policies, he remarked: 'If life is peaceful [*esli spokoino zhivetsa*], then Bolshevism is not needed. Absolutely not needed.' (*Sto sorok besed s Molotouym* by F. Chuev, Moscow, 'Terra', 1991, p. 312.)

It is impossible to answer all such questions within the ambit of a one-volume symposium. But they are there, in the minds, if not always in the pages, of all the contributors.

Epilogue

As Sergo Mikoyan rightly stated in his Epilogue, the remnants of stalinism finally perished along with the conspirators in the abortive coup of August 1991. This was also the end of Bolshevism, of Communist party rule and of the Soviet Union both as a political system and as successor of the Russian Empire.

Of course this was not Gorbachev's intention when he launched perestroika. I agree entirely with Mikoyan that he wanted big, and not just cosmetic, changes in the system he inherited. He wished to demolish the stalinist legacy, while preserving the empire, using the Party-dominated power structures, while changing the personnel. He also sought to make sweeping changes in the economy, introducing long-needed market forces, while preserving the dominant role of state property. Was this a viable package? He plainly underestimated the power of nationalism, released by glasnost. He only gradually came to terms with the logic of marketization, a logic understood neither by his own power-apparatus nor by the masses. By 1990 there was neither plan nor market, and the disintegration of the economy was paralleled and reinforced by the disintegration of central political authority. Criticism of Stalin's tyranny had by then been extended to wide-ranging attacks in the media on Lenin, Marx, the October revolution, i.e. the fundamental bases of the legitimacy of the Soviet regime itself.

The heirs of Stalin were doubtless profoundly convinced that Gorbachev had betrayed them. However, faced with the fact that the radical reformers were fragmented and disputatious, had failed to set up any alternative to the old power-structures, in the second half of 1990 Gorbachev executed his so-called 'right turn', sought support from the old power structures, appointed to key positions the men who wished to overthrow him in the August coup. We know he still wished to preserve the party of which he was still general secretary, while changing its nature and probably also its name, for he told us so at its last plenum in June 1991. In August everything fell to pieces, and Communism-Bolshevism came to an end, not even with a bang and with hardly a whimper.

What can be the feelings of Stalin's ghost as he surveys the wreck? One can imagine many variants on the theme of 'I told you so': the Union, or the Empire, could not be preserved under glasnost and *demokratizatsiya*. Gorbachev sought to prove that such a view was mistaken, that a more educated population would reject despotism, was now ripe for the emergence of a genuine civil society and legal order. The experience of the years of perestroika seem to have proved him wrong so far as the Union was concerned. But can Russia, shed of its 'colonies' and under Yeltsin's leadership, surmount its economic and social crisis and devise democratic power structures? Can she avoid chaos and a new authoritarianism? One can see Stalin's ghost shaking its head. I sincerely hope that the coming years will confound the pessimists. But I would not bet on it.

Index